Pro-Life Feminism:
Different Voices

edited by Gail Grenier Sweet

LIFE CYCLE BOOKS
Toronto, Ontario • Lewiston, New York

Pro-Life Feminism: Different Voices

Published by:

Life Cycle Books Ltd.
2205 Danforth Avenue
Toronto, Ontario
M4C 1K4
(416) 690-5860

U.S.A. office
Life Cycle Books
P.O. Box 792
Lewiston, NY 14092-0792

ISBN 0-919225-22-5

Printed and Bound by Hignell Printing Limited

Printed in Canada

Dedication

To Ted, Audrey, and George Grenier
Who taught me to cherish life.
And to children everywhere —
That they may grow up in a humane world.

— Gail Grenier Sweet

Table of Contents

SECTION FIVE: **Giving Life: Activism and Strategies**

EPILOGUE:

APPENDIX

Introduction

Pro-Life and Feminism:
No Opposition
by Paulette Joyer

Two great social movements have been evolving during the Seventies, the pro-life movement and the women's movement. Tragically, they are perceived as opposing movements. Many pro-life people fear equality for women as a dark threat to the family. Many feminists are willing to suffer the killing of their unborn daughters and sons in the name of an elusive freedom. But feminists also believe in family; pro-lifers cherish freedom.

The pro-life tenet is that each and every human being, pre-born or born, deserves the opportunity to develop into the best she or he is capable of; that each individual be respected, however minimal or great their development may be. And the feminist tenet? That each and every human being, woman or man, deserves the opportunity to develop into the best she or he is capable of; that each individual be respected, however minimal or great their development may be.

Introduction

by Gail Grenier Sweet

The women's movement and the technological revolution have grown up side-by-side in the twentieth century. American women won their right to vote in every state when the nineteenth amendment to the U.S. Constitution was passed in 1920. With that victory, feminists realized that they could get what they wanted...if they fought hard enough.

In the 1960's and 1970's, women demanded equality in job opportunity and pay. They insisted upon the freedom to choose their own lifestyles, unfettered by the stereotypes of the past.

Along with gaining some concessions in the workplace, women were handed a box of band-aids in 1973. Many women (and men) believed that the band-aids would bring about the total justice they sought. But instead, the band-aids only covered up major social ills that continued to flourish...and women kept their status as "second-class citizens."

The band-aids, of course, were abortion rights. What had happened was that with the maturing of technology, abortion became a safer, cheaper, "cleaner" procedure than ever before. So when women demanded reproductive freedom, this new improved technology was used to appease them.

The same pattern occurred when women struggled to take over their own birthing experience. They gained some concessions — fathers present at birth, homelike birthing rooms — but along with family-centered maternity care came new obstetric technology. Diagnostic ultrasound and fetal monitors had come of age; medical insurance made them affordable; and intrusions and interventions which had never been used before became routine. Cesarean rates rose while birthing retreated even further from the control of women.

Pro-life feminists, like environmentalists, believe that nature should be left alone. That's not to say that all technology is bad. Technology could end world hunger, if teamed with human intelligence and compassion. But unbridled technology threatens to destroy the environments *inside* and *outside* our bodies. Tragic examples like acid rain abound in the outside world. In our inner world, we can look again to the technologies of abortion and birthing for examples.

In recent years, diagnostic ultrasound has become almost a plaything of obstetricians. It's been heralded as much safer than X-rays, and all sorts of reasons have been thought up for using it. However, longterm biological dangers loom threateningly. There hasn't been enough time to study the possible effects — but studies thus far have been at best uncertain and at worst, frightening. Mutations are possible and ultrasound may prove to be the DES of the future.

Abortion is similar. There have been plenty of horror stories surrounding both legal and illegal "botched" abortions. Disregarding those, and assuming that the procedure has been perfected, we still know little or nothing about longterm biological effects. There are rumblings, however, that infertility is the specialty of the future for gynecologists. Infertility has become most epidemic, for many reasons. It is likely that abortion and intrusive devices like the IUD and the Pill have something to do with this epidemic.

Feminists, who demand control of their own bodies, should be very concerned about these chilling developments. They need to study with open eyes the biological effects of technologies which have become so commonplace. And yet there may be some who are willing to risk physical hazards for the sake of *liberation*. However, neither abortion rights nor obstetric devices have brought women the freedoms they deserve!

Pro-life feminists lead the fight for the long-sought-after liberation which has been kept from women. They seek the ultimate in justice: a society which bends to women's biological identity, rather than insisting that women change their biological identity through abortion. Pro-life feminists want a society which gives more than partial concessions, more than lip-service to women's equality. Here's what their "list of demands" might include:

*shared responsibility (with men) in fertility control

*easy access to safe, nonabortifacient birth control and natural family planning education

*sufficient maternity and paternity leaves

*job protection

*career options such as job-sharing and flex-time

*aids to women who wish to stay home to raise young children

*tax breaks and subsidies for those women (often single) who care for elderly relatives at home

*programs to enable divorcées raising children alone to actually collect their child-support payments

*community-based shelters for pregnant single women to enable them to give birth to their babies, to help them learn parenting skills, and to help them finish their education so they aren't trapped in the cycle of welfare

*upgraded pension plans to alleviate the poverty faced by many elderly women

*humane care of the handicapped and elderly in nursing homes

*options such as hospices for the terminally ill

*medical care for infants born with handicaps

*tough laws against pornography depicting sexual violence, incest, and child sexual abuse

*shelters for battered women and programs to help woman-beaters and child-abusers

*low-cost, high-quality childcare programs

*safety rules in factories dealing with toxins

*nutrition and health care for poor women who are pregnant

*support for handicapped children and their parents

*non-discriminatory housing for families with children, especially those headed by single parents

*an end to the exploitation of vulnerable Third World women through the export of unapproved drugs or the marketing of expensive products which they cannot use safely...

...The list could go on and on.

If feminists keep expending their time, money and energy protecting abortion rights, who will fight for these demands?

If you grab an abortion bandaid, you could blot out each of the demands just listed. But if you insist on human rights, you'll throw away the box of band-aids. Many pro-choice feminists retort, "Yes of course we all want those wonderful things, but the world isn't perfect, and until it is, we need the option of abortion." Pro-life feminists, on the other hand, believe that if we keep resorting to abortion to solve problems, we'll never achieve the quality of life that we all want. We'll keep fooling ourselves with a false liberation.

Slavery is a good analogy here. Slavery, like abortion, was a human rights issue. There were many convincing arguments for slavery, just as there are as many seemingly sound defences for abortion. What would happen to the slaves once they were free? Who would take care of them? Wouldn't their lives be miserable with poverty and starvation? And what would happen to the economy without their free labor?

It's true that abolition created very grave problems. But would anyone argue that slavery is a necessary solution to problems in an unjust world?

Feminists, like abolitionists, believe in the equality of all human beings. To argue that the fetus is not human life is biological ignorance. In traditional Western medical and social thinking, life itself was held intrinsically valuable. But along with the abortion mentality, there has developed a new ethic which values "quality of life" above life itself. The irony is that if you examine the quality of life argument, you'll see that it must create an opposite effect in the long run. To quote Dr. Landrum Shettles, "an ethic that makes any class of individuals expendable 'in the interests of society' ultimately imperils that entire society." I believe with Dr. Shettles that "the clearest-headed pragmatists and 'situational ethicists' *must* oppose abortion if they truly do prize the 'greatest good for the greatest number.' The Golden Rule is pragmatism of the highest order."*

The Golden Rule says "Do to others what you would like them to do to you." The abolition of slavery was evidence of the power of the Golden Rule (although there were other, less noble, reasons that slavery was abolished). There have been two other momentous exercises of the Golden Rule in recent times: the fight against child-abuse and wife-beating. In the past, these practices were commonly accepted by the general public. Not any more. What changed people's minds and hearts? What made people finally push for laws making these practices illegal? Why can a parent or teacher no longer whip a child with legal sanction?

The answer is: HUMAN RIGHTS. People recognized, after a long, long time, that it is everyone's right not to be beaten. Nobody owns anyone else; no one has the right to hit anyone else.

There will come a time when men and women realize that abortion, like slavery and beating, is an infringement of human rights. Pro-life feminists already see abortion as a roadblock to full rights for *women* as well as unborn children. Women aren't being told the truth about abortion. Pro-life feminists believe that if you respect women's intelligence, you'll inform them about fetal development and what actually happens in the abortion procedure — *before* they pay for their

*From *Rites of Life* by Landrum Shettles, M.D. and David Rorvik.

abortions! The U.S. Supreme Court has ruled *against* informed consent, so that we cannot require that women receive information on the risks of abortion. Yet women have fought for years for access to medical records and for information which will help them become intelligent consumers of medical care! The law says that the father need not be informed of an abortion. Suddenly after struggling to get men involved in family planning and childbirth, women are on their own again!

The pro-life feminist says, "Women can handle the truth; tell them the facts about abortion." The pro-life feminist says, "We have fought to get our partners involved in family planning — let's keep them involved." And also, "We've struggled for years to have pregnancy regarded as a normal, healthy process. Let's not return to regarding pregnancy as a sickness and an impediment to career."

The pro-life feminists who speak in this book see the whole picture. They realize that abortion is just one facet in a kaleidoscope of social ills which harden our hearts and destroy our planet — ills including infanticide, euthanasia, capital punishment, war, and pollution. These writers are like the earliest feminists who understood that civil rights meant recognizing the dignity of every human being, *especially* the defenseless. Those early women's leaders identified with the fetus because women too were defenseless and treated as property "owned" by husbands or parents.

What will it take for pro-choice feminists to become convinced that abortion is a violation of civil rights? Two things may help them to open their minds: first, they may get a chance to view former abortionist Bernard Nathanson's filming of ultrasound images of a very young fetus being aborted. Second, they may hear the loud voices of thousands of angry women like those who belong to WEBA (Women Exploited by Abortion). These are women who were told that their fetuses were "blobs of tissue," who were told that there were no physical or emotional dangers to this "simple procedure."

If more and more people listen to these ardent civil libertarians, the box of abortion bandaids will be thrown away. And humane alternatives will be found in place of infanticide and euthanasia as well...because they're all part of the same syndrome: seeing killing as a solution to problems.

Meanwhile, pro-life feminists will keep fighting, just as feminists have in the past, for true liberation and quality of life.

*   *   *

This book would never have seen print if not for the work of Susan Maronek and Denyse Handler; the financial donations of Milwaukee Feminists for Life and the Ted, Audrey, and George Grenier Foundation; the unremunerated literary contributions of the many authors; and the courage and foresight of Paul Broughton at Life Cycle Books.

What would normally be author's royalties will be channelled to the Grenier Foundation, a nonprofit nonsectarian charitable organization which funds pro-life efforts. One project of the Grenier Foundation has been HOPE Network, a grassroots support system for single mothers and   their children.

— Gail Grenier Sweet
1985

(Thirteenth anniversary year of the birth of Feminists for Life of America — and twelfth anniversary year of the U.S. Supreme Court decision legalizing abortion.)

Pro-Life Feminism:
A Historical Perspective
by Kathleen M. Glover

It's fascinating to straddle a political and moral fence. A pro-life feminist must defend her position on both sides. But she also has the right to speak up on both issues: women's rights and the right to life.

The history of feminism includes many women who first became concerned with basic human rights and then with their own lack of rights as women. Sarah and Angelina Grimke were among the first women to speak out publicly against slavery. They soon found that even their right of free speech was challenged, and that they could not function as equals with their male abolitionist friends. Sarah Grimke in a letter written in the 1830's "on the Condition of Women in the United States" sounds remarkably like a current feminist. She attacks the manifestations of "male superiority" in marriage as well as in the employment market. Similarly, after attending a World Anti-slavery Convention in London, where, even though they were U.S. delegates, they were not allowed to speak, Elizabeth Coady Stanton and Lucretia

Mott agreed on the need for a public meeting on women's rights. On July 14th, 1848, the first Woman's Rights Convention was announced in the Seneca, N.Y. *County Courier*. During this and subsequent conventions the early feminists recognized that the injustices could be resolved only if the basic right to make laws and choose rulers was secured.

Many members of Feminists for Life of America have arrived at their position via similar routes. I first became an activist in college. I was a member of the National Organization for the Advancement of Colored People, and protested the war in Vietnam. In 1971, I became involved with the pro-life movement in New York as a Birthright volunteer. At the same time, the women's movement was gaining momentum, but the National Organization of Women had a firm pro-abortion stand. When I moved to Wisconsin in 1977, I found a group with interests paralleling mine: Feminists for Life.

Since the basic tenet of feminism is equality and a belief in the dignity of each individual, I believe that feminism is the best possible platform from which to proclaim my pro-life beliefs. If we truly support the right to life of each individual child, we should also be concerned with the equal rights of each individual adult. The lack of concern for the rights of individuals is what constitutes prejudice. Overcoming prejudice is what the women's rights movement and the pro-life movement are all about.

In the past 150 years, men have found it increasingly difficult to keep women silent. Women have looked around, and seen that many of the accepted practices of their day violated basic human rights. These abuses were perpetuated largely by men, for financial gain. Perhaps women saw clearly what was wrong because the prevailing laws gave them very little share of any of these ill-gotten gains. Women did speak out and they agitated against the injustice of slavery; and against unfair labor practices in factories and mills, where women and children were among the most abused. They were pacifists, and protesters against the violence done to families by alcohol abuse. They became educators, health care providers, lawyers and lawmakers.

Among the many women involved in the struggle for human rights was Sojourner Truth, a former slave, who was a respected lecturer both on the abolition of slavery and on women's rights. Susan B. Anthony was a teacher involved in the temperance movement. She was not interested in women's rights until she tried to address the New York State Teachers' Convention about the injustice of paying women teachers one-fourth the salary paid to men for the same work. Two-thirds of the 500 teacher delegates were women, but she had to wait to speak until the male teachers took a vote on the advisability of allowing women to speak. Francis Willard was one of the most effective organizers of women in the late 19th century. Her Women's Christian Temperance Union had 10,000 local unions and more than 200,000 members across the country. The W.C.T.U. was more than just a temperance movement. Her goal was to expand the thinking of American women, and her motto was "Do everything". This meant suffrage, legislation for women and fair labor practices, health programs, welfare work in prisons, programs for Indians, Blacks and immigrant women, peace programs, mothers' problem circles and kindergartens to name a few. In 1917, Janet Rankin became the first woman elected to congress. She was an ardent pacifist as well as a member of the woman's suffrage movement. She voted against both World Wars, and at the age of 87 led 5,000 women to Capitol Hill to protest the war in Vietnam. These women were giants in the history of liberation of peoples, yet few of the general public are aware of their existence. The activities of half of our population have been ignored in our history books. Since before the Civil War women have been active in the struggle for equality, and against injustice to the individual. The 19th amendment (which gave women the right to vote) was first proposed in 1844. An immense amount of work by hundreds of women over a period of 72 years brought about passage of this amendment in 1920. Women today are largely uninformed about this struggle, and it's easy to take our right to vote for granted. The 19th amendment, however, *only* recognized women's right to vote. Sexism and inequalities were still deeply ingrained in every facet of our society.

During the Civil Rights movement of the sixties, women frequently found themselves making coffee instead of decisions. And again the women's movement gained momentum as a result. The Equal Rights Amendment was first introduced to Congress in 1923. It was re-introduced at each Congress until February of 1970, when the reorganized women's groups were able to force hearings on the matter. The amendment finally passed in May of 1970. It simply stated: "Equality of rights under the law shall not be denied or abridged by the United States or any state on account of sex." Rev. Fr. Hesburgh, president of the University of Notre Dame, noted that "...Ratification of the E.R.A. would demonstrate that we are a nation truly committed to equality. Ratification would go far toward ensuring that sex, like other immutable and irrelevant characteristics, plays no part in determining individual worth or opportunity."

Women working for passage of the E.R.A. have helped change traditional attitudes and the legal status of women. The Equal Pay Act of 1963 and the Educational Amendment of 1972 are just two examples. We have all benefited from these changes whether or not we agree with the activists in the women's movement.

Despite these laws, equal treatment and equal opportunities still do not exist for many women. Women are conditioned by the discrimination inflicted upon them every day to follow, to appease, to expect less of themselves. Literature has a profound effect on our culture. The only real goal in almost all "women's books" or magazines is still to catch a man or to keep him. The idiotic housewife portrayed in television commercials affects our self image as women, as well as men's view of women, and our children's idea of what a woman is. The acceptance or rejection of the "stereotyped woman" plays a large part in each woman's personal adjustment.

Studies show that sex stereotypes often affect medical doctors' attitudes and their professional treatment of women patients.[1] In 1981 more than 75% of all practicing physicians were men.[2] When a man goes to see a doctor, he is listened to, and his symptoms treated. When a woman goes to a doctor she is often merely given a prescription for tranquillizers. Moreover, although there have been great improvements over the old "Dick and Jane" readers, sex stereotypes still exist in our schools and our children's textbooks. This has a subtle effect on our daughters' expectations for themselves.

Employed women earn an average of 59¢ for each $1.00 earned by their male counterparts. The average pay for female college graduates still only equals that of male high school dropouts. Only 8/10ths of 1% of working women earn more than $25,000.00 a year.[3] The labor unions are a good example of how far we have to go to reach equality. The International Ladies' Garment Workers' Union with a membership of 322,505, had one woman on its Board of Directors in 1983.[4] Although more women are joining labor unions, the majority of women workers are unorganized and underpaid. Most women are still segregated into "women's jobs", and face the same patterns of discrimination that the early feminists spoke to. On salaries kept lower than men's, working mothers must also pay for child-care. And many women actually cope with two full-time jobs, one at home and one at work.

These startling economic facts have far-reaching effects. Twelve million children are dependent on women for their support and 60% of these children live in poverty.[5] Because a woman earns less money for equal work, it follows that she receives less social security credit, and has to manage with fewer benefits when she retires. There are over five million women living alone in this country. Half of them are living in poverty.[6]

As our divorce rate increases, so does the number of displaced homemakers. Middle-aged divorcees who have spent their time keeping house and raising children receive no financial or legal credit for this work, no social security, no insurance benefits, no credit rating; and are usually ill-equipped to compete in the job market. Widows often suffer from the same problems because federal and state inheritance laws generally assume that the homemaker makes no economic contribution to the family. Therefore a widow must pay an inheritance tax on her home or farm or business, as well as on her belongings that she thought she owned. A major theme of the women's movement has been an attempt to recognize individual achievement and needs. Women are in a stronger position in states such as Pennsylvania which have passed an Equal Rights Amendment, and where the contributions of homemakers are given equal credit.

These are just a few examples of the discrimination that does exist against women. We must also be aware of the gains made for all women by the feminists working for women's rights, during the past hundred years. As I climb back on my fence I note that many modern feminists are also working very hard to secure "abortion rights". In four states there have been attempts to use the state E.R.A. to justify Medicaid funding for abortions. In two of these cases the E.R.A. testimony was not considered, and one case is still pending. Most recently, in September of 1984, in Pennsylvania, a higher court judge *overturned* a lower court ruling in favor of Planned Parenthood and the Civil Liberties Union, which did cite the state E.R.A. Reproductive rights are important in the struggle for equality. However, I believe that the feminists of the last century would have used their tremendous ingenuity and willpower to find life giving solutions to this problem. I do not believe that they would have been willing to settle for this violation of the most fundamental right of the unborn child. And I think they would have been able to see clearly the abuse done to women by the violence of abortion.

I believe that respect for the individual is necessary to both the women's movement and the pro-life Movement. What we truly need is an Equal Rights Amendment that would guarantee the equality of each individual regardless of sex or stage of development.

1. Lauerson, N.H., "Remedies for medical sexism", *The Milwaukee Journal*, Nov. 4 (1979).
2. Kandel, Thelma, *What Women Earn*, (The Linden Press, Simon and Schuster. New York, N.Y., 1981), p. 69.
3. ibid., p. 9.
4. Bureau of Labor Statistics, (1983).
5. Scott, J. "Affirmative action for women: A practical guide for women and management", (Addison-Wesley pub. Co., Menlo Park, Ca., 1975), p. 9.
6. Ruckelshaus, J., " '...To form a more perfect union...' — Justice for American women", report of the National Commission on the observance of International Woman's Year, (U.S. Govt. printing office, June 1976) p. 104.

Challenging Alliances

by Sandra K. Mahkorn, M.D.

"Feminists for Life, what's that?" People often hear the name of our group and assume we are "hardcore" feminists committed by some occult oath or blood-letting bond to a life-long, militant struggle for female equality or perhaps even female superiority, not understanding that we are not referring to life in the chronological sense. When one explains that the real purpose of the group is to secure the civil rights of women as well as the unborn, the questioner is usually equally perplexed. We are an enigma to most — to the women's rights activists who assume that a pro-abortion position is a prerequisite for feminism, and to the right-to-lifers who equate the women's movement with abortion on demand.

If we are enigmas let us delight in our incapacity to be conveniently categorized! So many have abandoned individualism, succumbed to peer group pressure and become enslaved by labels. They define themselves as "liberal" or "conservative" and when confronting an issue consult a laundry list of so-called "liberal" or "conservative" positions to decide what their own beliefs should be. Free thinking and critical analysis succumb to the security of conformism. So, if I want to be a "feminist" I have to check to see what "feminists" think and say and do — and conform. It means allowing myself to be defined by someone else. Rather than liberation, such obsequious behavior merely substitutes a dominant group for a dominant male. I have grown to despise labels — categories that enslave the mind and dampen the quest for truth.

But, the question remains, "What is Feminists for Life, and what women would be attracted to such a group?" Certainly not the conformist or those whose insecurity makes the questioning of former alliances impossible. Feminists for Life appeals to those women whose abhorrence of violence necessitates a break with those embracing abortion. Feminists for Life singles out those whose commitment to human rights is wide and penetrating enough to encompass even the impotent and unwanted and not merely the powerful and privileged. In the introduction to her book *Women, Resistance and Revolution*, Sheila Rowbotham writes, "the liberation of women necessitates the liberation of all human beings."[1] Perhaps then, what Feminists for Life has to offer is liberation in the fullest sense.

"Liberation", "freedom", "justice", "rights" — declarations so profound yet so subject to rhetorical manipulation. In a 1979 article in *The Practitioner*, Gardner writes, "Those who are quick to deny that the fetus has any rights are the first to claim that it has the right to be wanted."[2] The belief that an individual's worth is dependent upon their degree of wantedness or how pleasing they are to another conflicts with both the feminist and the pro-life philosophy. Just as a woman's value is independent of her ability to please or attract men, so an unborn child's value is independent of how "wanted" he or she is by his or her parents. To believe otherwise is to embrace a utilitarian ethic, a dehumanizing philosophy which can only result in making objects of us all.

Women attracted to Feminists for Life have proven to be those whose sense of self is tenacious enough not to be threatened by an *all-encompassing* commitment to liberation — broad enough to include even our unborn brothers and sisters; women who reject the reactionary method of problem-solving — violence against the human person; women who are not afraid to challenge former alliances, in sum women who *are* liberated. Perhaps *true* liberation is merely a byproduct of self-actualization: "for you can only be free when even the desire of seeking freedom becomes a harness to you, and when you cease to speak of freedom as a goal and a fulfillment."

1. Rowbotham, Sheila, *Women, Resistance and Revolution*, Vintage Books, New York, 1972. introduction.
2. Gardner, R.F.R., "The Ethics of Abortion," *The Practitioner*, Vol. 223, Aug., 1979.
3. Gibran, Kahlil, *The Prophet*, Alfred A. Knopf, New York, 1973, essay "On Freedom."

Reflecting
As FFL Celebrates
Its Tenth Birthday

by Cecilia Voss Koch

Ten years ago Feminists for Life was born out of the deep dissatisfaction of two feminists with the pro-abortion stance of existing women's rights groups. There was no voice for feminists who were committed to the "life" causes, so Pat Goltz and Cathy Callahan of Columbus, Ohio acted to fill that void. Since then, local chapters throughout the United States have joined in a coalition called Feminists for Life of America. We are one of the bridges that have been built in recent years between the pro-life movement and other movements in the country. Although we are concerned with a number of issues, pro-life feminists are basically promoting justice for women and the protection of human life. To that end we support an Equal Rights Amendment and a Human Life Amendment, because we believe these two amendments to be complementary in their concern for human life.

Our philosophy is firmly rooted in the conviction that human life has inherent value; therefore, its destruction is a serious matter. Without this conviction, that life itself has value, there is little personal security, since then one's value depends on the attitudes of others. The "life-itself-has-no-value" philosophy necessitates that a person prove personal worth through endless goal-oriented activities, in an unsatisfying drive to achieve greater and greater worth, never quite sure how much is enough. When we positively affirm the principle that life, including our own, has value and dignity, we have good reason to love ourselves, and the consequence of loving others develops naturally and logically.

Pro-life feminists do not espouse the "quality-of-life" ethic which is so popular in Western society today, but rather the "value-of-life" ethic. I must admit that at first glance the "quality-of-life" argument seems very attractive, but upon closer scrutiny it discloses a serious danger. Inherent in this philosophy is the idea that a life must have a certain amount of quality to justify its continued existence. Persons lacking the prescribed minimum amount of quality are considered "unfit" and lose their claim to life. But who shall be the arbiter — the judge of the minimum of quality? Shall an IQ of 30 be the lowest permissible standard? What about the hopelessly insane? The German euthanasia program began with the insane, and within two years hospitals were exterminating World War I amputees and children who were chronic bedwetters or had misshapen ears. The German people gave the power of life and death to their doctors, judges and government officials. To whom shall we entrust the lives of our "devalued" people?

Can we honestly say that the world would be a better place if all the so-called "unfit" were eliminated? *I fear* for a society without the burdensome. In the void created by their absence, would our narcissistic tendencies find fertile soil and give birth to a monster that would eventually devour us? We must not listen to the voices that tell us there aren't enough of the world's resources to go around. Those voices belong to the greedy who are consuming more than their share of those resources, and the powerful who will not loosen their grip on the powerless. If you listen very carefully to those who insist that it is cruel to bring into the world an imperfect human being, you will hear the insidious master-race philosophy creeping in ever so silently, like a wolf disguised in sheep's clothing. Elitism has always been with us; we must not let it fool us because it is wearing a new dress of humanitarianism.

Being pro-life means not being selective about whose life we defend. Can we say we will fight for the life of an unborn child but not care about the child once he is born and needs adequate shelter or child care? Do we remember those with twisted bodies and forget those with twisted minds, including those who sit on death row? Do we champion the cause of the handicapped but neglect the political and religious captive? Is the life of a dying cancer patient worth less than the life of a war victim sprayed with napalm, or the life of a malnourished child less than that of an old woman at death's door? Who can say? Society is playing a deadly game when it chooses to support one type of life over another.

We do not necessarily propose that a human being has the right to complex life-sustaining machinery, but we do propose that each has the right to certain basic necessities. We consider sustenance and relief of pain during terminal illness to be such necessities. But we condemn the active termination of a life. Each time we actively terminate a life (except to save the life of another) we cheapen it. And every time we cheapen someone else's life, we cheapen our own and place it in jeopardy. Not one of us knows when she will be helpless — completely dependent on the whim of some powerful arbiter.

One might ask why, given our strong pro life stance, we Feminists for Life are not simply members of a larger Right to Life organization. How are we different? The answer is that we are basically a feminist group and our pro-life philosophy arises logically from our feminist convictions.

Many pro-life groups have long opposed the ERA for fear that its passage would permanently embed legal abortion into the Constitution. Until recently Feminists for Life worked for the passage of the original ERA, and held to its position that there is no *logical* legal connection between ERA and abortion. Many legal experts testified to that effect, notably the Senate Judiciary Committee, which said the ERA "does not require that women must be treated in all respects the same as men. 'Equality' does not mean 'sameness'." (S. Rept. 92-689, p. 12) In addition, J.W. Heckman, Jr., Chief Counsel of the Subcommittee on Constitutional Amendments of the U.S. Senate says the ERA "provides simply that government may not in its laws or official actions discriminate on the basis of sex. Since abortion by its nature concerns only women, sex discrimination in this area is a biological impossibility. The...(ERA), if ratified, therefore, would have no applicability whatsoever to the question of abortion."

In a similar vein, Attorney Ruth M. Ferrell, writing in a journal of the American Bar Association, argues, "The Equal Rights Amendment...prohibit legislation dealing with physical characteristics unique to one sex...The Equal Rights Amendment (will not) have any effect on laws regulating or prohibiting abortion..."

We still maintain that there is no *logical* legal connection, but there definitely is an *illogical* one, and it was used recently when the Pennsylvania Supreme Court ruled that that state's ERA *necessitated* abortion funding. Because of this and other similar judicial decisions, our position has been altered to support only an abortion-neutral Equal Rights Amendment. Unfortunately, the staunch opposition of mainline feminist groups to any modification of the "virgin" ERA dooms its passage in the foreseeable future.

The twisting of logic employed by pro-choice people in Pennsylvania was a blow for FFL, but it should not have been so surprising when we consider that all the arguments used in favor of abortion are gross distortions of reason.

But what of the attitudes displayed by some right-to-life activists towards feminist issues in general? So often I hear women who are pro life say, "Of course I want women to get the same pay as men, but other than that, I just can't buy all this women's rights babble. I enjoy being a woman." Invariably, these are not women who have had to shift for themselves or who have felt the sting of prejudice. Those who simply are not aware of any real prejudice will do well to listen to the words of Thomas I. Emerson, professor emeritus of the Yale Law School:

> "Discrimination against women persists in many areas of our law. It is particularly acute in the fields of family law, social security, welfare and criminal law. Most of our public institutions, such as governmental agencies, educational systems and the military, retain many of the attitudes and practices that throughout the ages have relegated women to the status of second-class citizens. And in private employment, education, business and the professions, women still largely play a secondary and subordinate role. Thus, while some progress has been made in recent years, the problem of achieving equal status for women in our national life remains unsolved."

A vague fear haunts many tradition-minded people that somehow the Equal Rights Amendment will alter their family structure and deprive them of the kind of life they know and enjoy. For them I quote the words of Monsignor John J. Egan, Director, Center for Pastoral and

Social Ministry, Notre Dame University:

> "I believe that the Equal Rights Amendment will allow women complete legal equality *without infringing on their private lives or family relationships.* I think our country needs the resources of women and therefore should not inhibit their potential by any legal discrimination."
> (Emphasis added)

The role of women has traditionally been homemaker. Since the domestication of fire, someone was needed to stay near it to keep it burning, and since woman was the one who bore the offspring, she was the logical choice. But today technology eliminates the fire-tending duty. Husband and wife are equally capable of turning on the stove and the furnace. We cling strongly to our biological job of childbearing and the related nurturing duties. We defend that role, rejoice in it, thrive in it, relish it, and believe that that role has given us a unique perspective. But we need to break out of the restrictions of our immediate homes and share that perspective with the community, whether local, national or worldwide. Other aspects of technology have released women from total commitment to the home. The lengthening of our life span has left many of us wondering what to do with the rest of our lives after the children are gone. Child care facilities and several innovative employment practices enable career women to continue to contribute their special talents to the world.

It is also interesting to note that for centuries the poorer women in Western societies have had to work outside the home to support their families, and in many other cultures women's food-gathering and agricultural skills saved their people from extinction. The role of husband as sole supporter is relatively new, and only possible in affluent societies.

The term "feminism" is much maligned these days because it is so often confused with femininity. A great fear exists in some minds that the aim of feminism is to deprive women of their intrinsic characteristics. We all have our own cherished notions of that abstract idea "femininity," whether it be graciousness, gentleness, meekness, compassion, tenderness or benevolence. We are wary of taking on the worst of what we consider masculine traits, such as aggression, ruthlessness, cruelty, callousness, malevolence and viciousness. History, however, reminds us that there have always been women who, while on the surface were amorous, demure and charming, were basically cruel, ruthless and vindictive. On the other hand, millions of people have described Jesus Christ as gracious, gentle, meek, compassionate, tender and benevolent. Quite clearly, a person does not possess a quality by virtue of his or her sex, but deliberately develops it. A feminist (male or female) is simply one who advocates for women the same rights, economic and political, that are granted to men. It's as simple as that. The doctrine of feminism has nothing to do with femininity, as such.

The reader may ask, since we Feminists for Life feel so strongly about feminism, why aren't we aligned with larger women's rights groups? We are — on true feminist issues. At this time we are participating with the National Organization for Women (NOW) in their Message Brigade to help implement the passage of the E.R.A. But we refuse to join them totally because they seek to solve the world's ills through the violent means of abortion. Feminists for Life consider the fanatical insistence of certain women's rights groups on abortion to be a sell-out of the feminist cause. They have sold out to the male dominated abortion industry (and it has been documented that the greatest majority of clinics are businesses owned by entrepreneurs) and to the playboy philosophy which sees women as exploitable commodities for male convenience and profit.

Abortion is the destruction of human life and energy that does nothing to eradicate the very real underlying problems of women. The pregnant welfare mother begs for decent housing, a decent job and child-care or respect for her child-nurturing work. Instead, she gets directions to the local abortion clinic and is told to take care of "her problem." How convenient. Much less time and trouble than teaching her about authentic reproductive freedom and reproductive responsibility. Much cheaper than attending to her real problems: her poverty, her lack of skills, her illiteracy, her loneliness, her bitterness about her entrapment, her self-contempt, her vulnerability. After the abortion these problems will all be there and another one added besides: her guilt.

By encouraging society to consider a woman's child as a disposable piece of property, abortion reinforces the image of woman herself as disposable property and reusable sex object — a renewable sexual resource. It is no coincidence that the biggest single financial contributor to the cause of "abortion rights" is the Playboy Foundation. When abortion is available to all women, all male responsibility for fertility control has been removed. A man need only offer a woman money for the abortion and that's it: no responsibility, no relationship, no commitment. And there we are ... recycled and used again!

While pro-life feminists condemn the anti-life influences so prevalent today, we do not, in any way, condemn a woman who has had an abortion. That is neither our job nor our wish. Our aim is to spread our philosophy, listen to a woman's problems, give of our time and money, extend our hands and above all, our hearts in understanding.

Juli Loesch, President of Pennsylvania Feminists for Life, writes so persuasively (*Our Bodies, Their Lives*):

> "The development of feminist (cooperative, fertility-aware) sexuality and pro-woman, pro-child support structures is something that society must do on a massive scale. We deserve, demand, have a right to — can create — something better than the abortion industry's "cure" for our unique condition of impregnability, whether that abortionist be in the back alley or in the plush front office."

And Jo McGowan, a pro-life feminist writer, appeals eloquently in *The Body as Battleground*:

> "What we need now is a race of woman who will stand up and say NO! The violence ends here. The misogyny ends here. The destruction of our children ends here. No longer will our bodies be used to write messages of fear and hatred. We hold within our bodies the power of creation, the power to nourish and sustain life. We shall not pervert these powers to serve death."

At the National Right to Life Convention in 1978, the Feminists for Life of America set forth their resolutions. The preamble to those resolutions speaks for all of us:

> "We, as pro-life feminists, offer a return to the roots of feminism in this country, a feminism which is a loving, nurturing response to any human suffering...be it the suffering of a woman, a man, or an unborn child. We reject the violence which is the world's way. We believe that our non-violence and our embracing of life where we find it must extend to the entire human family, and beyond the narrow confines of our biological families. We proclaim that we are homemakers — that the world is our home and we make it — loving, nurturing and pro-life."

Originally published as "The Pro-Life Feminist Movement" in the Fall 1981 issue of *Heartbeat*, 2606½ West 8th St., Los Angeles, CA 90057. Reprinted with permission.

Section One:
How we differ from the National Organization for Women (NOW)

This section answers the questions

- What do Feminists for Life say about the ERA? About a HLA?
- What do Feminists for Life say about abortion?
- What do pro-life feminists say about the Left and the Right?

Flunking Again: ERA Lessons Not Learned

by Paulette Joyer

Pro-life feminists have to live in the real world and our position on many strategies for justice are constantly evolving. This cannot always be said about most of the mainstream pro-abortion feminist leadership. On one of the most critical issues of the decade, the Equal Rights Amendment, they have learned nothing from their failures. After ten years, the period allowed for ratification ran out, failing to win the support of three-fourths of the states.

Did *status quo* feminists rethink their strategy in light of their failure? In a word, no. In June of 1983, following the expiration of the old ERA, the same old ERA was re-introduced into Congress. The exact same wording that had failed to get the needed support of the states was used. And there it sat through the summer, with no momentum.

Then, in October of that year, participants at the National Organization for Women conference passed a resolution "that the National Organization for Women serves notice on Congress that we will accept no amendments to the ERA and that any sponsor willing to accept amendments should remove his or her name from the list of sponsors. That we demand a vote on the ERA before the 1984 primaries. And we pledge that the ERA will be a central national domestic issue for the 1984 elections — not only will we remember in November but we will make sure the nation does also."

They got the vote they wanted — and lost it. Apparently looking for ways to aggravate the "gender gap" to his own party's self-interest, House Speaker Tip O'Neill seized the opportunity and on November 15 he used a parliamentary privilege usually reserved for minor or non-controversial bills: he gave "each side" twenty minutes for debate, then forced a vote on the Equal Rights Amendment with no consideration of amendments thereto. The proposed constitutional amendment failed to garner the needed two-thirds majority by six votes; the count was 278 for to 147 against.

By adamantly refusing to debate questions of the possible effects of the ERA, which would have necessitated considering amendments, the NOW leaders, Tip O'Neill and their supporters again jeopardized its ratification. By not allowing congressional discussion of the possibility of mandatory abortion funding if ERA passes — and other related issues which cause anxiety to many Americans — the ERA lobby allows clouds of doubt to continue to shadow its efforts on behalf of women. Shifting responsibility for the effects of the ERA onto the federal courts does nothing to allay the suspicions and fears of citizens who oppose abortion policies imposed by the U.S. Supreme Court, and don't want the Court's influence in this area expanded. Unless the effect of the ERA regarding abortion is clarified, there is little hope of building the needed citizen enthusiasm for ratification.

Representative James Sensenbrenner prepared to make a motion to amend the ERA to make it abortion-neutral: "Nothing in this article [the ERA] shall be construed to grant or secure any right relating to abortion or the funding thereof." A fair and open debate on the ERA is needed and must include consideration of the Sensenbrenner amendment.

When it considered the Hyde Amendment which would prohibit federal funding for abortion, the House voted 231 to 184 for the Medicaid abortion restriction. We believe that this Hyde vote in 1983 and the ERA vote in November of the same year reflect the position of most Americans, that is, opposition to abortion-on-demand as well as support for equal rights for women. We shouldn't have to settle for either no ERA or one which may entrench abortion-on-demand; the ERA needs the Sensenbrenner amendment.

From *Sisterlife* 12/83, the journal of Feminists for Life of America, 811 East 47th St., Kansas City, Mo. 64110. Reprinted with permission.

Pro-Life, Pro-E.R.A.

by Juli Loesch

I'm for the Equal Rights Amendment. But a number of women whom I respect are not. Are they devotées of Marabel (*The Total Woman*) Morgan? Or captives of some decrepit political boys' club? No. They are thoughtful individuals, explicit or implicit feminists, who would have supported the E.R.A. gladly a few years ago. They've backed off for one reason, and one reason alone: abortion.

Now, I've read articles that say there is some sort of link between the E.R.A. and abortion, but I hold with those that say there isn't. The only logical link I can perceive is that if men can't have abortions, then women can't either. A silly line of argument.

But although there is no intrinsic connection between the issues, the feminist movement has been portrayed by the media as having two goals on its legislative agenda: the E.R.A. and abortion. So there's a tendency on both sides to say, "if abortion is a woman's 'right' and the E.R.A. will strengthen all of women's rights, then the E.R.A. is pro-abortion."

As I said, I'm pro-E.R.A. I see legal equality between women and men (blacks and whites, etc.) as a matter of simple justice. But if, after its hopeful success, the E.R.A. campaign droops and then dies, I hope it will be understood that it was the abortion issue that killed it. Abortion is such a liability as an issue that it should have been rejected as a priority by the women's movement on pragmatic political grounds alone.

The E.R.A. forces, I am convinced, could have swept the state legislatures with a mighty, united wave of women if the abortion issue had never been broached. Even conservative women's groups, like the Catholic Daughters of America, are opposed to discrimination against women, want their own daughters to have the fullest opportunities and wholeheartedly support principles of equality such as equal pay for equal work. It took an issue like abortion to split this potentially unstoppable sisterhood into two bitter and distrustful camps.

Abortion divides white people from black and third-world people. It is no secret that the poor non-white people, often designated the "beneficiaries" of abortion, have been the most distrustful of the whole issue. Many see abortion as a racist strategy pushed by white "planner" types who get queasy when thinking of an America that is increasingly brown and black. It's bad enough that the anti-E.R.A. forces are aggressively (and successfully) chaining the two issues together in the public mind. The fact that many pro-E.R.A. organizations have also announced "abortion rights" as a priority will tend to make everything else they stand for a nonpriority among many concerned black and brown people.

We who want the equality of women and men to become part of the United States Constitution should avoid antagonizing the two or three largest religious groups in the United States. The abortion issue — with notable exceptions — pits Catholics, Baptists and evangelicals against Unitarians, Jews and agnostics. Religious, pacifist pro-lifers (like me) are pushed toward the arms of conservative coalitions, which are also anti-E.R.A.

What I am saying is that it is strategically suicidal for any group to be linked to "abortion rights" if they also wish to generate and sustain support for the E.R.A.

Abortion is, or ought to be, completely separated from the equal-rights question. It's a political liability. But I will go one step further. I would say abortion is inconsistent with the rest of the feminist agenda. It is anti-feminist, wrong on principle.

Most feminists favor a more equal sharing by men and women for the responsibility for children. We approve when men learn to be babysitters as well as baseball players. We're glad when a father is attentive and nurturing to his children, and not just a remote breadwinner/authority figure. This expanded scope of male involvement is undermined when babies are defined at some stages of their lives as the mother's sole and individual property, and the father is denied any accountability for the life of his own child.

Collective responsibility is eroded by abortion. Society at large can say: "Lady, we feel no particular responsibility for your little problem because there is nothing to feel responsible for; so just terminate your problem and everybody will breathe easier." Lacking the secure base of a caring community, women whose pregnancies are an emotional, social or financial burden are thrown onto the demands of a rather heartless individualism.

To say that the conception of a child is a private matter that does not implicate father, sisters, brothers, grandmothers, grandfathers and all the rest of us, is a rejection of our social and communal responsibilities. To say that pregnancy is one of those female problems and to offer gallantly to scrape it out rather than burden the poor, individual woman is to abandon that woman to the most painful alienation.

The pro-choicers I know are concerned men and women with good, functioning consciences. They're not callous. I am absolutely certain that they do not mean to deny the human dignity of any child.

The same goes for the pro-life women who are against the E.R.A. They don't mean to deny the human dignity of any women.

It doesn't seem impossible to me that women could get together (disregarding their "right-to-life" and "pro-choice" labels) and hammer out a common agenda that would bring women of all colors, religions and classes together. I realize that this is what was supposed to happen at the International Women's Year Conference in Houston in 1975; but the presence of a sizeable counter-rally shows that that sort of dialogue often does not take place.

I decided to go to the Right-to-Life Convention in St. Louis, at the end of June to promote dialogue on the E.R.A., and then to the E.R.A. rally in Washington, D.C., on July 9 for dialogue on the right to life. I didn't want to prove anybody wrong, but to strive for more inclusive solutions on the belief that, as the old slogan says, "Women united can never be defeated."

Of course, I had expected the Right-to-Life Convention to be rather conservative socially and politically, especially since their powwow was being held at the patrician Stouffer's Riverfront Towers. (Stouffer's is a wholly owned subsidiary of Nestlé, a corporation then under severe criticism by some groups for its policy of promoting baby formula in developing nations.) Our liberal sisters would not have been guilty of this blunder, I hope. I noticed a STOP E.R.A.-Eagle Forum literature table, but no Feminists for Life table; I noticed the Cardinal Mindszenty Anti-Communist Crusade, but no Maryknoll or Network. A few people who sported "Democrats for Life" buttons felt like leftists, leftovers and left-outs.

I resolved simply to keep my eyes and ears open, and I prayed with all sincerity for a spiritual disposition of openness, of learning, of being sensitive to the other person's point of view. And I learned. Mostly, I learned that I cannot dismiss with a flippant one-liner the possibility of an abortion/E.R.A. connection.

The most disturbing thing about the E.R.A. is not what the right-to-lifers are saying about it, but what many pro-abortion feminists are saying. Many of the organizations that are throwing money, leadership or ideological support behind "abortion rights" (groups like NOW, Planned Parenthood, A.C.L.U., National Lawyers' Guild and others) have emphasized to their constituencies that the E.R.A. is important, perhaps essential, to reach their goals. Attorney Sarah Weddington, who successfully argued the case before the Supreme Court that resulted in the 1973 abortion decision, has insisted that the E.R.A. means the right to choose abortion. Significantly, she is one of the very people who would be most capable of engineering a platoon of test-case precedents to ensure that the E.R.A. will mean exactly what she says it will.

So it wasn't dumb gullibility that led many prolifers to believe there's an abortion/E.R.A. hook-up. They got their analysis from the pro-abortion E.R.A. faction.

All this made my head reel with ambivalence. I knew at some point I'd have to say either, "I don't care how much evidence there is: I will not accept that there's an abortion/E.R.A. link, because I don't want there to be a link" (a variation of "Don't bother me with facts, my mind's made up"); or else I would have to say, "I'd have to reconsider."

The Right-to-Life Convention did turn out to include a small but ardent Feminists for Life caucus. Their approach was to pass a resolution calling for a new amendment combining both the E.R.A.

and the H.L.A. (Human Life Amendment), a sort of Equal Human Life Rights Amendment: to "ensure equality of rights under the law for all persons, regardless of sex, from fertilization to natural death."

That made them and me feel clever to the max, like the inventors of the catamaran. But I was still dissatisfied. Out there in the real world, the fight would still be presented in terms of the E.R.A. without nuance: Take it or leave it.

The E.R.A. march didn't do much to intensify my feelings of solidarity. I was passing out the same old leaflet ("Pro-God, Pro-Life, Pro-E.R.A.") but the resistance was phenomenal. Right off the bat, a parade marshal told me I would not be allowed to pass out literature. ("Gee, I didn't get to see a newspaper this morning. They suspended the Constitution?") I ignored her prohibition and kept on working the crowd; but although I was festooned with feminist buttons, both women and men would take one look at the leaflet's headline and rebuff me as if I were a counter-demonstrator. It was grim.

I finally found a little knot of people with "People of Faith for E.R.A." buttons, Mennonites, Brethren with Catholic Women's Ordination people, who at least comprehended where I was coming from. Gratefully, I fell in with them for a while. It was like enjoying the solidarity with Feminists for Life in St. Louis: What a relief to be in cahoots. I'm not crazy; or, if I am crazy, I'm not alone.

I have withdrawn my argument that there is no connection between the E.R.A. and abortion, but I have not entirely recanted my pro-E.R.A. position. Instead, I'm using my catamaran as a shuttle between the two big ships that I believe must eventually dock together: the feminist movement and the prolife movement. Or, rather than a catamaran, I'd say I, and people like me, form a pontoon bridge, struggling to keep fingernail- and toenail-holds on both sides of the chasm. Our integrated prolife-feminist movement is small, but growing and developing rapidly.

In other words, we're an embryo. And we do have a right to live.

Judi Loesch is the founder of Prolifers for Survival, which opposes nuclear proliferation and abortion. P.O. Box 3316, Chapel Hill, NC 27514.

HLA *and* ERA —
Inedible Alphabet Soup?

by Gail Grenier Sweet and Nancy Randolph Pearcey

Feminists for Life of America supports both a Human Life Amendment and an Equal Rights Amendment. In some people's eyes the two may seem incompatible, the attempt to harmonize them producing a jumble of contradictions — an inedible "alphabet soup." In the eyes of many pro-lifers, the ERA is an open door to abortion on demand and no pro-life group can support it. To pro-choicers, the HLA would administer a blow not only to abortion rights but also to many other women's rights and no feminist can support it. Is pro-life feminism a hopelessly muddled position?

In fact neither amendment needs to produce the more extreme effects predicted by its opponents. Let's examine some specific allegations.

The HLA — is it Anti-Women?

Planned Parenthood and the National Abortion Rights Action League (NARAL) have waged massive campaigns against the HLA. These organizations have spent tens of thousands of dollars on full-page notices in major newspapers predicting the alarming effects a HLA would have on women. The following are some of the most common. Let's see how they stand up under scrutiny:

The HLA would criminalize women.

A constitutional amendment cannot in itself criminalize anything since the Constitution is not a body of criminal law. What the HLA would do is provide a constitutional foundation for the *states* to enact laws regulating abortion.

What kinds of laws the states would pass depends on how they interpret the amendment. We can make some educated guesses, however: since the HLA simply creates a return to pre-1973 conditions, we can look to former laws as a guide to predicting what effects it would have.

Prior to 1973 abortion was illegal under some conditions in all fifty states. But it was not legally defined as murder. That is, abortion was treated as an offence separately from the state's homicide statutes. Under former laws, moreover, women were not prosecuted — the one who was "criminalized" was the abortionist, not the mother. It is reasonable to predict that laws passed under a HLA would be similar.

The HLA would outlaw contraception.

The HLA is intended to protect the life of the unborn; obviously it cannot come into effect until *after* there is life to protect.

Contraception, on the other hand, occurs *before* there is life. The definition of contraception is that which prevents the beginning of life. Therefore any contraceptive agent (condom, diaphragm, spermicidal foam, and some forms of the Pill) would be unaffected by a HLA.

Women using the Pill or IUD would be prosecuted for murder.

This allegation rests on the fact that the IUD and some forms of the Pill are *not* contraceptive but abortifacient (i.e., they act *after* conception). At their 1984 caucus held at the National Right to Life convention, Feminists for Life of America resolved that:

> "Where birth control pills act to prevent implantation of the fertilized egg, such pills should be clearly labelled as abortifacients. All forms of birth control which may be abortifacient should be so labelled."

Under a HLA abortifacient drugs or devices could be regulated in some way or taken off the market, depending on how the amendment is interpreted.

The use of these products, however, does not fit any of the legal criteria for murder, no matter how the amendment is interpreted. A charge of murder requires at a minimum that there be a body for evidence. If a product works prior to positive proof of pregnancy there can be no way of knowing that a victim even existed. To predict that women using abortifacient drugs or devices will be prosecuted for murder is sheer scaremongering.

The HLA would prohibit research on new, safer forms of birth control.

Since it would inhibit research on abortifacients, the HLA would actually *increase* research on products that are truly contraceptive. FFLA supports such research, as well as education in natural family planning.

If this allegation refers to new forms of birth control which are abortive, however, it is true.

Chemical abortifacients, such as prostaglandins, which work after positive proof of pregnancy, would be outlawed. FFLA has long supported a boycott of Upjohn pharmaceutical products since Upjohn is a pioneer in the development and testing of "do-it-yourself-at-home" abortion drugs.

The HLA would intrude the government into private family planning decisions.

The HLA would not infringe on anyone's private life, which is protected already by the Fourth Amendment. What it would accomplish is to prevent the right to privacy from overriding the right to life.

The HLA would eliminate all legal abortions, even when the mother's life is in danger.

As before, the most reasonable predictions are made on the basis of previous abortion laws and their effects. Before 1973 all states, even those with the most restrictive laws against abortion, did allow it to save the life of the mother.

The ERA — Does it Support Abortion?

Having defined abortion as a woman's right, pro-choice feminists would have us believe that anyone who supports women's rights must support abortion. Pro-life feminists disagree. Women's rights, like the right to privacy, cannot supercede the right to life.

Logically, the ERA should have no impact on abortion. Its purpose is to prohibit discrimination on the basis of sex; anything which affects women only (such as pregnancy) or men only cannot be the basis for discrimination *between* men and women. A law regarding vasectomies, for example, could not generate prejudicial treatment of men in contrast to women, since only men would be affected. The same holds for a law regarding abortion.

On March 9, 1984, however, the Pennsylvania Commonwealth Court ruled that its state ERA entitled women to state funding of abortion. Classifying abortion as a "medical procedure," the Court argued that women were being denied funding for a medical service on the basis of sex. "Once the legislature has decided to grant financial assistance to the medically needy," Judge McPhail ruled, "it cannot exclude persons from that grant on the basis of sex."

Because of this decision, many members of FFLA feel that clarifying language should be added to the federal ERA before it is passed. Although some members still support the amendment in its original form (and there is room within our ranks for varying opinions), a majority now believe neutrality toward abortion should be written into the ERA.

There are two possible means of accomplishing this: either 1) introduce a new ERA which is explicitly abortion-neutral, or 2) support an amendment to the present ERA, such as the Sensenbrenner amendment, which reads:

> "Nothing in this Article [the ERA] shall be construed to grant or secure any right relating to abortion or the funding thereof."

Ironically, pro-choice feminists have consistently opposed the insertion of abortion-neutral wording. Yet they acknowledge that the reason our nation has remained in a deadlock over passage of the ERA for so long is precisely the abortion controversy. Many people would support an equal rights amendment if they were assured that a vote for the amendment is not a vote for abortion rights.

Resistance to abortion-neutral wording will undoubtedly be interpreted by ERA opponents as confirmation that many supporters intend to use it as a tool in the abortion struggle. Concern for passage of the ERA should prompt all its supporters to facilitate its progress by making it clearly and explicitly neutral toward abortion.

Synergy

Properly understood, the ERA and HLA do not contradict but actually strengthen and support one another. The ERA cannot enhance women's dignity at the expense of someone else's dignity (and life) — that of her *in utero* offspring. The attempt to do so is to women's own detriment: the attitude abortion produces toward women and their childbearing function is profoundly anti-feminist.

Easy abortion allows a woman's awkwardly unpredictable reproductive capacities to be subject to the ideology of control and domination which has been at the core of Western Humanism since the Enlightenment — which turns first nature and then human beings themselves into mechanisms to be used for economic ends. In practical terms, abortion ensures that a woman's pregnancy need never inconvenience her employer or interrupt her education. Women and their pre-born children are both subordinated to the overriding demands of economic interests.

In repudiating abortion we are saying that we will not be truly equal until our institutions respect women enough to accommodate to them — instead of demanding that they deny their femaleness and sacrifice their children in order to participate in society. Thus the HLA is actually supportive of women's dignity in the fullest sense.

Conversely, the HLA will not be effective without the support of the ERA. Most women who get abortions feel unwilling or unable to pay the price society exacts of mothers: in caring for young children, a woman faces the loss of job and education opportunities, the loss of income and peer contact, the loss of mobility and social involvements. Although childbearing has its own rewards, a woman whose pregnancy was unexpected and whose financial and social resources are already low (or whose career goals are high) may feel the cost is too great.

We cannot effectively discourage abortion unless we also initiate social changes that make motherhood less costly. A woman who is confident of continuing economic, educational, and social opportunities is less likely to resort to abortion to avoid the stresses of childrearing. The ERA is a step toward ensuring that, within the bounds of the law, society will accommodate itself to women and not force them to choose between motherhood and participation in society.

The abortion mentality encourages women to devalue motherhood in favour of career or social goals, to consider pregnancy expendable to other gains. In opposing abortion we stand against society's devaluation of women as mothers and commit ourselves to giving women the support they need to bear children with dignity. A full-orbed feminism thus envisions the HLA and ERA working together for the rights of all people.

Quiz

Under current U.S. law, which is not a person?...
(a) A Supreme Court judge.
(b) A corporation.
(c) An unborn child.
HINT: Who can hire the fewest lawyers?

Taken from a pamphlet distributed by Milwaukee S.O.U.L. (Save Our Unwanted Lives).

The ERA and Clarifying Language

by Susan Maronek

Feminists For Life of Wisconsin must express a difference of opinion with some members of the pro-life movement on the meaning of the Equal Rights Amendment. We do not believe that it will erode the right to life, but rather that the E.R.A. will enhance it. Feminists For Life of Wisconsin believe that abortion is one result of the historic and deep exploitation of, and discrimination against, the female. We believe that when this exploitation and discrimination end, the practice of abortion will also end. Therefore we believe in the necessity for an Equal Rights Amendment.

We call ourselves radical feminists. A "radical", by definition, gets at the "root" of a social problem. (Latin "radix" = root) We therefore note that not all radical feminists are against national right to life legislation since we actively support and work for the passage of a Human Life Amendment. We believe that if abortion is ended, and sexism remains, other evils will spring from this root. To be pro-life is to be for all human life and the enhancement of this life. The Equal Rights Amendment supports the full dignity and rights of the female.

It is a strange irony that other, pro-choice feminists, embrace abortion and define it as a fundamental feminist right instead of seeing it as a fundamental and devastating exploitation. Such a feminist embraces and cooperates in her own oppression.

Abortion, in the final analysis, works to the advantage of the exploitative male, not for the female. It provides an end to any and all financial, legal or social obligation which comes with childbirth by eliminating the possibility of birth. Abortion provides the ultimate rationale when pressing for sexual favors. It makes the female a perpetual and re-usable sex object. When an unwanted pregnancy occurs, the female is potentially left without any social support as all other persons, by legal definition, are irrelevant in the abortion/childbirth decision. The male can remove himself from the situation, physically or mentally, because abortion is "her" right. The female is left with the sole and final legal responsibility for killing their offspring. It is her body and mind which bear the scars of this destructive operation and experience.

The "Akron" decision by which the Supreme Court ruled that informed consent legislation is unconstitutional, made it abundantly clear that it is not the female who has the ultimate voice in the abortion decision but the abortionist. He determines what medical information is "necessary" for her "welfare". The abortionist has the ultimate power as he controls the necessary medical information pertinent to the abortion decision. Abortion is a male sexual fantasy come true. All that is necessary is that reality be denied — and denied it is.

An explanation as to why pro-choice feminists have adopted so anti-feminist a position is that they have been shut out of institutions that believe in the value of absolute good and thus of absolute worth. Institutional religion has excluded and failed to support feminists. Law, family, business — society generally, our history, — have similarly failed to give support to the female.

Deprived of support by institutions holding historic, traditional and long-standing values, fundamental beliefs and values can be shaken and replaced. Deprived of support from basic institutions in our society, many feminists have found a home in pro-choice gatherings. *They will not lightly jeopardize the one support group which has welcomed them.*

Abortion can be viewed as a statement that one's value and worth as a fully developed human being takes precedence over that of a being "in the making". It underscores the female's worth. Abortion also provides an escape from "motherhood" — a definite and sometimes permanent impediment to the attainment of social mobility. Abortion does allow a woman to compete for societally-defined "success" by eliminating the "burden" of children. Other perspectives can be found for the acceptance of abortion in pro-choice circles. Our point is to note that we believe that *abortion springs from sexism.*

A matter under dispute is whether there is anything in the Equal Rights Amendment which supports abortion. Feminists For Life of Wisconsin believe that there is not. We believe that the E.R.A. is "abortion neutral". Can the Supreme Court use the Equal Rights Amendment to support and advance abortion? As the Supreme Court has drawn the justification for abortion out of the thin air, it can use anything to support and advance abortion — and indeed does. The "right" to an abortion comes from *Roe vs. Wade*, the U.S. Supreme Court's abortion on demand decision of 1973. No one has the right to kill innocent human life (unless such killing is a by-product of unavoidable self-defense), or to make a decision which has the clear potential of killing innocent human life. *Roe vs. Wade* is murderous or clearly potentially murderous and hence should not be legal. In *Roe vs. Wade* the Supreme Court abrogated its responsibility; therefore the decision should have no legal authority. The Supreme Court, or any other body, or person, has no legal or moral authority to make this kind of ruling.

The argument of whether the E.R.A. will or will not be used to advance the practice of abortion hinges upon the question of whether the Supreme Court will approach the E.R.A. as an issue of due process or as an issue of sex discrimination.[1] "The Court's choice of a legal theory is crucial in determining whether it will find a constitutional violation and, if it does, what corrective steps it will require."[2] There is a Court history which demonstrates a preference for treating the E.R.A. as an issue of due process rather than of sex discrimination. However Court histories and Court philosophies do change. *Roe vs. Wade* made it very clear that at birth, the states did have a legitimate and legal interest in the treatment and welfare of the newborn. Thus one could reasonably believe that the full rights of the Constitution applied to any baby who survived the birth process. Yet Baby Doe, Baby Jane Doe, Philip Becker and others demonstrate that many courts view the "quality of life" standard reflected in *Roe vs. Wade* as superceding the application of the other rights of the Constitution to individuals. No one would have suspected that this application could be made, given the result, given that *Roe vs. Wade* granted more state interest in the protection of older children. Yet handicapped infants and adults are dying with the tacit or stated approval of the Court. This fact makes any past Court history or preference too tenuous to be trusted. And if the Supreme Court should immediately or eventually take a "sex discrimination and equal protection" approach to the E.R.A. — then legislation against abortion would indeed become difficult.

Since the nonlegal ruling of *Roe vs. Wade* has resulted in the deaths of millions of unborn children, the Supreme Court does have a vested interest in shielding itself from the consequences of its action. It seeks to give *Roe vs. Wade* an ever greater credibility as a valid legal ruling. The Equal Rights Amendment can be used to this end. But since *Roe vs. Wade* is not a legal ruling, the E.R.A. is thus illegally and improperly used. The E.R.A. does not promote abortion; it is the Supreme Court (in *Roe vs. Wade*) which is promoting abortion. Unfortunately the Supreme Court and pro-choice forces can "swallow the E.R.A. whole" to use it to advance unrestricted abortion on demand. Protective and clarifying language such as the Sensenbrenner Amendment thus becomes a necessity. I believe that with such clarifying language, passage of the E.R.A. would be guaranteed.

Feminists For Life of Wisconsin has always believed that feminist rights are undermined when the rights of any other person or group, including the unborn, are denied or destroyed. The rights of people are intertwined and buttress one another. This is especially true of the mother and her child, born and unborn. The female's fundamental make-up involves life-giving processes, often in a very physical manner.

The passage of an Equal Rights Amendment and a Human Life Amendment continue to be Feminists For Life stated goals. We continue to be committed to these goals. We therefore continue to cooperate and work to protect the unborn. We continue to believe, however, that the welfare of the female and the welfare of the unborn are intimately connected and to promote the dignity of one is to promote the dignity of the other. We believe that the passage of an E.R.A. and an H.L.A. is necessary to promote the dignity and protection of the born and unborn.

[1]Elizabeth Alexander and Maureen Fielder, "The Equal Rights Amendment and Abortion: Separate and Distinct", *America*, (April 12, 1980), 314-317.
[2]*Ibid.*, p. 316.

Pro-Abortionists Poison Feminism

by Rosemary Bottcher

Support for abortion rights is generally considered to be the *sine qua non* of feminism. Gloria Steinem has flatly stated that it is impossible to be a pro-life feminist; it is a contradiction in terms. I disagree. In fact, I believe it is hypocritical for feminists not be pro-life, and that the pro-abortion stance of the orthodox women's liberation movement is poisoning the roots of feminism.

The basic tenet of feminism is that human life can take forms other than that of a tall, dark, handsome Caucasian male and that all classes of human being have innate value and ought to have equal rights. Feminism is, properly, merely part of a larger philosophy that values all human life.

Feminists deeply resent the discrimination women have suffered at the hands of men. Men have used their power to deny women some basic rights. The price of men's privilege has been paid by women, and the price is too high. Feminists believe that rights must be ranked; one cannot demand a right that deprives another of a more important right. A woman's right to lead her own life, fulfill her own potential, is more important than a man's right to special privilege. Decency requires that men make some sacrifices to prevent larger sacrifices being unjustly imposed upon women.

This is a reasonable position, but the pro-abortion feminists dilute the force of its persuasiveness by hypocritically refusing to grant the unborn the same rights they demand for themselves.

Pro-abortion feminists resent the discrimination against a whole class of humans because they happen to be female, yet they themselves discriminate against a whole class of humans because they happen to be very young. They resent that the value of a woman is determined by whether some man wants her, yet they declare that the value of an unborn child is determined by whether some woman wants him. They resent that women have been "owned" by their husbands, yet insist that the unborn are "owned" by their mothers. They believe that a man's right to do what he pleases with his own body cannot include the right to sexually exploit women, yet proclaim that a woman's similar right means that she can kill her unborn child.

The rhetoric of pro-abortion feminists is also damaging the cause of women's rights. The shrillness and anger they often display does nothing to dispel the myth of women as irrational and emotional. Besides mangling the language, contorting logic, misrepresenting the facts and steadfastly refusing to face the real issue, their bombast presents a very unflattering view of women.

Faye Wattleton, president of Planned Parenthood, states, "If we don't win (the abortion fight) millions of women will be forced to bear unwanted children, and many of them will be condemned to lives of trauma, abuse, hopelessness and despair." Does she think women are incompetent, incapable of handling stress and cannot be good mothers except under ideal circumstances?

Pro-abortionists then contradict themselves by saying that making abortions illegal will not reduce their numbers; women will have them anyway. Does that mean that women are irresponsible and undependable, that they cannot be counted on to obey the law; they never have and they never will? We are told that they will be "forced" to seek illegal abortions. Does that mean that they are weak and witless and cannot resist this "force"?

According to one feminist writer, women fail to control their sexual behavior because, "We are told we cannot say no because we will be called prudes, frigid or cruel...or beaten up." Does she think that women are so insecure that they will risk unwanted pregnancies to avoid displeasing men?

The suggestion that women bearing unwanted children could surrender them for adoption is greeted with indignant outrage. The implication is that women cannot be expected to conform to a standard of minimal decency, much less one of selflessness.

It is ironic that feminists have made abortion the symbol of their liberation, because two major supporters of abortion rights are those bastions of male chauvinism, the Playboy Foundation and the medical establishment.

Playboy's attitude toward women is well known, and it is stubbornly anti-feminist. Hugh Hefner once ordered an attack upon feminists in a memorandum to his editors that declared, "These chicks are our natural enemies." The playboy has no sympathy for feminism because feminism elevates women to the status of persons. It is not really surprising, then, that he is such an ardent fan of abortion, because abortion reduces women to the status of sex machines — which can be "repaired" if necessary.

Abortion helps ease his anxiety about sex and relieves him of the last vestige of responsibility. At last sex is really free! Abortion negates the one awesome power that women have: The power to nurture new life.

Abortion reduces women to the level of the playboy: shallow, callow and fallow. Abortion represents the "castration" of women.

The medical literature also frequently expresses a frankly contemptuous view of women having abortions. One journal editorialized against the Akron, Ohio ordinance that requires that a woman have explained to her the characteristics of her fetus before she has an abortion, because, "This information merely adds to her stress". In another journal, a physician recommended the dilitation and evacuation procedure for a woman having a late abortion because, anesthetized, "She is allowed to continue her pattern of denial." A woman having a salt poisoning abortion actually delivers a dead or dying baby, and this "forces her to come to terms with the significance of her decision". In other words, he seems to be saying, keep her ignorant. If she knew what she was doing, she might become upset.

It seems as though pro-abortionists are agreeing that women are helpless, cowardly, submissive, hysterical and empty-headed. Women are incapable of resistance and are forever being forced to do things. They are forced to engage in sexual activity, forced to become pregnant and forced to seek illegal abortions. This reinforces the traditional concept of women as having "diminished responsibility". They cannot be held to the same standards as men because they are not as competent as men.

The law expects and requires that a man provide for his children, even though doing so may cause him much inconvenience. He cannot demand that he be excused from his obligation because his career, schooling, health or emotional well-being might suffer. He knew what he was doing when he did it and should expect to be held accountable. Men are expected to be mature, and the mark of maturity is the willingness to accept the consequences of one's actions, even though doing so may cause sacrifice and even hardship. Women who want equality can demand no less of themselves.

Taken from the *Tallahassee Democrat*, P.O. Box 990, Tallahassee, Florida 32302-0990. Reprinted with permission of the author.

Feminists: Developing a 'Party Line'

by Richard Cohen

A woman called the other day and stated her credentials: She was a feminist. She had headed up this organization and that organization. She had been to all the required conventions and she subscribed to all the proper magazines and she has read all the required books. Her standing in the ranks of feminists was secure, yet she opposed abortion.

This, she argued, did not strip her of her standing as a feminist. But some people, she said, thought it did. She and others like her were constantly being lumped in with women and men who were not feminists, who not only opposed abortion, but also the Equal Rights Amendment and conscription for women and birth control and maybe — just for good measure — the 20th century. She resented this.

The woman went on. She was a liberal. She had been raised in a liberal home and liberal causes were her causes. She had marched. She had protested. She has sat-in and sat-down and opened her purse for civil rights and civil liberties. She was a union maid from way back, but just because she was opposed to abortion she was being called a conservative — a virtual reactionary. She was more than upset. She was angry.

She had a right to be. For too long now, abortion has been the *sine qua non* of a whole lot of movements. To many, it seems impossible that someone could be both a feminist and opposed to abortion. On the other hand, to many conservatives, it is just the other way around. The furor over Sandra O'Connor, President Reagan's Supreme Court nominee, is almost entirely over abortion, which is, after all, only one issue — and maybe an issue that has already been settled. No matter. To some people, there is no way to be a conservative as long as you are soft on abortion.

It is the same with feminists. There is a certain validity to the view that abortion is sometimes opposed for what could be called anti-feminist reasons. Some people clearly think of pregnancy as punishment for sex, especially sex outside of marriage. In this view, anything that would eliminate pregnancy as an inhibiting factor — abortion, birth control, sex education — is to be opposed.

Similarly, there are some men who consider abortion threatening. They think it means a loss of the traditional control men have had over women. This may be the emotional force behind attempts to forbid abortions that are not approved by fathers or husbands. And this may also be why some women revert time and time again to what is now a cliché about control over their own bodies. Abortion, of course, has to do with their own bodies, but it also has to do with someone else's body — or the potential of one.

Still, there are people who want no control over women, who are not threatened by female sexuality, but who are nevertheless morally and ethically opposed to abortion. And to say, fine, hold that position but don't try to impose it on others begs the question. If I considered abortion to be murder, I would try through the political process to ban it. This is how I feel about capital punishment, and no one is going to tell me that I shouldn't use the political process to try to abolish it.

Politics is the proper forum for the abortion controversy. But abortion is not the one and only political issue — not the one issue that defines who you are politically. The insistence that it be that weakens not only the conservative movement, but feminism as well. It is reminiscent of attempts throughout history to impose a doctrinal purity on large ideological or religious movements. People have always been told that they could not be what they wanted to be — Christians or Jews or even Whigs — if they did not believe such and such. When the Communists attempted to do this, all they really succeeded in doing was to contribute the term "party line" to the language.

Well, feminists, especially the more doctrinaire ones, are developing their own party line. They are attempting to define a movement very narrowly: You can't be against abortion. You can't be blasé about pornography. You have to be blind to the real differences between men and women. You have to be this and you have to be that. But the fact of the matter is that all you need to be a feminist is to believe in, and work for, the equality of women. It's my club, too — and anyone can join.

What Things Have Come To

by Paulette Joyer

In the beginning there seemed to be a lot of talk about the Sisterhood and women helping women. We were going to find our own identities; to claim equal opportunities in education, work and politics; we were going to eliminate sexism. And, oh, yes, we were going to secure our reproductive freedom.

"Reproductive freedom" is a term that early on got mis-defined to mean the "right" to "terminate" our unborn children, popularly known as "products of conception," "blob of cells," and "contents of the uterus." Or, if space was short, "the pregnancy" as in "terminate the pregnancy."

Abortion has now become THE FOCUS of the old guard feminists' movement. They are positively rabid in their insistence that if you don't want to work for abortion "rights" they don't want you. In an effort to purify "their" movement, so-called feminists leaders are attempting to eliminate from the ranks any would-be supporters who don't support a woman's right to kill her unborn child.

In 1981, Minnesota Feminists For Life was rejected from the Minnesota Women's Consortium (MWC) and by the Take Back the Night rally organizers. But even before that many letters from us offering our help on ERA-related activities have gone unanswered by women's groups with whom we have much in common.

In an October 1981 article recounting MFFL's woes with the MWC and the Take Back-people, *Twin Cities* magazine asked MWC coordinator Gloria Griffin about her flip-flop posture toward MFFL. Griffin, you will remember from this summer's newsletter, had stated publicly that MFFL would be accepted into the Consortium but then wrote us a letter of rejection.

'Originally, that was the way I felt,' Griffin [said] about her radio remarks. 'I really had hoped that all women could work together.' But, others, she said, told her, 'Wait a minute.'...Freedom of choice on abortion is basic to being a feminist, said Griffin.

In an article in the September 1981 *Ms.* magazine ("Abortion Rights: Taking the Offensive") Naomi Weisstein, a brain scientist at State University of New York, urges feminists not to build coalitions. "This time, we can't afford to waste our energies and our passions beseeching a recalcitrant Left to keep the faith with us." And to what should feminists be devoting all of our attentions? Abortion! She writes, "If feminists retreat from a focused defense of abortion rights — one of our most dramatic and popularly supported victories — we will be falling into [a] trap. We will narrow the permissible social options and broadcast to the public that we ourselves think there's something shamefully un-American about wanting our basic rights — in this case, abortion on demand."

Something new in Minnesota from the feminist old guard was Project 13. The "13" stands for the number of states needed to stop ratification of a Human Life Amendment once it is passed out of Congress. In a *Minneapolis Tribune* article ("Abortion-rights group to try to pack caucuses") Project 13 organizers describe their "high-visibility, big-budget ($200,000) political education effort." But do not call them *single issue.*

"That's what people say about us when they don't want to take a stand," Koryne Horbal said. " 'This is not a single issue to women — this is a real right.' " (October 2, 1981)

Will this new hit-them-over-the-head strategy accomplish anything? We think not. As one pro-life feminist said in her letter to MFFL, "When people become more concerned with expelling heretics than with building coalitions, they usually are on the way out."

We would tend to agree with MFFL member Carol Wold Sindt who was contacted by the *Tribune* in her position as DFL Pro-Life Caucus leader for a reaction to Project 13.

"The feminists outnumber us only when they have several issues in mind. They won't see all their members jumping into this one. Will Project 13 change the Minnesota legislature? Fat chance."

The old guard feminists have failed to understand mainstream American women and that failure has resulted in a doomed ERA. They are doomed again. The only people more out of touch with the real world than the old style feminist leaders are their followers.

For example, I was out for a social evening recently with a friend and a pro-abortion feminist in our group, learning that we oppose abortion, attempted to stop us in our tracks with this piercing question, "Do you believe in survival of the fittest?" *Do we believe in survival of the fittest?* Whatever happened to civilization and the fit taking care of the unfit? Do *you* believe in survival of the fittest?

We were invited in to speak to a Women's Studies class at the University of Minnesota during the summer session. The entire class rejects that the fetus is human or alive. These college women can't really say what *it* is but they don't *believe* it's human and alive. For 55 minutes we talk biology (but of course, we would) and they talk belief (don't you understand?).

A letter to the editor in the *Minneapolis Star* (Oct. 6, 1981) from an Abortion Rights Council booth staffer defends certain historical cultures for controlling their populations through infanticide. In a rambling, disjointed letter she expresses exasperation that "civilized, religious Western types" view infanticide as immoral. Children are starving all over the world. "We do the humane thing: We force people into life and then show no mercy when they suffer and starve."

In the pro-abortion feminist scheme of things one can't care for the woman *and* her child, born and unborn. In the pro-abortion feminist world view one can't care for the hungry *and* the small. By their reasoning it is better to kill the babies than let them die. Other alternatives don't count.

Tunnel-visioned pro-abortion feminists cannot see to help develop real alternatives to abortion, programs of support for women with hardship pregnancies, a change in society's attitude toward pregnant women so that young women won't automatically think that, once pregnant, they can never attend college, never pursue a career, not go on living. Pro-abortion feminists are part of the problem — they contribute to a "pregnancy as disease", "fetus as cancer" attitude that turns a normal, natural function of a woman's body into something to be attacked with curette and vacuum. Is this creative thinking? Is this women supporting women? What kind of "sisterhood" have we wreaked upon ourselves?

But there is hope. "Julie" is a young, Smith College student with whom Barbara Grizzuti Harrison spoke when researching her October *Harper's Magazine* article, "What Do Women Want?" What does Julie want?:

"I want to be a writer. But first I want to work for a world where nobody ever has to have an abortion. I want to get birthright organizations established, you know, like day-care centers. Society doesn't make room for unwanted children, so women have to kill them. I hate that so much. I see abortion as a symptom of women's oppression. Gosh, I'm afraid to tell the feminists at the Women's Resource Center that I think that."

First published in *Minnesota Feminists for Life Newsletter*, September/October 1981. Reprinted with permission.

Feminism and Abortion —
The Great Inconsistency

by Daphne de Jong

In the same way that many opponents of slavery and racism have failed to apply their principles to the question of women's rights, so feminist writers have a peculiarly dense blind spot about the unborn.

No argument in favor of freely available abortion is tenable in the light of feminist ideals and principles. And all of them bear an alarming resemblance to the arguments used by men to justify discrimination against women.

Principally, the arguments are: that the fetus is not human, or is human only in some rudimentary way; that it is a part of its mother and has no rights of its own; that a woman's right to control her body supercedes any rights of the fetus; that those who believe the fetus is a human being with human rights should not impose their beliefs on others through the medium of the law.

Biologically, the fetus is not only human, but an individual human by virtue of its unique genetic inheritance. Six weeks from conception it looks like a very small baby, with a functioning heart, brain and nervous system. The appearance and behaviour of very early foetal infants show definite individual patterns. After implantation of the fertilized ovum (and many would say from the first fusion of the parent cells), scientists are unable to pinpoint any stage at which something "subhuman" becomes a human being.

Regardless of arbitrary legal definitions, the concept of a definitive moment when humanity becomes present is simply the ancient religious theory of "ensoulment" rephrased in pseudo-philosophical jargon. Medieval theologians postulated "ensoulment" at 40 days for boys and 80 days for girls. Even in the 19th century, philosopher Otto Weininger wrote: "In such a being as the absolute female there are no logical and ethical phenomena, and therefore the ground for the assumption of a soul is absent...Women have no existence and no essence; they are not; they are nothing."

Weininger described Jews in similar terms. Eva Figes, author of *Patriarchal Attitudes*, comments on those views: "It soon becomes possible to deny such inferiors basic human rights. The implication is that these inferiors are not human at all."

Kate Millett recognized the same phenomenon in *Sexual Politics:* "The rationale which accompanies that imposition of male authority euphemistically referred to as "the battle of sexes" bears a certain resemblance to the formulas of nations at war, where any heinousness is justified on the ground that the enemy is either an inferior species or really not human at all."

Women were not, of course, "nothing" because Weininger believed them to be so. Neither is the fetus just a collection of matter because others do not accept its humanity. It is only the latest in a long line of human beings who throughout history have been denied human status because of their "different" appearance. They include Blacks, Jews, dwarfs, the handicapped — and women.

Feminist writers clearly see the link between feminism and racism. "It should," Figes says, "teach us a valuable lesson about the dangers of attempting to categorize people on the basis of physique — whether it is a matter of sex or skin color."

Perhaps it should also teach us something about categorizing people on the basis of immaturity. Especially since alleged immaturity or "childishness" has been the excuse for sexual discrimination, too. Idealist philosopher Schopenhauer found women "In every respect backward, lacking in reason or true morality... a kind of middle step between the child and the man, who is the true human being."

The unborn, particularly in the embryonic stage, bears little resemblance to the "norm" of the adult white male. Feminists ought to be sensitive about arguing the non-humanity of the fetus on the grounds of its physical appearance or size, or ability to function independently.

Jessica Starr, visiting New Zealand to preach abortion on demand, contemptuously characterized the two-month fetus as "a thing the size of a cashew nut." She might have been wise to remember that size has always been a factor in the supposed superiority of the male. Not to mention all those careful measurements of male and female brains. Even now misogynist writers deny women the potential for genius because of "smaller brain capacity." (Fetal brains have similar configurations to adult brains, and EEG tracings have been made at less than six weeks gestation.)

Until this century, the laws of both Britain and America made women a "part of" their husbands.

"By marriage, the husband and wife are one person in law...our law in general considers man and wife one person." (Blackstone's *Commentaries,* 1768).

The one person was, of course, the husband, who exerted absolute power over his wife and her property. She had no existence and therefore no protection under the law. The only thing a husband could not do was kill her.

The earliest feminist battles were fought against the legal chattel status of women. Many feminists were among those who overturned the U.S. Supreme Court decision of 1857, that a black slave was "property" and not entitled to the protection of the constitution. Feminism totally rejected the concept of ownership in regard to human beings. Yet when the court ruled in 1973 that the fetus was the property of its mother, and not entitled to the protection of the Constitution, "liberated" women danced in the streets.

A fetus, while dependent on its mother, is no more a part of its mother than she a part of her husband. Biology is constant; not subject to the vagaries of law. The fetus lives its own life, develops according to its own genetic programme, sleeps, wakes, moves, according to its own inclinations. The RH negative syndrome which occurs when fetal and maternal blood are incompatible, is one proof of its separate life.

That a woman or a doctor does not perceive a fetus or embryo as human is not sufficient reason to put abortion outside the context of morality and law. Most people find babies more attractive than embryos, as most of us prefer kittens to cats, and as Hitler found Aryans more attractive than Jews.

To define humanity on the basis of one's emotional response is to rationalize prejudice.

To allow any person or group to define that certain human beings are to be regarded as less than fully human, is to construct a basis for discrimination and eventual destruction.

"Liberated" women who object to being "sex objects" may not care to examine too closely their conviction that embryos and fetuses are expendable objects which become less so as they grow more visually attractive.

There have always been "lawful" exceptions to the universal ban on taking human life; notably self defense and abortion to save the woman's life. The mainstream feminist movement rejects most other exceptions, such as warfare and judicial retribution. Feminism opposes the violent power games of the male establishment, the savage "solutions" imposed by the strong on the powerless.

The feminist claim to equality is based on the equal rights of all human beings. The most fundamental of all is the right to life. If women are to justify taking this right from the unborn, they must contend that their own superiority of size, of power, or of physique or intellect or need, or their own value as a person, transcends any right of the unborn.

In the long history of male chauvinism, all these have been seen as good reasons for withholding human rights from women.

The temptation to dominate is the most truly universal, the most irresistible one there is; to surrender the child to its mother, the wife to her husband, is to promote tyranny in the world. (Simone de Beauvoir: *The Second Sex.*)

To claim that the unique interdependence of the fetus and its mother is sufficient to give her absolute rights over its life, is to claim a right which society in general, and feminists in particular, do not concede to anyone else — the arbitrary right to terminate a human life. Women who will not accept that a woman's value be measured by how far some man wants her body or needs her services, now demand that the unborn be judged by the same standard — to be allowed to live or die on one criterion, its sentimental value to its mother.

Since Nuremberg, the world has accepted that those who perceive the humanity of groups defined as "subhuman" have not only a right but a duty to protect their human rights. Those who are unconvinced by medical and biological science have a right to try to persuade others to their view. But they must recognize the obligation of those who believe in the human-ness of the fetus, to oppose them. Not to do so would be "...truly irresponsible. To abdicate one's own moral understanding, to tolerate crimes against humanity." (Germaine Greer: *The Female Eunuch.*)*

How many feminists would defend the right of a man who sincerely believed in the inferiority of women, to beat, rape and terrorize "his" woman? Should the law allow him his right to choose who is to be regarded as fully human?

---

*Greer was writing in general terms. Like other feminist writers notably de Beauvoir, who was enraged at the callousness of lovers and society toward pregnant women, she fails to see the radical injustice of inflicting abortion on them as a "solution" to their problems.

This article was originally published in the *New Zealand Listener*, January 7, 1978, and is reprinted here with permission of the author.

How Do Pro-Choicers "Fool" Themselves?

by Rosemary Bottcher

When I first emerged from the closet about 10 years ago my friends were aghast. "We can't believe it!" they wailed, "You're so liberal!"

I have always thought it peculiar how the liberal and conservative philosophies have lined up on the abortion issue.

It seemed to me that liberals traditionally have cared about others and about human rights, while conservatives have cared about themselves and property rights. Therefore, one would expect liberals to be defending the unborn and conservatives to be encouraging their destruction. This apparent irony has caused me to change my opinion of conservatives and to wonder how liberals could have arrived at their illogical position.

It seems to me that there are basically two types of people who favor abortion on demand:

The smaller group is made up of cynical, cold-blooded utilitarians who believe that society's attitude toward its citizens should be like that of a farmer who cares for his livestock only as long as they produce wealth for him. Sentiment must never interfere with profit. They are well aware that abortion is killing, and they believe that killing is a useful social tool.

Some are just now beginning to suggest that killing for the sake of expedience should not stop at the unborn; prudence demands that all "useless eaters" be destroyed: the handicapped, the chronically ill, the criminal, perhaps even the dissident. Those who hold this view are basically evil people devoid of compassion or sentiment, and barring a religious experience, they will not change their minds.

The majority of pro-abortionists are good people. Many are involved in missions of mercy and expend great effort in helping the disadvantaged, the helpless, the unwanted.

So how can it be that they approve of abortion?

They lie.

They go to elaborate lengths to deceive themselves and others. They use such phrases as "mass of cells" and "pregnancy tissue" to refer to a perfectly formed human being.

Suction abortion "vacuums out the uterus", merely a housekeeping chore. Saline causes the uterus to "reject what's in it." Hysterotomy is a surgical procedure to remove the "products of conception."

I asked an avid pro-abortionist if she was disturbed by the suffering of the Weaver baby, a three-pound baby girl who was allegedly strangled after she survived a bungled abortion. The kind lady assured me that she was not at all bothered by that sort of thing, because "That wasn't a baby; it was an abortion."

A physician was quoted in the *American Journal of Obstetrics and Gynecology* as saying that he preferred the risky saline abortion, because it did not require that he ever see the baby. The D & E technique is safer and less traumatic for the mother, he agreed, but it required that he cut a live baby to pieces, and "I don't like to think of myself as killing babies." Such sophistry would be funny if its consequences were not so grim.

The same people who wax hysterical at the thought of executing, after countless appeals, a criminal convicted of some revolting crime would have insisted on his mother's unconditional right to have him killed while he was still innocent.

The same people who organized a boycott of the Nestlé Company for its marketing of infant formula in underdeveloped lands would have approved of the killing of those exploited infants only a few months before.

The same people who talk incessantly of human rights are willing to deny the most helpless and vulnerable of all human beings the most important right of all.

Apparently these people do not understand the difference between contraception and abortion.

Their arguments defending abortion would be perfectly reasonable if they were talking about contraception. When they insist upon "reproductive freedom" and "motherhood by choice" they forget that "pregnant" means "being with child." A pregnant woman has already reproduced; she is already a mother.

Robert Jay Lifton, an American psychiatrist, is conducting a fascinating psychological study of the Nazi doctors who planned and managed the notorious German death camps.

How could German physicians, heirs to Europe's proudest medical tradition, participate in mass slaughter? How could they preside over killings while viewing themselves as idealists?

He concluded that most of these men were not maniacs. They were ordinary people who were led by circumstances to commit extraordinarily evil acts.

They justified their execrable activities in the following ways: First, they allowed themselves to be seduced by the "If it's legal, it must be moral" fallacy. Secondly, they denied that those who were being killed were fully human; the Jews were referred to as "Untermenschen." Thirdly, they talked compulsively about technical matters to avoid confronting the reality of the horrors around them. The killing was projected as a medical operation. Finally, they convinced themselves that while what was being done was unpleasant, it was necessary and, in the long run, for the good of mankind.

Incredibly, they saw genocide as a health measure. Lifton calls this elaborate lattice of self-deception "psychic numbness."

The analogy to the abortionists' logic is obvious, but I do not mean to compare the average American who approves of abortion to Nazi doctors. Most pro-abortionists know nothing of fetology, have never even seen an aborted baby, and do not appreciate the humanity of the unborn. Yet there does seem to be a definite reluctance to learn, a deliberate ignorance.

The truth is suspected, but the truth is painful; it cannot be confronted. This in itself is a form of psychic numbness.

It will be very difficult for good people to admit to themselves that they have condoned the killing of eight million human beings. But every day that we fail to face the wrenching reality of this modern day Holocaust, more than 4,000 American children will be put to death — without trial, without appeal — for the crime of being unwanted.

Taken from the *Tallahassee Democrat*, P.O. Box 990, Tallahassee, Florida 32302-0990. Reprinted with permission of the author.

Abortion: The Left Has Betrayed
The Sanctity of Life

by Mary Meehan

The abortion issue, more than most, illustrates the occasional tendency of the Left to become so enthusiastic over what is called a "reform" that it forgets to think the issue through. It is ironic that so many on the Left have done on abortion what the conservatives and Cold War liberals did on Vietnam: They marched off in the wrong direction, to fight the wrong war, against the wrong people.

Some of us who went through the anti-war struggles of the 1960's and early 1970's are now active in the right-to-life movement. We do not enjoy opposing our old friends on the abortion issue, but we feel that we have no choice. We are moved by what pro-life feminists call the "consistency thing" — the belief that respect for human life demands opposition to abortion, capital punishment, euthanasia, and war. We don't think we have either the luxury or the right to choose some types of killing and say that they are all right, while others are not. A human life is a human life; and if equality means anything, it means that society should not value some human lives over others.

Until the last decade, people on the Left and Right generally agreed on one rule: We all protected the young. This was not merely agreement on an ethical question: It was also an expression of instinct, so deep and ancient that it scarcely required explanation.

Protection of the young included protection of the unborn, for abortion was forbidden by state laws throughout the United States. Those laws reflected an ethical consensus, not based solely on religious tradition but also on scientific evidence that human life begins at conception. The prohibition of abortion in the ancient Hippocratic Oath is well known. Less familiar to many is the Oath of Geneva, formulated by the World Medical Association in 1948, which included these words: "I will maintain the utmost respect for human life from the time of conception." A Declaration of the Rights of the Child, adopted by the United Nations General Assembly in 1959, declared that "the child, by reason of his physical and mental immaturity, needs special safeguards and care, including appropriate legal protection, before as well as after birth."

It is not my purpose to explain why courts and parliaments in many nations rejected this tradition over the past few decades, though I

suspect their action was largely a surrender to technical achievement —
if such inventions as suction aspirators can be called technical
"achievements." But it is important to ask why the Left in the United
States generally accepted legalized abortion.

One factor was the popular civil libertarian rationale for freedom of
choice in abortion. Many feminists presented it as a right of women to
control their own bodies. When the objection was raised that abortion
ruins another person's body, they respond that (a) it is not a body, just
a "blob of protoplasm" (thereby displaying ignorance of biology); or
(b) it is not really a "person" until it is born. When it was suggested that
this is a wholly arbitrary decision, unsupported by any biological
evidence, they said, "Well, that's your point of view. This is a matter of
individual conscience, and in a pluralistic society people must be free to
follow their consciences."

Unfortunately, many liberals and radicals accepted this view
without further question. Perhaps many did not know that an eight-
week-old fetus has a fully human form. They did not ask whether
American slaveholders before the Civil War were right in viewing
blacks as less than human and as private property, or whether the
Nazis were correct in viewing mental patients, Jews, and Gypsies as less
than human and therefore subject to the final solution.

Class issues provided another rationale. In the 1960's, liberals were
troubled by evidence that rich women could obtain abortions
regardless of the law, by going to careful society doctors or to countries
where abortion was legal. Why, they asked, should poor women be
barred from something the wealthy could have? One might turn this
argument on its head by asking why rich children should be denied
protection that poor children have.

But pro-life activists did not want abortion to be a class issue one
way or the other; they wanted to end abortion everywhere, for all classes. And many people who had experienced poverty did not think
providing legal abortion was any favor to poor women. Thus, in 1972,
when a Presidential commission on population growth recommended
legalized abortion, partly to remove discrimination against poor
women, several commission members dissented.

One was Graciela Olivarez, a Chicana who was active in civil rights
and anti-poverty work. Olivarez, who later was named to head the
Federal Government's Community Services Administration, had
known poverty in her youth in the Southwest. With a touch of
bitterness, she said in her dissent, "The poor cry out for justice and
equality and we respond with legalized abortion." Olivarez noted that

blacks and Chicanos had often been unwanted by white society. She added, "I believe that in a society that permits the life of even one individual (born or unborn) to be dependent on whether that life is 'wanted' or not, all its citizens stand in danger." Later she told the press, "We do not have equal opportunities. Abortion is a cruel way out."

Many liberals were also persuaded by a church/state argument that followed roughly this line: "Opposition to abortion is a religious viewpoint, particularly a Catholic viewpoint. The Catholics have no business imposing their religious views on the rest of us." It is true that opposition to abortion is a religious position for many people. Orthodox Jews, Mormons, and many of the fundamentalist Protestant groups also oppose abortion. (So did the mainstream Protestant churches until recent years.) But many people are against abortion for reasons that are independent of religious authority or belief. Many would still be against abortion if they lost their faith; others are opposed to it after they have lost their faith, or if they never had any faith. Only if their non-religious grounds for opposition can be proven baseless could legal prohibition of abortion fairly be called an establishment of religion. The pro-abortion forces concentrate heavily on religious arguments against abortion and generally ignore the secular arguments — possibly because they cannot answer them.

Still another, more emotional reason is that so many conservatives oppose abortion. Many liberals have difficulty accepting the idea that Jesse Helms can be right about anything. I do not quite understand this attitude. Just by the law of averages, he has to be right about something, sometime. Standing at the March for Life rally at the U.S. Capitol last year, and hearing Senator Helms say that "We reject the philosophy that life should be only for the planned, the perfect, or the privileged," I thought he was making a good civil-rights statement.

If much of the leadership of the pro-life movement is right-wing, that is due largely to the default of the Left. We "little people" who marched against the war and now march against abortion would like to see leaders of the Left speaking out on behalf of the unborn. But we see only a few, such as Dick Gregory, Mark Hatfield, Richard Neuhaus, Mary Rose Oakar. Most of the others either avoid the issue or support abortion. We are dismayed by their inconsistency. And we are not impressed by arguments that we should work and vote for them because they are good on such issues as food stamps and medical care.

Although many liberals and radicals accepted legalized abortion, there are signs of uneasiness about it. Tell someone who supports it that you have many problems with the issue, and she is likely to say, quickly, "Oh, I don't think I could ever have one myself, but...." or "I'm really not pro-abortion; I'm pro-choice" or "I'm personally opposed to it, but...."

Why are they personally opposed to it if there is nothing wrong with it?

Perhaps such uneasiness is a sign that many on the Left are ready to take another look at the abortion issue. In the hope of contributing toward a new perspective, I offer the following points:

First, it is out of character for the Left to neglect the weak and helpless. The traditional mark of the Left has been its protection of the underdog, the weak, and the poor. The unborn child is the most helpless form of humanity, even more in need of protection than the poor tenant farmer or the mental patient or the boat people on the high seas. The basic instinct of the Left is to aid those who cannot aid themselves — and that instinct is absolutely sound. It is what keeps the human proposition going.

Second, the right to life underlies and sustains every other right we have. It is, as Thomas Jefferson and his friends said, self-evident. Logically, as well as in our Declaration of Independence, it comes before the right to liberty and the right to property. The right to exist, to be free from assault by others, is the basis of equality. Without it, the other rights are meaningless, and life becomes a sort of warfare in which force decides everything. There is no equality, because one person's convenience takes precedence over another's life, provided only that the first person has more power. If we do not protect this right for everyone, it is not guaranteed for everyone, because anyone can become weak and vulnerable to assault.

Third, abortion is a civil-rights issue. Dick Gregory and many other blacks view abortion as a type of genocide. Confirmation of this comes in the experience of pro-life activists who find open bigotry when they speak with white voters about public funding of abortion. Many white voters believe abortion is a solution for the welfare problem and a way to slow the growth of the black population. I worked two years ago for a liberal, pro-life candidate who was appalled by the number of anti-black comments he found when discussing the issue. And Representative Robert Dornan of California, a conservative pro-life leader, once told his colleagues in the House, "I have heard many rock-ribbed Republicans brag about how fiscally conservative they are and then tell me that I was an idiot on the abortion issue." When he asked why, said Dornan, they whispered, "Because we have to hold them down, we have to stop the population growth." Dornan elaborated: "To them, population growth means blacks, Puerto Ricans, or other Latins," or anyone who "should not be having more than a polite one or two 'burdens on society.' "

Fourth, abortion exploits women. Many women are pressured by spouses, lovers, or parents into having abortions they do not want. Sometimes the coercion is subtle, as when a husband complains of financial problems. Sometimes it is open and crude, as when a boyfriend threatens to end the affair unless the woman has an abortion, or when parents order a minor child to have an abortion. Pro-life activists who do "clinic counseling" (standing outside abortion clinics, trying to speak to each woman who enters, urging her to have the child) report that many women who enter clinics alone are willing to talk and to listen. Some change their minds and decide against abortion. But a woman who is accompanied by someone else often does not have the chance to talk, because the husband or boyfriend or parent is so hostile to the pro-life worker.

Juli Loesch, a feminist/pacifist writer, notes that feminists want to have men participate more in the care of children, but abortion allows a man to shift total responsibility to the woman: "He can buy his way out of accountability by making 'The Offer' for 'The Procedure.' " She adds that the man's sexual role "then implies — exactly nothing: no relationship. How quickly a 'woman's right to choose' comes to serve a 'man's right to use.' " And Daphne de Jong, a New Zealand feminist, says, "If women must submit to abortion to preserve their lifestyle or career, their economic or social status, they are pandering to a system devised and run by men for male convenience." She adds, "Of all the things which are done to women to fit them into a society dominated by men, abortion is the most violent invasion of their physical and psychic integrity. It is a deeper and more destructive assault than rape...."

Loesch, de Jong, Olivarez, and other pro-life feminists believe men should bear a much greater share of the burdens of child-rearing than they do at present. And de Jong makes a radical point when she says, "Accepting short-time solutions like abortion only delays the implementation of real reforms like decent maternity and paternity leaves, job protection, high-quality child care, community responsibility for dependent people of all ages, and recognition of the economic contribution of childminders."

Fifth, abortion is an escape from an obligation that is owed to another. Doris Gordon, Coordinator of Libertarians for Life, puts it this way: "Unborn children don't cause women to become pregnant but parents cause their children to be in the womb, and as a result, they need parental care. As a general principle, if we are the cause of another's need for care, as when we cause an accident, we acquire an obligation to that person as a result....We have no right to kill in order to terminate any obligation."

Sixth, abortion brutalizes those who perform it, undergo it, pay for it, profit from it, and allow it to happen. Too many of us look the other way because we do not want to think about abortion. A part of reality is blocked out because one does not want to see broken bodies going to an incinerator, in those awful plastic bags. People deny their own humanity when they refuse to identify with, or even acknowledge, the pain of others.

With some it is worse: They are making money from the misery of others, from exploited women and dead children. Doctors, businessmen, and clinic directors are making a great deal of money from abortion. Jobs and high incomes depend on abortion; it's part of the gross national product. The parallels of this with the military-industrial complex should be obvious to anyone who was involved in the anti-war movement.

And the "slippery slope" argument is right: People really do go from accepting abortion to accepting euthanasia and accepting "triage" for the world hunger problem and accepting "lifeboat ethics" as a general guide to human behavior. We slip down the slope, back to the jungle.

To save the smallest children and to save its own conscience, the Left should speak out against abortion.

Reprinted by permission from *The Progressive,* 409 East Main Street, Madison, Wisconsin 53703. Copyright © 1980, The Progressive, Inc. Taken from the September, 1980 issue, *Vol. 44, No. 9.*

January Thoughts on Single Issue Groups

by Paulette Joyer

In the things we do and say, we try hard to promote a consistent pro-woman, pro-life philosophy that embraces many issues. This posture sometimes makes us outsiders in the two major movements we regularly frequent. Sometimes we hear outrageous statements in huge groups of people and yet we're the only ones who sigh.

For example: The New Year begins and we are invited to a meeting of pro-lifers to discuss various ways representatives from different groups may cooperate on upcoming events of shared interest. This meeting becomes a classic illustration of people who have ceased to focus on the issues and now waste energy expressing profound dislike of feminist women and men. A woman turns out to have used her maiden name with her married name? Though no one knows her, everyone knows all they need to. Someone is connected with the University? Write them off. And if we *ever* hear the word "flakes" again, we're going to scream.

Then, a Monday night some time later and Gloria Steinem charms a capacity crowd at the Urban YWCA. Advertised as "MS in the Eighties" it was a big hype for *Ms. Magazine.* That's fine, even at $4 a ticket. Question and answer time: A young woman is so frustrated she can hardly share her question, "This being an election year, and all those anti-abortion people being one issue, and we being multi-issue, what can we do?" Gloria emotes, "They are *single issue.* It's terrible. But we have to remember that *reproductive freedom is a fundamental human right and we should not support any candidate who doesn't support that.*" Thanks, Gloria. We never appreciated the difference before....

Then comes Saturday and back to the Y for a day-long conference, "Exploring the New Right." Some of it was very affirming, like the panel of political scientists who admitted that abortion is not merely a conservative issue but one that cuts across all groups. One professor read a poll indicating that in Minnesota 50% oppose abortion except to save the life of the mother. Keynote speaker former New Hampshire Senator Thomas MacIntyre, a supporter of legal abortion, confessed, "You read a book like *Aborting America* by Dr. Bernard Nathanson and it kind of tugs at you."

Afternoon, though, found us with the same old tired pro-abortion spokespeople. At the workshop on "Political Process from a Feminist Perspective" we heard these gems:

> "Abortion is the umbrella for anti-public school, anti-sex ed, anti-labor."

> "It's easy to criticize Mormons, but the real force are the Roman Catholics."

> "We have to lie, cheat and steal (to win at the precinct caucuses). We must make up our own rules."

> "The issue is freedom and "we will be violent to defend ourselves."

> So much for extremism and one-issue groups.

January 22 comes and we are reminded what it's all about. It's not about liberals and conservatives. It's not about feminists and fundamentalists. It's that seven years ago the Supreme Court ruled that in America we can kill babies to solve our social problems. *That* was an extreme decision.

Taken from the January/February 1980 issue of *Minnesota Feminists For Life Newsletter*, 2815 West 38th Street, Minneapolis, MN 55410 Reprinted with permission.

Pro Life Liberals
What Effect Can They Have?
by Denyse Handler

One significant change that has been taking place in the pro-life movement in the United States in the last few years has been the establishment of a small but viable "liberal" wing. In the U.S., 'liberal" means "left-wing"; the refusal to use the latter term may be a holdover from the McCarthy era, or the earlier phase of the Cold War. In Britain and Canada left-wing pro-life groups have long been established (cf. Life Labour Committee and New Democrats for Life). Their membership has tended to consist of members of local pro-life groups who also band together on a national level on the strength of party conviction, as the names of the groups suggest.

No Rallying Point

What is happening in the U.S. seems to be somewhat different and may prove quite significant in changing the way in which the pro-life cause is perceived, all over the Western world. In the first place, with its entrenched two-party system, the U.S. offers comparatively few official choices. Most American pro-lifers tend to be Democratic voters though ironically that is the less sympathetic of the two parties. (Of course, the same holds true in Canada and Britain. In Canada most pro-lifers are Liberals. The Liberals are their nemesis on the pro life issue. In Britain most pro-lifers are Labour party supporters but the party itself is three degrees worse than bad on these issues.) At any rate, there seems to be less incentive for American liberal pro-lifers to organize around a party affiliation; instead they identify themselves simply as "pro-life liberals" gaining respectability primarily from their participation in avowed "liberal" causes such as nuclear disarmament, draft resistance, etc.

The Catholic Plot

Conventional wisdom in the media has it that pro-lifers are always "conservatives" regardless of their political or social views, whereas pro-abortionists are always "liberals" — even when their actual statements are elitist or Malthusian! The pro-abortionists have come to depend heavily on this because, while they have been gaining legal ground, they have been losing ideological ground. Their philosophical base was never more than a patchwork of convenient transient ideas, offered for quick sale. Now the old alliances are breaking up: philosophical defections like Bernard Nathanson's have become common (though few were as public), and none of the utopian prophecies has come to pass. Hence the pro-abortionists in the U.S., setting the tone for the ones here and elsewhere, have come to depend primarily on name-calling. Even the legal arguments before superior and supreme court justices depend to an amazing degree on the assertion that it is all a Catholic plot.

So far, the pro-abortionists' position has not been weakened because they are still holding all the cards in the courts, in the medical schools, on boards, councils and committees. But ideological weakening is important nonetheless, because it reduces greatly the capacity of the group to respond to new challenges. This is precisely what pro-life appears to be starting to present.

Pro-Life Week At the Pentagon?

The first time liberal pro-life groups came to public attention was when they started getting arrested for handing out leaflets and providing on-the-spot counselling at abortion clinics.

P.S. — Prolifers for Survival, has been drawing many of them together. This anti-war pro-life group once organized a "Pro-life Week at the Pentagon". They distributed 15,000 copies of "Against War on the Unborn" at the Jan. 22 March for Life in 1980, "gaining a very friendly reception and several interviews".

"Depredation" by Dolls

Says Juli Loesch, founder of P.S., "We also maintained a daily leafletting and bannering presence at the Pentagon that week. On Jan. 25, we did two 'symbolic actions' in the context of prayers for life and peace. The first, on the steps of the River Entrance, used abortion as a metaphor for war. The second, in the public concourse area, represented childbirth as a celebration of resistance and peace. It was startling and lovely.

They read Exodus 1, 15-21:

"Then the king of Egypt spoke to the Hebrew midwives, whose names were Shiprah and Puah. 'When you are attending the Hebrew women in childbirth,' he told them, 'watch as the child is delivered and if it is a boy, kill him; if it is a girl, let her live.' But they were God-fearing women. They did not do what the king of Egypt had told them to do, but let the boys live. So he summoned those Hebrew midwives and asked them why they had done this and let the boys live. They told Pharaoh that Hebrew women were not like Egyptian women. When they were in labour they gave birth before the midwife could get to them. So God made the midwives prosper

and the people increased in numbers and in strength. God gave the midwives homes and families of their own, because they feared him." (*New English Bible*) "Three P.S.'ers were arrested and will be tried on February 22 for 'Depredation of Government Property'. We did not intend to 'depredate' their property with our plastic dolls and blood; there's a chance we might be acquitted.", Juli notes.

Political Support

But much of the liberal pro-life activity is taking place at the level of intellectual discussion and serious politics rather than confrontation drama. Mary Meehan, a Washington-based writer, whose work has appeared in *Inquiry, the Nation, Washington Post*, and other journals, considers herself a 'liberal' pro-lifer. Writing recently in *Commonweal* (Jan. 18/80), she notes that many well-known American politicians who were sponsors of human life amendments, were also liberals. She cites Harold Hughes, an Iowa Senator, Mark Hatfield, an Oregon Senator, and also Joseph Biden, Thomas Eagleton and William Proxmire, as well as many Congresspeople. Noting the growth of such "liberal" groups as Feminists for Life (about 1,000 members) and National Youth Pro-Life Coalition (about 5,000 members, mostly under 25) Meehan makes the point that they are peculiarly well fitted to deal with the argument that defending the right of the unborn child to live is "imposing one's morality on others."

Slavery

She writes: "Because pro-lifers believe there are decisive arguments against abortion on secular grounds, they are not worried by the pro-choice battle cry, 'Don't impose your morality on me!' They think that imposing morality, in the sense of defining one person's obligations to another, is what the law is largely about. Senator Hatfield says that 'belief in life's fundamental right to be has inevitable corporate consequences.' He notes that, in opposing American intervention in Vietnam, 'I did not merely believe it would be wrong for me, as an individual, to fight there. I believed that no American should fight there, which compelled me to propose legislation expressing that conviction.'

"Juli Loesch, a pacifist and pro-life feminist, speaks of women in the peace movement: 'It would never occur to us to say, "For private moral reasons I don't personally condone nuclear arms, but I really can't impose my feelings on my fellow citizens who don't hold the same religious beliefs — and certainly each nation has the right to choose to incinerate its enemies if it wishes,' "

"And Jesse Jackson (prominent black civil rights leader) said that the idea that life is private and that one may do with it as one wishes, 'was the premise of slavery. You could not protest the existence or treatment of slaves on the plantation because that was private and therefore outside of your right to be concerned.' "

Meehan also mentions that "Writer and activist Jay Sykes, who led Eugene McCarthy's 1968 antiwar campaign in Wisconsin and later served as head of the state's American Civil Liberties Union, wrote a 'Farewell to Liberalism' several years ago. Sykes cited several areas of disagreement and disillusionment, then added, 'It is on the abortion issue that the moral bankruptcy of contemporary liberalism is most clearly exposed.' He said that liberals' arguments in support of abortion 'could, without much refinement, be used to justify the legalization of infanticide.' "

Try to Understand

Many other pro-life liberals have chosen to try to help other liberals understand what the issues are, rather than resign. It is not easy. Writing in the Feminists for Life Newsletter, Judy Shea notes ironically that the outcry in the National Organization of Women about Sonia Johnson being excommunicated from the Mormon Church smacks of hypocrisy. In 1974, NOW kicked out the only vocal pro-life feminist in their organization. Pat Goltz was ousted essentially because she would not "keep (her) mouth shut", as a local executive member put it, about the right to live. The same newsletter quotes some elegant thoughts from pro-abortion feminists at a recent conference: "We have to lie, cheat and steal (to win at the precinct caucuses). We must make up our own rules." "We will be violent to defend ourselves". (*Newsletter*, Jan./Feb. '80). It sounds as though these people would make it very tough indeed for pro-life feminists if they got the chance.

The Raspberries

The media seems to be discovering the pro-life liberals to some extent. A nationally syndicated columnist, William Raspberry, talked recently about a liberal pro lifer, Bill Smith, who was walking from San Diego, California, to Washington, D.C. for the March for Life on January 22nd. (*Detroit News*, Jan. 28/80) Smith, he proclaimed, was "your quintessential liberal" — except that he is opposed to abortion. Spending the rest of the column explaining this to readers, he quotes Smith: "I consider my position very liberal. A lot of my liberal friends who are in the anti-nuclear movement will acknowledge that there are

a lot of uncertainties about nuclear energy, but they still insist we ought
to err on the side of safety and shut 'em (nuclear plants) down. Why
can't they reach the same conclusion with regard to abortion clinics?

"I remember what one of the Save-the-Whale people said when they
cut open a dead whale and found a rather large baby whale inside:
'Those SOB's killed two whales, not one.' Why can't they look at
human beings the same way?"

Friction?

Raspberry also persistently questioned Smith about the friction that
sometimes develops between "liberal" and "conservative" pro-lifers.
The latter are not a majority, but rather a vocal minority. Most pro
lifers are "moderates" on most social issues. Friction is inevitable,
since each camp views pro-life as an outgrowth of its own otherwise
conflicting ideas..Thus, for example, whereas a liberal may have
become a pro-lifer through pacifism, a conservative may have become
one through a belief that his country was selling out to the ideology of
national enemies and that a military and moral rearmament was
needed. The right to live is so fundamental to the Western concept of
the human being that it can actually draw together very disparate
groups.

A liberal pro life Congressman, Nick Nolan, writing for **American
Citizens Concerned for Life**, a liberal pro life legislative lobby, talked
about one of the unfortunate results of this friction. (**ACCL Newsletter**,
Vol. 6, No. 1) A colleague told him that in a recent vote he had voted to
allow abortion only in hard cases: "That's the strongest pro life vote I
can cast and still deal with the realities facing those I represent, to say
nothing of being re-elected. Now the anti-abortionists want to defeat
me. We should be working together, but I've just about given up."

Part of the problem that brings these situations about is an
important difference in outlook. The conservative pro-lifer insists on
unilateral opposition to all abortions on the grounds that any
slackening will open the floodgates. There is plenty of evidence to
support that position. The liberal pro lifer on the other hand, believes
that, when society is hooked on abortion, it must be weaned away from
it by degrees. There is also lots of evidence to suggest that fundamental
social changes do take time to occur; one could point to gradual
improvement in the civil rights and acceptance of blacks, Catholics and
women. It is tragic when the two groups fall out over the timetable of a
victory that they have not yet started to win.

Hope

Despite this, liberal pro lifers, as well as others, are hopeful: Bill Smith notes: "It's my impression that this is a one-way street. I keep hearing about pro-abortion people who change their minds but I never hear about anti-abortion people changing theirs."

If you would like to get in touch with some of the groups mentioned:

American Citizens Concerned for Life
6127 Excelsior Blvd.
Minneapolis, Minn.
55416

Feminists for Life of America
811 East 47th St.
Kansas City, Mo.
64110

National Youth Pro Life Coalition
735 Eleventh St. N.W.
Washington, D.C.
20001

Pro Lifers for Survival
P.O. Box 3316
Chapel Hill, NC
27514

Post Script:

The "illiberal" aspect of the pro-abortion movement is well-illustrated by a recent article, one among many, in the *Spokesman Review*, of Spokane Washington, titled "Wrong People are Producing Most Children" (Oct. 25/79). This article purports to show the need for a "new sense of urgency" in the debates about abortion, birth control and public welfare, because the poor and uneducated are having more children than the rich and educated so that "America in the next century will be a poorer place to live". Unless something is done, of course. And we can guess what that 'something' is going to continue to be.

Most interesting is the fact that this complaint about the wrong people having all the kids is, literally, from time immemorial. See back to our quote from the Book of Exodus; that's what Pharaoh was uptight about! The cry had been taken up by uncharitable multitudes through the centuries. If you were to believe them, you would have to suppose that the "quality" of the human population has decreased greatly since 3,000 B.C., when this complaint was first made, no doubt. Does anyone really believe that?

Taken from *The Human*, April, 1980. Reprinted with permission.

Abortion and the Left

by Juli Loesch

In September, 1980, *The Progressive* ran articles for and against "abortion rights." Expecting flack for printing Mary Meehan's pro-life article, Editor Erwin Knoll was astonished when the letters flooded in, split *nearly 50-50*. The Left, he found, is profoundly divided on abortion.

More indications: in October, 1980, *Pax Christi USA*, a Catholic peace organization that includes feminists and socialists, approved an anti-abortion resolution at its national assembly by virtually unanimous vote.

Weeks later *Sojourners*, a Christian peace/justice magazine, featured Daniel Berrigan, Shelley Douglass, Jesse Jackson and others arguing for opposition to abortion integrated with a more radical commitment to non-violent feminism and human dignity.

Possibly abortion never was a Left/Right issue. Soon after the 1973 *Roe v. Wade* abortion decision one of the most progressive Senate Democrats, Harold Hughes, joined one of the most progressive Republicans, Mark Hatfield, in co-sponsoring a Human Life Amendment (HLA). Both were opponents of the Vietnam War. Both opposed abortion because of, not despite, their other political convictions.

But those who soon got out in front of the largely working class, lower-middle class, ethnic-Catholic, traditionally Democratic "Right-to-Life" constituency — who provided an analysis, a language of political expression — were conservatives (like black surgeon Dr. Mildred Jefferson) and New Right spokesmen (like lobbyist Paul Weyrich.)

I attribute this to the default of the Left. Michael Harrington once called pro-life one of the only true grassroots movements to emerge from the '70's. These millions have not been "taken in" by the Right so much as pushed out by the Left — booted toward the eager arms of conservative coalitions.

The rift between "pro-choice" and "pro-life" seems unbridgeable if only the extremes are heard. On the one hand, there are those who would like to ban contraceptives. On the other, there are those who want the Supreme Court's concept of human non-personhood to encroach still further, to five days after birth, so that both parents have a fuller opportunity to "terminate" unwanted children legally.

Most of us are between those two extremes.

We would be upset to witness one of the 60,000 or more abortions from the fourth through the ninth month performed legally since 1973, that have destroyed perfectly recognizable children by lethal injection and dismemberment. But we are opposed to criminalizing the 1,100,000 pregnant women who annually choose abortion as a felt need.

What we need — desperately — is a reworking of the argument to express the legitimate value judgments of the opposing camps when they are at their best.

This is what I would like concerned people of the Left to do: Drop the increasingly untenable notion that we must champion "abortion rights" at all costs and that anyone who has a problem with that should be abandoned to the Right. Admit that many of us have mixed consciences, and initiate a season of dialogue.

Pro-choicers have exposed the fact that in this society women's life choices can be crippled by an untimely pregnancy. Pro-lifers have reminded us of the dignity of new life. Even the heat of the debate is a sign of people's certainty that the oppressed and the weak must be afforded justice.

One "bridge" group that has practical experience with dialogue is *Feminists for Life*, a thousand-member pro-ERA, pro-HLA group. Another, which does *not* endorse legislation but which links concern for the unborn with opposition to nuclear weapons, is *Prolifers for Survival*. These and other groups have resources we could all use.

Originally appeared in *Religious Socialism, Vol. V*, No. 2, Spring, 1981.

Confessions of an Anti-Choice Fanatic

by Ginny Desmond Billinger

I've decided to leave the closet. Though prudence would have me dodge the accusation indefinitely, scruples impel me at last to come out and claim a leadership role in the movement so handily dubbed "anti-choice."

Yes, it's time to 'fess up; I can no longer stifle the evidence. So step right up, pro-choicers, and allow me to confirm your suspicions. Let me fuel your fire of fury with some exclusive inside dope on the anti-choice mentality.

Until now, of course, you've directed the indictment only at our position on abortion, but you'd be foolish to stop there. Let's take a look at just a few of the other issues that I, as an avowed antichoicer, am ready to address:

Spouse and child beating — Here, my position is unhesitatingly anti-choice. My perspective as a spouse, a parent, and a former child qualifies me to support all measures to remove from people the freedom to choose to abuse their family members — even in the privacy of their own homes.

Drunk driving — Again, anti-choice. I'm afraid I must impose my morality on those who would choose to operate life-threatening machines while influenced by alcohol, and ask them to temporarily abstain from one or the other.

Gun control — Despite the big-bucks, "constitutional rights" lobbying by the NRA, I remain consistently anti-choice on this issue. The memory of a friend, forces me to reject any justification for handgun ownership without strict regulation.

Endangered species protection — Faced with a whale-hunter or seal-clubber, I'll take a hard line anti-choice stand every time.

Hazardous waste disposal — We're talking about the rights of corporate America vs. the average Joe here, but my anti-choice position still applies. The right to choose efficient business practices must always be weighed against the public's right to a safe environment. Ditto for occupational safety and health issues.

I expect that these declarations will leave me open to censure; I will no doubt be labelled a heretic. The American principle of personal liberty would surely suffer with the propagation of my anti-choice philosophy. Nonetheless, I would have felt sinister had I not revealed my convictions, and I have a reputation to maintain, however despised.

So, call me what you will: pro-life anti-choice, fetus-worshiper, anti-abortion. A thousand labels will never alter the certainty that the road to freedom cannot be paved with the sacrificed rights of others.

This article was originally published in the September/October 1982 Newsletter of Minnesota Feminists for Life, Inc., 1815 West 38th Street, Minneapolis, MN 55410, and is reprinted with permission of the author.

Section Two:
Abortion:
We've Been There

This section chronicles how abortion has affected women's lives. Perhaps not all of the women whose stories are recounted here would regard themselves as feminists. But they are our sisters and all have been hurt by abortion.

Where are the Pro-Life Feminists Anyway?

by Judie Gillespie

A week ago I received a phone call from a high school teacher concerned about one of her students, one of her "brighter" students, who had an abortion recently and is now suicidal. As a pregnancy counselor, I had not dealt with a single woman who thought about aborting her baby because *she* thought it was best. No, it was her parents who thought it was a good idea, or a boyfriend, or a husband, or a boss, or a frowning, judgmental society which was too much for her to withstand.

The only woman (to the best of my knowledge) who had an abortion after spending time with me, discussing her options and her wish to have her baby, was not 16, but 36, was not a minority race member but white, was not poor, but far from it, married to an ambitious business executive; no, this woman who had an abortion was not like some of the others I had counseled, not like Heidi, the 19-year-old alcoholic, or Margie, whose father beat her mother and called her a slut. No, my abortion victim had two children she was crazy about and wanted another, but her husband said no way...they had a Caribbean cruise planned, not time for a pregnancy. It was the baby, he said, or it was him. Choose. So she did. They split up about a year later, and she struggles through each day.

Do abortion clinics hear stories like these? Do they have women (whose babies they have killed) coming back to *them* to talk about how crazy they are now, how desperately they want to die? What is the abortionist's response to the 8,000 women who have joined Women Exploited by Abortion in the past year? How much longer can women who claim that to be feminist is to be pro-abortion espouse a philosophy responsible for the severe physical and psychological damage to millions of women each year?

Sooner or later, though, it's going to happen. The abortion movement will bury itself, as more and more women who have suffered the unending grief and desperate humiliation when some stranger is paid $200 to kill their baby, killing a part of them in the process. But in the meantime, pro-life feminists, we must be visible, must be vocal, must spread the message that to be feminist is to be nurturers, life-givers, justice-seekers, peacemakers. We have the responsibility of letting the world know it...true feminism *is* pro-life!

Taken from the November 1983 issue of *Feminists for Life of Wisconsin Newsletter*, 1503 N. 47th St., Milwaukee, WI 53208

Who are the Victims?

by Monica M. Migliorino

Donna is a friend of mine and she had an abortion. This was in 1974. One year later, Saturday mornings found Donna standing outside the same abortion clinic in Chicago to persuade women not to go through with the scheduled procedure. She says she does this in order "to help women. To spare them the suffering I endured."

Donna had an abortion because, like so many other young women seeking abortions, she found herself pregnant and unmarried. She was scared. She didn't know what she wanted. She didn't know where to turn. Afraid of the pregnancy, afraid of giving birth, afraid of motherhood, abortion seemed to be the only solution. She believes that if only one person had talked with her, calmed her fears, extended a helping hand, guided her to an alternative, her child would be alive today. No one did, however, least of all those who label themselves "pro-choice."

Donna visited a woman gynecologist referred to her by the American Medical Association. "I wanted to find out if I was really pregnant," says Donna, "but more than this I really needed to talk to someone about being pregnant." This talk never took place. The gynecologist said to Donna:

"You didn't plan this pregnancy, did you?"

"No," replied Donna.

"Well, we'll get rid of it for you."

The gynecologist never asked for Donna's opinion. Donna was frightened and vulnerable with the gynecologist already setting up an appointment for an abortion. "I didn't know what to say," said Donna. "She was already making the decision for me. I was confused. Upset. I didn't know what I wanted. I knew, however, that I didn't want to talk to her about my pregnancy because to her there was no choice in the matter. She didn't give me any support. When I went to the nurse to confirm the appointment she told me it would cost $230.00. She and the doctor just assumed this was what I was going to do. Two hundred and thirty dollars was a lot of money and I looked at the nurse in disbelief. She said to me "Well, really, Donna, you have no choice.' "

Because of the expense and because of the doctor's brisk, uncaring manner Donna decided not to return to her for the abortion. She didn't know exactly what she was going to do except that perhaps for the first time she actually began to consider going through with the pregnancy. Donna then received a phone call from the woman gynecologist.

"Why didn't you show up for the appointment? You haven't decided to keep the baby, have you?"

"No," replied Donna, because, in fact, she hadn't decided anything.

"Well, for heaven's sake, what is the problem?"

"It's...expensive," replied Donna, not knowing what else to say.

"Well, if that's the only reason I can refer you to a good clinic, but you have no time to lose. You've got to do something now. You're seven weeks pregnant."

The gynecologist referred Donna to the Concord Medical Center in Chicago. This clinic was cited by the Chicago *Sun-Times* series on abortion profiteers as providing non-exploitive, compassionate and safe abortion. Donna asked, "Is there counseling there? I need someone to talk to." The gynecologist replied, "Oh, yes. Don't worry about it."

Donna called the clinic and an appointment was made for an abortion the following day. Donna asked the woman on the phone, "Do you have counseling?" The woman answered, "Oh, yes. You'll have plenty of time to talk to someone. We'll tell you all about it."

When Donna arrived at the clinic with her boyfriend there were forms to fill out. The forms asked "Do you want counseling?" Donna replied, "Yes." The forms also asked "Are you sure you want this abortion?" Donna replied, "No."

Donna told me, "I wanted to know the facts about abortion. I wanted to know how it would affect me physically and mentally. I wanted to know if the fetus was human."

Before Donna received any counseling, she, along with the other women, first *paid* for the abortion, had her blood test taken, was told to undress and given a hospital gown to wear. In other words, she was "prepped" for an abortion she had indicated on the forms she wasn't even sure she wanted!

Donna states: "They treated us like guinea pigs. The whole manner of treating their patients is set up to make the woman unthinkingly follow one step after another. Their attitude was one of 'Now, let's behave properly,' like we were naughty children who had committed a wrong act and were now going to have to go through the necessary surgery to clear up the problem we had caused. The counseling was at best inadequate. It consisted of a woman who supposedly had an abortion herself describing the procedure of a suction abortion. She said, 'Abortion is simple. A tube is inserted and you'll feel a gentle suction. Afterwards you'll lie down for a while and then go home.' No mention was made of any possible physical complications except for 'You can expect a little cramping — something like menstrual cramps.' Of course, absolutely no mention was made of the fetus."

"I felt I couldn't talk with the counselor. I felt intimidated by her and for this reason I asked no questions. The woman was obviously no counselor. She was not a trained anything. She was not sympathetic to my problem. She had not a stitch of compassion in her even though she'd had an abortion. I felt there was nothing I could do. I couldn't go back. Couldn't say no. There I was in my gown ready for an abortion. It's hard to explain. Once you're in there you don't get out. You're there. What's the answer? If you leave, what do you do?"

Donna never saw the doctor before the actual abortion even though she had signed a form which stated: "I have seen the doctor and he has explained the abortion procedure to me." When the doctor finally did appear one of the first things he said to Donna was, "Who was your partner in crime?" "As if being pregnant was a crime" Donna told me. "As if pregnancy were a crime against humanity."

"The abortion was horrible. I was grasping the nurse's hand in a vice-like grip. She said, 'My goodness, but you're upset.' As if she couldn't believe I would be upset about having an abortion. I moved on the table, it hurt so much. The doctor may not have waited for the anesthetic to take effect. In a few minutes it was over. I got off the table. I could hardly walk. I was hanging onto the nurse. They put me in bed. I couldn't move. I felt paralyzed from the waist down. I was in a state of total shock. During the procedure it finally hit me that I was destroying my baby."

Donna is one of the approximately twelve million women in America who suffered severe repercussions from abortion. There was physical pain for her, but most of all there was mental anguish and distress — a deep feeling that she had been exploited and violated. She states:

> One's ability to reproduce is the most personal part of you and I felt they just went in there and ripped the fetus out and said, 'Okay, you can go home. It's all over.' I didn't feel they cared. They had a utilitarian attitude — like, let's get it done as fast as possible with no complications, with no complaining. I was not told what to expect in the way of

physical pain or in the way of emotional anguish, and most
of all I feel the abortion deprived me of that pregnancy.*

Women as Victims

I felt it necessary to begin this article not with statistics or with what
doctors have to say about the complications of abortion, but rather
with a woman's own experience of abortion. Why? Because abortion
is perhaps more than anything else the story of women seeking a
solution — indeed seeking what appears to be a liberty. For many,
many women abortion is a solution that hurts and a false liberty that
does not make them free. One does not have to search very far to find a
woman who has been made a victim of abortion. It is the few who
escape totally unscathed. I personally know four other women besides
Donna who, having had abortions, consider it a very negative and
degrading experience, an experience they regret and from which they
need healing.

It may be helpful to clarify what I mean when I say that women are
victims of abortion. The *Oxford English Dictionary* provides the
following definition of the word *victim*. A victim is:
  (A) One who is reduced or destined to suffer under some oppres-
      sive or destructive agency.
  (B) One who perishes or suffers in health, etc. from some enter-
      prise or pursuit voluntarily undertaken.
  (C) In a weaker sense: One who suffers some injury, hardship, or
      loss, is badly treated or taken advantage of, etc.
Women have been made victims of abortion in all the ways des-
cribed above.

---

*Donna currently lives in Chicago. Since her abortion she has become quite active in the pro-life movement. Most of
her pro-life activity involves counseling women with problem pregnancies and helping them seek alternatives to
abortion.

"If You're Gonna Get Sick, Get Out Of Here"

by Denyse Handler

In 1973, when Tanya Hughson was 17, she was just finishing high school and asked to be left behind when her parents moved to B.C. "Like most girls, I had access to birth control. I had a prescription for the pill on my dresser when I got pregnant." She felt she could not tell her parents. Her boyfriend offered to marry her but she knew that getting married would not be a good idea.

She went to a doctor. He asked her "What do you want to do about it." She replied, "I don't know". When she brought up abortion, the gynecologist just laughed and said that she could not abort at 17 without her parents' consent. It was then that Tanya went to the Calgary Birth Control Association, which was then called Abortion Information Centre. They said that they could get her into a hospital in Calgary, without her parents' knowledge or consent, listing the abortion as a "D&C". But when they discovered that she had been to a gynecologist, they were unwilling to do this, for he knew that she was pregnant.

Somewhere Else

The counsellor and her boyfriend made the decision that Tanya would go to a clinic in Bellingham, Washington. Tanya reports feeling a curious sensation, shared by other aborting mothers that she has spoken with, that she was not really sitting there in a chair with the others in the room, but rather, "somewhere else", uninvolved and simply watching the scene. This made it possible for her to passively allow others to make all the decisions, so that she would not have to feel that she was accepting responsibility for what was done.

The counsellor told Tanya to bring $90.00, and take two enemas. They recommended hotels close to the clinic. "All I had was a suitcase full of pads and a nightgown."

All that the doctor at the clinic did was abortions. Tanya was his first appointment in the morning. And, when she got in, he told her, "Oh, and by the way, we don't give you any anaesthetic...we have found that many women experience guilt and we want you to feel you are a part of it". Tanya was very nervous at this point, whereupon she was asked about her religious beliefs. "Heavy religious innuendos" were alleged to be the cause of her fear and trembling. She did not want to go through with it. Then the staff asked her, "Do you want to go out and face your boyfriend after all this and tell him you haven't even had the abortion?" She gave in and it was done.

"If you're gonna get sick, get out of here."

She staggered out of the clinic and went to fill a prescription. She mentioned in the adjoining drugstore that she felt ill, whereupon she was rudely told, "Well, if you're gonna get sick, get out of here." My boyfriend was very upset when I was crying on the plane and he threatened to leave me", A half year later, he did.

Tanya had health problems in the ensuing years and when she met her husband, and became pregnant again, she started to hear babies crying at night and all the pain came back to her. (She had phoned Abortion Information Centre because she had felt so badly, but they did not want to deal with the situation.)

"Friends for Life" — to Help Others

Coming to a resolution abut how she felt was not easy for her or her girlfriend, Laura McCaughey, who had also had an abortion. One day they saw some pictures of unborn children in some display material put out by Calgary Pro-Life. Tanya recalls that at first she hesitated about writing to Diane Molloy, president of the group, fearing that she would be "hostile". But Mrs. Molloy was very sympathetic and suggested that perhaps Tanya and Laura could consider helping themselves by helping others, for there were many women in their position. Out of this grew the "Friends for Life" group, a self-help group for women coping with the after-effects.

When most young girls ask for an abortion, Tanya said, they are really saying, "I'm pregnant and I don't know what to do". "Almost every girl I have talked to did not know that it was a baby. It is referred to as pregnancy tissue, a fetus. All these things conjure up in a young girl's mind something she can disassociate herself from. Ninety per cent would not abort if they could see such pictures or hear the heartbeats."

"It's very hard for women to talk about it" Tanya explained to the **Human**, "It's even hard for me to talk about it. Sometimes I can get women to write it out, but then only for me, not for anyone else to see." This was strikingly illustrated on a radio talk show Tanya was on, when a woman called up to insist that she was glad to have had an abortion — but was in tears by the time she rung off.

Much Hostility Encountered

Tanya and Laura did a very brave thing when they decided to go public, using their own names. They received much hostile comment; a popular attitude among men has been, "Why can't you just forget it; we all have problems". This attitude, however, ignores the basis of the problem, the fact that a woman is not "supposed" to feel sorry or guilty about aborting an unwanted baby in our society. If she is, she is discouraged from talking about it, very often by men who wish she would just "forget it", — with the result that she may develop psychosomatic or emotional problems.

Tanya has not just "forgotten" what happened. She encourages all of us to be understanding and loving towards women who are scarred by abortion, inviting people who may have had a similar experience to talk to her. She may be reached at:

Tanya Hughson
Box 3077, Stn. B,
Calgary, Alta.
T2M 4N7

Taken from the July 1980 issue of *The Human*, Reprinted with permission.

"Abortion...I Have Lived To Regret It..."

(The following is a true experience of a Vernon, B.C. woman.*)

I am writing this to share an experience that I have had that has totally affected my life. I am a woman who has had an abortion and who has lived to deeply regret it.

No one except the woman who has actually been there can truly understand the horror of the word "positive" when a pregnancy is unplanned and unwanted. Believe me I have experienced that horror. This is my story of how I felt when my pregnancy was confirmed.

Me? Pregnant? No! It couldn't be. I was a professional person with an excellent job. Pregnancy just couldn't fit into my plans. I wasn't married. I'd be scorned by all my colleagues. I thought, the nurse must be wrong. My doctor will have an answer when I go back to see him. I am crying and he seems uncomfortable. I feel so alone and discouraged and deserted. If only I knew where to go or what to do. Yes, he does have an answer — abortion. He seems so sure it is the only solution for me. And he should know — he's the doctor.

But abortion? Isn't that killing this little life I have inside me? No, it's not life. It's not human. It's just a blob of cells. Don't think of it as a baby. Keep thinking this. If you ever start to think it could be a baby — your baby — you're done for. I start to pray, "Dear God, don't let this be happening to me. Help me." No, I better not pray. There's that thing about "thou shalt not kill". Better not get God into this. Might change my mind. This isn't life — keep remembering — it's just a blob of protoplasm.

Oh God, hurry this thing up. How long do I have to wait for the call to say my bed in the hospital is ready?

My tummy doesn't show any change but my breasts are getting fuller. I'm horribly sick every morning and sometimes at work. There is definitely some change going on in my body. Just very, very occasionally I get a sort of thrill — wow — there's a baby growing in my tummy. I often put my hand on it.

What really is going on in there? Maybe it is a baby? What if I kept it. There's adoption — no; how could I bear giving my baby away to some strangers never to see it again?

No — I love it too much. Love — how could I speak of love? Me, who was about to kill my baby. Perhaps if I could have a fall — I do everything I can think of to abort myself. No luck. A flash thought of wonder crosses my mind at the determination this baby seems to have to stay inside there. There I go again — don't think of it as a baby.

The day has finally come, I have to be in the hospital by 8 a.m. I sign some sort of a consent form. I'm lying in a hallway to be wheeled into O.R. Why don't they get me in there and get this thing over with? Finally the anaesthetist is there. Just as I'm slipping into unconsciousness I ask him, "Do you think I am...?" The last part of my question never gets asked.

I'm just waking up. Where am I? What's happened? Suddenly, I know. My hand reaches for my tummy. I shall never forget the feeling of horror and emptiness I had at that moment. It was gone. I was pregnant no longer. It was all over. "Oh, God," I cry, "I've killed my baby. I've killed my baby." A nurse comes quickly and gives me a shot. Everything goes black.

I wake up back in the ward. I hardly ever consciously think about my abortion again. Life carries on. I've hardly missed a step. Or have I?

Months later I begin to be plagued with periods of depression. They get worse and worse. I never know when they will come. The only way I can describe it is like a black cloud suddenly totally encompassing me. The most terrifying part is not knowing why this is happening. Am I going crazy? Even the simplest of tasks suddenly becomes monumental. I wonder how much longer I can cope with this life.

Finally I see a doctor about it. "I did have an abortion," I tell him. "But I know this has nothing to do with how I'm feeling. It didn't bother me." He never questions further about the abortion. He takes a leave of absence and I tell the doctor who replaces him the same thing. He also never questions further. This one puts me on a series of anti-depressant drugs. They don't help at all. My depression is becoming a living hell. I want to sleep but I can't. I look around at other people and wonder if anyone in the world has ever felt as isolated as I do. And I never think about the abortion.

In a roundabout way I hear of a doctor who helped an acquaintance through her depression. In desperation I go to him. "I did have an abortion," I again repeat. "But it never bothered me." "You had an abortion?" he probes. We talk and talk and in the intervening hours I come to the realization of the unconscious grief and guilt I have, and the aching in my heart and arms for the baby I had never let be born. Yes, abortion had taken its toll. Me who had been so ready to say, "There's nothing wrong with abortion. It's a woman's right. It was the best thing for me. I never looked back." Me, who had been so incensed by those stupid ads, "Did you know that at three weeks the unborn baby's heart begins to beat?" My mind had been closed.

It had been easy to talk of "terminating a pregnancy" or "destroying a fetus". I had avoided at all costs accepting that it was a developing living baby in my womb. If I ever had consciously accepted that fact — that it was human life — could I ever have killed it?

But it was life. From the moment an egg is fertilized, life exists. It is just a question of nutrition and time and development. A four month old unborn baby develops into a week old child, who develops into a teenager, who develops into a mature adult. At no stage is life any less there. Yes a woman does have the right over her own body, but the unborn baby is, in no real way, a part of her body. He is a complete person in himself with his own heart, blood supply and other organs. He can even be of opposite sex and how can male sex organs be part of a woman's body? The truth is, the fetus is someone else's body. If given time it will grow, (just as will a child and a teenager), into a mature adult.

But my story isn't over. It's later now. I'm happily married and my husband and I want to have children. But something is wrong. I can't seem to carry a baby to term. I'm sent to a specialist. I am told my cervical muscle has been permanently weakened by my abortion. An increase in prematurity and tubal pregnancies are two common subsequent complications of abortions I learn. No, mine wasn't a "backstreet butcher" abortion. No, it was a legal "therapeutic" abortion that was performed in one of the largest hospitals in Vancouver.

Why didn't anyone tell me this could happen? What have I done to my as yet unborn babies I so long to have? The social judgment I so fear would have been a small price to pay for the life of the baby I killed and the ones I now can't carry.

I'm not saying that every young woman is going to suffer a severe depression such as I did. I'm not saying that every woman who has an abortion won't be able to carry her babies to term afterwards or will have premature babies.

I am saying that statistically reliable medical studies confirm that abortion does carry with it many complications. I am saying that no one told me there were any possible after-effects, and if you are considering an abortion I want you to know about them. I am saying that if you haven't considered that it is human life in your womb that you must open your mind to both sides of the story. You owe it not only to yourself but also to your unborn baby. Don't deny it, as I did, without thinking about it. It is upon this question, "Is this human life?", that the whole abortion issue hinges.

If you are pregnant, I know how you feel. It seems like there is no single thing in the entire world that could have happened to you that could be worse.

But, looking back on my experience I know I could have managed, had I let my baby live. There were answers. I really couldn't see the forest for the trees. I have found many times since in life, that when one is in the midst of the darkness of some seemingly insurmountable problem, it is very easy not to see clearly.

However, looking back when the darkness lifts and my vision clears, often there were long-range solutions I never, in my anguish, saw.

There will be pro-abortionists who read this article and dismiss it as a neurotic woman trying to rid herself of her guilt. No, I will always regret what I did, but I have come to terms with my guilt. I have no need to pour out my soul to anyone.

My hope is that by my sharing my story, just one as yet unborn baby's life will be saved, just one woman will be spared the anguish I have suffered. If this happens, my unborn baby will not have died in vain.

(*To contact the author write to: Vernon Birthright, Suite 4, 3315B-30th Avenue, Vernon, B.C. V1T 2E1)

Women Form WEBA to Fight Abortions

by Tom Diaz

(The following article appeared in the Washington Times, *August 3, 1983)*

Nancyjo Mann on the horror of having an abortion, and of the mission of Women Exploited By Abortion.

Every year for the past 10 years, 1.5 million women have had an abortion. For many, according to Nancyjo Mann, founder and president of Woman Exploited By Abortion (WEBA), having an abortion only began their problem. Mann was interviewed by Washington Times staff writer and columnist Tom Diaz.

Q: Tell us about your experience with abortion and its consequences.

A: My experience goes back to 1974, the month of October, 30th day — the day that I killed my baby girl. It was a second trimester abortion. I was 5½ months pregnant.

I went to the doctor because family members had pressured me, had encouraged me. There was no "Nancy maybe you should reconsider," because it was not my idea in the first place, it was theirs.

My husband had walked out the door and deserted us. The responsibility of three children was just too much for him. I went to my mother and my brother and asked, "What am I going to do?" And my mother said "It's obvious, Nancy, no man's going to want you with three children, let alone the two you already have. You're probably not going to amount to a hill of beans and you're probably going to be on welfare for the rest of your life."

And following those three positive, uplifting statements, she said "You're going to have an abortion." Then she called one of the leading ob/gyns in the Midwest, and he said, "Absolutely, no problem. Bring her on in."

Q: Did he know at the time how far you were along?

A: Absolutely. He does all kinds of second trimesters, no problem.

I went in and I asked, "What are you going to do to me?" All he did was look at my stomach and say, "I'm going to take a little fluid out, put a little fluid in, you'll have severe cramps and expel the fetus."

I said, "Is that all?" He said, "That's all."

It didn't sound too bad. But what that doctor described to me was not the truth.

I went to the hospital and 60 ccs of amniotic fluid were drawn out, and a saline solution injected. Immediately the needle went through the abdomen I hated Nancyjo, I hated myself. With every ounce of my being I wanted to scream out "Please, stop, don't do this to me." But I couldn't get it out.

Once they put in the saline there's no way to reverse it. And for the next hour and a half I felt my daughter thrash around violently while she was being choked, poisoned, burned and suffocated to death. I didn't know any of that was going to happen. And I remember talking to her and I remember telling her I didn't want to do this, I wished she could live. And yet she was dying and I remember her very last kick on her left side. She had no strength left.

I've tried to imagine us dying that kind of death, a pillow put over us, suffocating. In four minutes we'd pass out. We'd have that gift of passing out and then dying. But it took her an hour and a half just to die.

Then I was given an intravenuous injection to help stimulate labor and I went into hard labor for 12 hours. And at 5:30 a.m. on the 31st of October I delivered my daughter whose name is now Charmaine Marie. She was 14 inches long. She weighed over a pound and a half. She had a head of hair and her eyes were opening.

I got to hold her because the nurses didn't make it to the room on time. I delivered my girl myself. They grabbed her out of my hands and threw her, threw her, into a bedpan. After they finished and took her away in the bedpan, they brought a lady in to finish her last hour of labor lying next to me. She had a healthy baby boy.

That was tough.

I liked Nancyjo, I liked me, prior to the abortion. But shame and remorse and guilt set in — I mean, when you get a hold of your own daughter and you see what you did. She was not a "fetus." She was not "a product of conception. She was not a "tissue adhering to the uterine wall." So those are cheap, inhuman words to use around me.

I chose to be sterilized because I couldn't cope with the idea that I could possibly kill again. It was too devastating. It was not something you go around telling people, that you just killed your baby, no problem. I was ashamed, totally ashamed.

Q: But some people would say that although this experience obviously had a great impact on you, it is not characteristic of most other women who have abortions. Is your case unusual?

A: No, my case is not unusual at all. People want to say "Oh, but Nancy, you're the extreme." That's not true. In fact there are so many more of us than there are the other. The emotional hurt is so deep. You do not discuss your abortion, the suction machines and the needles and everything else, over a cup of tea and a cookie. Women just don't do this. The pain is just too deep and too great.

I'm sure there are women out there who are never fazed, never, by their abortion. But I would say that 98, 99 percent of them are fazed, whether it's for a small period of time or for the rest of their life, whether they suffer only a small degree or die from their abortions.

Q: How did WEBA — Woman Exploited By Abortion — get started?

A: About one year ago I was talking to another recording artist who was pro-life. I asked what pro-life meant and he said he was anti-abortion. I said "Hank, I had an abortion in 1974. I was 5½ months pregnant. It hurt so bad for so long."

He just about drove the car off the road. And he said, "Nancy, you've got to tell the story." So, a year ago I went public, founded WEBA.

Q: What are some of the effects of abortion on women?

A: I have women who cannot vacuum their carpets. They have to have the neighbor or their husbands do it while they're at the grocery store, because of the suction sound. You see, the suction machine (used in many abortions) makes that sucking sound — it's 29 times more powerful than the vacuum we use in our home. The majority of the women aren't put to sleep. It's done without being put to sleep. It's heartbreaking to me that they can't run a vacuum cleaner — that's a deep wound.

One psychological effect we see almost all the time is guilt. Others are suicidal impulses, a sense of loss, of unfulfillment. Mourning, regret, and remorse. Withdrawal, loss of confidence in decision-making capabilities. They feel that maybe they've made a wrong decision, maybe they can't make another decision right in their life. Lowering of self esteem. Preoccupation with death. Hostilities, self-destructive behavior, anger and rage. You can lose your temper quickly. A despair, helplessness, desire to remember the death date which is really weird but you do that. You remember these dates very strongly. A preoccupation with the would-be due date or due month. My daughter was due in early March, so in early March it's there.

An intent interest in babies but a thwarted maternal instinct. Women really are interested in babies, but I have many members who can't hold children. A hatred for anyone connected with abortion. Lack of desire to enter into a relationship with a partner, loss of interest in sex, an inability to forgive self, feeling of dehumanization, nightmares, seizures and tremors, frustrations, feelings of being exploited. And child abuse. We see a lot of child abuse.

I want you to understand that I do not come from any right to life organization. We are connected with no one. We remain neutral. But we are the ones they are all arguing about and discussing and debating. We are the voice of experience.

I told Congressman (Henry A.) Waxman, D-Cal., at a recent hearing, "Have you ever had your cervix dilated and the womb ripped open? Have you ever had tubes stuck inside of you and everything sucked out? Have you ever had needles stuck through your abdomen? Have you ever felt your baby thrash around and die? Have you ever had hard labor, delivered and held your baby? Because if you haven't, sir, you can't intelligently talk to me about this. We are the voice of experience. We've all had this done to us."

And that's a fact. So we hold our own ground, our own turf, our own territory.

Q: What is it that your organization does as a voice of experience?

A: We are a support group for those women who hurt — physically, emotionally, mentally and spiritually — from their abortions. We are there when the phone rings at 3 in the morning and someone is suicidal because maybe it was four years ago on that day and they still can't cope with it. We cry with them and talk with them. We are a support group. We also are a political group. I am classified as that, and I guess the strongest thing of what I intend to do — I intend to shut the abortion industry down. I intend to shut the abortion-on-demand industry down.

Q: You talked about political activity. What's been your experience here in the Congress?

A: I testified two weeks ago before Rep. Waxman, Barbara Mikulski and a few other congressmen. It was a stacked hearing — 14 to 1 doesn't sound very balanced to me. But I went in very open and honest with them, they sat very intently and very amazed at the story I had to tell about my organization, myself and my constituency, WEBA.

Barbara Mikulski said "I've never heard this side." I said, "No, Pandora's box got opened up 10 years ago and now you're just starting to see it." I predict that in five years we will see an epidemic of mental and nervous breakdowns among the women of this country. People are not going to know why and I'm going to be able to tell you why: because they've had an abortion, that's why.

It's a quick solution. Abortion is not an ending of problems, it's the down payment for a whole new set of problems. That's what it is. It doesn't get rid of them.

Q: Have your congressmen been exposed to your view, the voice of experience?

A: No. I hear time and time again, "I've never heard this side before." "Are there many more like you?" they ask. And my answer is this. Take the 15 million of us who have, by legal abortion-on-demand, killed our babies. I will give 2 million or 3 million to Planned Parenthood, NOW or whoever they want. I will give another 2 million or 3 million who have two or three abortions without open remorse.

And justification to oneself is important here, by the way. I don't know how many women I told to go have abortions. Justification. It's like, if you can have a few more, go do what you did and kind of justify it, it makes it better. It makes it not quite so bad.

That still leaves 9 million of us who've been hurt in one way, shape or form or the other — psychologically, physically, emotionally or spiritually.

Q: So you believe that there are — by conservative estimate — perhaps 10 million women who suffered as you did?

A: I believe by very conservative there's 8 million who have been hurt.

Q: Where can people write for more information?

A: They can write W.E.B.A. P.O. Box 267 Schoolcraft, Mich. 49087.

The Hidden Mourning After Abortion

by Denyse Handler

One day a young woman was brought to the emergency department of a west Toronto hospital. She had overdosed herself, apparently out of the blue. The attending psychiatrist could not figure out why. After several counselling sessions the woman told the psychiatrist that she had overdosed on the expected date of delivery of a child aborted some months earlier.

A twenty year old woman had an abortion two months prior to calling the Pregnancy Aftermath Helpline in Toronto. She was single, living with her boyfriend who was a law student. She was four and one half months pregnant when she underwent a saline abortion. Although her boyfriend was supportive throughout, she felt that he couldn't talk about what happened. She found her own behaviour had become somewhat erratic. She felt guilty and angry with her boyfriend, blaming him somewhat, and found difficulty having intercourse with him.

A twenty-two year old woman was brought to the emergency department of a southwestern Ontario hospital by ambulance, following an overdose. After 48 hours in Intensive Care she was transferred to a psychiatric unit. A history obtained from family members indicated that she had been a happy, well-adjusted person. No cause could be found for the overdose.

A month later she came back to the psychiatrist and explained that six months earlier she had had an abortion at 12 weeks gestation. During that six month period she felt regrets and guilt at various times. But approaching the expected date of delivery, her remorse became so great that she decided that suicide was her only answer. (See Dr. L.L. Barry deVeber, **Care of the Dying and the Bereaved**, p. 112)

Over the last few years, enough case reports of severe grief following abortion have accumulated that some clear outlines are beginning to emerge. Back in the early Seventies, studies showing that mothers had no significant psychological reactions to induced abortion were quite fashionable and were often cited by those making a case for less protective abortion laws. However, in recent years, psychiatrists have become increasingly critical of many early studies. Said a formidably footnoted article in the **CMA Journal** in 1981, "A search of the literature on the psychiatric aspects of abortion revealed poor study design, a lack of clear criteria for decisions for or against abortion, poor definition of psychologic symptoms..., absence of control groups in clinical studies, and indecisiveness, and uncritical attitudes in writers from various disciplines." (**CMA Journal**, September 1, 1981, Vol. 125)

Some of these studies relied on questionnaire responses; not too surprisingly, few women indicated any serious problems on questionnaires. Then, in 1977, Dr. Ian Kent reported on a study at the Canadian Psychiatric Association meeting in 1977. There were two groups of women in the study. One group had filled out a questionnaire wherein the majority said that they felt only relief at having an abortion though some reported mild trauma or emotional numbness. However, the other group of 50 women had come for psychiatric treatment of various complaints, not apparently related to a previous abortion. But during therapy for these problems, deep, unresolved pain, bereavement and a sense of identification with the fetus became evident. (**Medical Post**, October 25, 1977)

Dr. Elizabeth O'Brien, a psychiatrist who practices in west Toronto agrees with the **CMA Journal** article that the psychiatric profession's literature on abortion is poor. But she points out that it is very hard to do controlled studies because abortion patients don't often go back for follow-up. If asked for a general obstetrical history by a psychiatrist, many women omit to say they have had an abortion; they have to be asked specifically about it. Thus, most information available on this subject is anecdotal. With over half a million abortions being done in Canada since 1969, there are a multitude of such anecdotes and they are beginning slowly to shape themselves into patterns.

Grief

The primary psychological reactions to an abortion are grief and guilt. These should not be considered in themselves unhealthy; they are quite natural. Severe psychological problems occur when they are prevented. They are prevented in cases where it is socially unacceptable to mourn the aborted child, to talk about the child or express regret. People sometimes attempt to comfort by saying, "No, no, don't think about that" or "You could never have coped with a baby anyway." While kindly meant, such comforts do not help because they tend to censor rather than air the feelings of the grieving woman. Thus she may become stuck at that level of grief or guilt and fail to work through it to a resolution.

Taken from the Feb. 1983 issue of The Human. *Reprinted with permission.*

Japan:
Mourning the Lost Ones
by Denyse Handler

"Tsubasachan, I'm sorry I couldn't give birth to you. I would have loved to put my arms around you even once....Please go to heaven and live happily there. Your Mother."

So reads a little note near a small statue in a vast Buddhist temple in Japan. It is surrounded by a multitude of other statues, along with candles, toys, flowers and letters. All are gifts — gifts for aborted children.

As Urban C. Lehner's recent article in the *Wall Street Journal* (Jan. 6 1983) points out, the Japanese don't quibble about whether the unborn child is a human life. Dr. Toshiko Seto, one of Japan's more than 11,000 licensed abortionists, explains that the rising popularity of these atonement areas in temples comes from people "feeling bad about killing their babies."

Abortion was legalized after the Second World War, to reduce the high birth rate in drastic economic times. But now that about one in three women has had an abortion, there is a proliferation of these Jizos or commemorative statues of infants. The statues are often accompanied by rituals; the package costs about $115.00. This has led to some charges of commercialism on the part of the temples.

Birth control advocates claim that Japan's failure to legalize the Pill is to blame for all this. But it should be noted that Japan's current abortion rate is not much higher than that of the U.S. which promotes almost every conceivable form of birth control. Japan is considering changing its laws to offer more protection to unborn children.

The little statues, commercial gimmicks or not, probably serve a valuable psychological purpose: they enable the bereaved parent to objectify the mourned child and therefore to focus and work through grief and guilt, which might otherwise come out in less healthy, hidden ways.

Taken from the March 1983 issue of The Human. *Reprinted with permission.*

Alarming Testimony Given in Council

A surprise witness, Meta Uchtman, regional director for Suiciders Anonymous spoke in support of the Parental Notification ordinance before the Cincinnati City Council on September 1, 1981. "Suicide is assuming frightening proportions", she said. "In the USA in 1978 there was one attempt every 16 minutes, today there is one attempt every minute. Adult suicide is up 400%, teenage suicide 500%. In 1978 there were 60,000 successful suicides.

"The Cincinnati group has seen 5,620 members in *35 months*. Over 4,000 were women of whom *1,800 or more had had abortions*. The highest suicide rate is in the 15 to 24 age group. There is a direct linkage between suicide attempts and this ordinance", she said, "it is an act of cruelty to remove parental duties and rights during the abortion crisis.

"Suicide is an act of violence against the structure of society, and it causes great suffering to those near and around them. Families should be included, not omitted" (from the abortion decision). "Critical moments come equipped with taloned claws, tearing time itself into raggedly bleeding pieces before and after an abortion. Pain pushes and truth pulls. Any experience that forces an individual to feel that sense of lonely isolation and complete abandonment *is a crisis* and when you exclude someone (parents) who can reach a hand out to you, someone who cares — *the crisis is worsened.*

"Without the strength and help from a family — you are actually giving birth to suicide". She repeatedly spoke to the need for bringing this pregnant child to her parents to share the problem and to share support. She spoke eloquently of the "panic and distress that grips them after an abortion, because feelings are allowed to remain shadowy — ominous — ghostlike. They are 'shapes' dancing around the edges of their consciousness. They commonly postpone the moment of truth as long as possible. But when the subconscious throws it forward, they go through mental hell. The critical moment comes when the chilling reality overwhelms them — cold reality numbs their spirit and casts them into those dark pits of despair and pain. Feelings cannot be denied and repressed without doing violence to every area of their living and of all those they touch."

She said much more. During her testimony there was dead silence in the room. She asked Council members to place themselves "physically on that cot — were you ever involved in an abortion? — I want to put you there with me the counselor, with the victims and families." Parents "must be involved" — otherwise "you are stacking the cards against them" — why force a "substitute authority" — is it fair to "punish all parents and their daughters because of an unproven allegation that a rare parent will abuse?"

---

*The above article was taken from the Right to Life Committee of Greater Cincinnati, Inc. Newsletter (September, 1981). Reprinted with permission.

Precious in my Sight

by Paula Sutcliffe

In 1961, when I was 16 years old, my mother told me never to come home pregnant — she would rather I had an abortion. I was only slightly surprised at this statement — but not worried. After all, I was already quite aware of artificial contraception, and used it. "No" wasn't necessary for me. Besides, I was living my life as if it were a grade B movie — if I became pregnant, well, baby and I would do fine by ourselves without parental help, thank you.

I had ambivalent feelings about abortion. I would never have one; but maybe it was right for other women. I had worked one summer as a volunteer at a large New York City hospital's gynecology floor. I encountered many women who had been admitted due to "botched up" abortions. I had friends who thought they might be pregnant, and lent one money when she needed an abortion.

I went to nursing school, and in 1973 when the Supreme Court ruled abortion was a private matter, I worked in an abortion clinic. Sex and procreation needn't be linked together anymore — and I applauded this. I took the job in the clinic to act out my support to my sisters in distress.

I found much distress in the clinic — but it involved not only the women. I saw the pain of the babies who were born burned from the saline used for late-term abortions. I saw the bits of feet, the bits of hands, the mangled heads and bodies of little people. I saw pain and I felt pain. Most of the patients weren't 14-year-old girls who had been seduced by some insensitive boy. Most of them were — they said — happily married women who just didn't want the hassle of another baby.

I quit the clinic after working there for two weeks, and I quit thinking abortion was the answer for unwanted pregnancies. Well, almost. I did not truly know what I would do if I became pregnant. I just stopped thinking about the whole subject.

Many things happened to me in the next few years. I grew closer and closer to Jesus, decided it was time to "clean up my act," and became a Christian. Not long after my conversion I became the wife of a man who was studying for Holy Orders in the Episcopal church. David said abortion was wrong. I agreed — except of course in cases where the baby would be deformed or in any way not quite "right." It wouldn't be fair to the baby, would it?

Our marriage was happy. We had one baby — Joshua was just perfect. Then another baby — this baby was not "quite right." He wasn't breathing at birth and he was in such a bad condition the doctors said he would probably die, or end up a vegetable.

Ben did not die, nor is he a vegetable. He has cerebral palsy. He does not walk or sit unassisted or have any fine motor abilities, and he is non-verbal. He is very intelligent, but will always be dependent on others for his physical needs. When Ben was an infant I would look at him and think *this is the type of baby I used to think would have been better-off aborted.* I didn't think that anymore.

Despite the abortion clinic experience...despite my faith in God...I hadn't completely internalized the fact (and for me it is a fact) that it isn't *what you can do* that matters, it is *who you ARE* that counts...and that is as the children's song says, "All are precious in His sight."

My son taught and still teaches me valuable lessons about what it means to be human. Through Benjamin, we have come to know many children and adults with physical and intellectual limitations. It hasn't always been a comfortable experience, but then most worthwhile experiences rarely start out by being comfortable. Ben is exceptionally loving and has a great sense of humor; he doesn't feel handicapped. What he does feel is LOVED. His presence in this world has let my husband and myself minister more effectively to the people around us.

We can deal with a real compassion that sees that what might seem to be the easiest answer to a problem may be in the end the most painful answer of all.

Abortion seems to be an easy answer to the problem of unwanted pregnancy, or a pregnancy where a baby with a "problem" is involved. But it is misplaced compassion to think that by the process of abortion we can pretend that child never existed.

Ben's existence in this world — and his very full part in our lives and the lives of many others — has shown me that *I* have all sorts of coping powers and that God has all sorts of transforming powers that I never knew existed. And I never would have known that these powers existed if Ben was not in our lives. With Benjamin's birth, I stopped being a "closet prolifer." Every baby who was aborted because of a genetic defect — why, it could have been Ben. Every newborn starved to death because it wasn't the baby his parents dreamed of — why, it could have been Ben. No longer can I relegate human beings to being precious only in God's sight. They — we — have become precious in my sight too.

Some people become thoroughly convinced of the prolife message as soon as they learn of fetal development. Some of us take a long time coming to what then seem to be the most obvious conclusions. Life is a gift. Violence is no more acceptable when committed on a preborn baby, than it is on a wife or a child or on someone whose skin color or beliefs are different than ours. It isn't always easy being consistent, but consistent I must try to be. Along with the horror stories of this world, along with the brokenness and pain — there is an awful lot of love. We must learn to reach out for that love. We must learn to give it.

Section Three:
What Kind
of World
Are We Creating?

- Abortion and Health
- Abortion and Economics
- From Abortion to...Where?

Sterilization Rather than Workplace Reform

*by Gail Grenier Sweet
and Nancy Randolph Pearcey*

According to a 1980 *Chicago Sun-Times* article, many U.S. industrial companies are telling women to sterilize themselves...to accept lower-paying jobs in less hazardous areas...or to leave. These "options" are offered to women employees, rather than the companies removing toxic hazards in the workplace.

Anthony Mazzocchi, described as the "Ralph Nader of industrial safety," made these accusations at a meeting of the Chicago Area Committee on Occupational Safety and Health.

"Companies are moving to alter the workers, not the workplace," he charged. He named one company (American Cyanamid Co.) which requires sterilization for women who are exposed to lead compounds.

Is this pro-*choice*?

Abortion and the Rights of Women in the Workplace

by Consuelo Beck-Sagué, M.D.

It was easy to anticipate that the unrestricted, constitutionally defended access to abortion through the second trimester would provide a real point of unity to the new right. After all, the other rallying "causes" such as school prayer and restriction of civil liberties of sexual minorities could hardly rally much support in the climate of tolerance of the seventies. But with abortion they had their own legitimate civil and human rights issue, and they were going to use it for all it was worth. But it was hard to anticipate what it would do to women's rights in the workplace.

Certainly other tragic events of the late 70's and 80's contributed to the attrition of these rights. The feminization of poverty and of the working poor are the products of many well known social and political events. But the focusing of feminist energy towards defending and expanding abortion rights has certainly had a foreseeable impact on these rights. This very ironic adverse impact accompanied the loss of the broad base of support enjoyed by the E.R.A., in part a reaction against its perceived association with abortion.

The ironic effects of abortion on working women's rights are best illustrated by an event that took place in California in 1984. A woman worker, after completing a six-week employer-approved maternity leave found her job had been taken during that time. She took her case to the courts and the lower court ruled in her favor. The employer appealed the ruling and the higher court struck down the lower court's ruling, finding that the maternity leave constituted a privilege on the basis of the employee's gender and was discretionary. The woman appealed to the A.C.L.U., which assured her that the birth was freely chosen and that she had no legally defensible right to the promised leave. The N.O.W. (National Organization of Women) declined to take the case, as they felt that a statement in support of guaranteed option of maternity leave would justify restriction of employment opportunities for women. The pregnancy, since it could have been "interrupted", became solely her responsibility, and her failure to use the back-up method of "contraception" represented a waiving of her right to compete in the workplace.

As might have been expected, while this case did not get much publicity, employers did take note. Many non-statutory informal agreements with women workers regarding maternity leave and daycare (and with men workers regarding paternity leave and daycare) represent an area which was formerly a feminist issue. Now that we have abortion, we don't need to be in the fight for those rights. The organizations that were formerly pioneers for working women's rights feel that abortion alone has been the great equalizer.

Soon, we may not even need suffrage.

Nature's Double Standard

Though God always forgives and men and women sometimes, nature never does. When it comes to health and sex, nature makes it a double standard, with the woman always paying.

In New Zealand there has recently been reported a fourfold increase in cancer of the cervix among younger women. A medical campaign for publicity in the UK aimed at encouraging sexually active younger women to take smear tests, reports 2,000 deaths a year from this cause.

In Christchurch, Dr. McLean, who uses a laser beam at the Women's Hospital, the only one in New Zealand, says that the increase is due to "more and more girls having multiple partners and starting their sexual career at a young age." The other day a new VD clinic opened in South Auckland, for the present rate of 10,000 visits a year has overburdened the existing service.

The woman always pays; for some, it is a sentence of sterility and possible early death. Do you hear the Family Planning Association broadcasting these warnings?

From *Women For Life Newsletter*, P.O. Box 38-137, Howick-Auckland, New Zealand, April 1982. Reprinted with permission.

Women Die From Legal Abortion

by Monica M. Migliorino

Since the legalization of abortion on demand in 1973, women dying from legal abortion have replaced those who died from illegal abortion. This is the conclusion of an in-depth study by Hilgers and O'Hare. Their study shows that since 1940 maternal deaths due to criminal abortion have steadily decreased, though by no means have they been entirely eliminated even with the legalization of abortion on demand. On the other hand maternal deaths due to legal abortion have increased. This parallels the decrease in criminal abortion deaths. They state:

> As a result, there has been no detectable change in the relative frequency of abortion-related maternal death due to induced abortion in the United States in the last 30 years. It is extremely important that there has been *no* significant impact on the relative frequency of abortion related maternal death due to induced abortion in the United States since the legalization of abortion. The reason for this appears to be quite simple. While maternal deaths due to criminal abortion appear to be decreasing, *they have been replaced, almost one for one, by maternal deaths due to legal abortion.**

---

*Thomas W. Hilgers, M.D. and Dennis O'Hare, "Abortion Related Maternal Mortality: An In-Depth Analysis," in *New Perspectives on Human Abortion*, ed. by Thomas W. Hilgers, M.D., Dennis J. Horan, and David Mall (Frederick, Maryland, University Publications of America, Inc. 1981), p. 84.

Abortion: Solution to Poverty and Starvation?

by Juli Loesch

I just got a letter from a group promoting a supposedly "humane" population-control, anti-poverty program. They claim that stepped-up contraception, sterilization and abortion for the poor is needed to cure the world hunger problem because there are "too many" poor people on earth and not enough food. They are asking for my donation.

They are not going to get it.

I don't want to get into the various forms of birth control (some of which may be quite acceptable) or the various reasons for abortion (some of which are morally agonizing). But I would like to criticize the notion that abortion and sterilization are good anti-poverty measures, and that famine is caused by overpopulation.

First, this group called for funds to ensure that poor women will have the opportunity to kill their offspring before they see the light of day. It was suggested that, for some classes of people, non-existence is preferable to existence. Abortion was offered as a solution for a sociological problem (poverty), as if to say, we can eliminate poverty by eliminating the poor.

This is not even "right to choose": no woman is exercising "free choice" if she is driven by poverty to wish that her unborn children (and even her born children) were dead. This hardly affirms her glorious "reproductive freedom" and certainly doesn't cure her poverty!

With its family planning budget of $250 million, HEW freely pays ninety per cent of the costs of sterilization for "low income women." They have aggressively promoted sterilization among Native American women, finding it more efficient than other birth control methods. And Puerto Rico's Population Studies Department reports that almost forty per cent of all Puerto Rican women of childbearing age have been sterilized!

The attrition of the poor by abortion and sterilization — both in this country and Asia, Africa and Latin America — is being offered as an anti-hunger tactic. But t'aint necessarily so: hunger is not caused by over-population.

Basic food self-reliance is possible for every country in the world.

Frances Moore Lappé, co-director of the Institute for Food and Development Policy (IFDP), calculates that even during the "food crisis" of the early Seventies there was plenty of food to go around — enough in grains alone to provide everyone on earth with 3,000 calories per day, plus ample protein.

Every African nation suffering from acute famine, actually produced enough grain to feed its total population, even during the worst drought year. In fact, agricultural exports from the Sahel (West Africa) rose dramatically during the early Seventies according to the U.S. Food and Agricultural Organization.

Yet thousands of people did die of starvation. Why?

Not because of population, but because of injustice. People starve in the midst of plenty because that "plenty" is owned by groups who are aiming at maximization of profits rather than serving human needs. They starve because the land is owned by a handful of landlords, corporations or a corrupt government monopoly. They starve because they lack the political power to control their own lives.

For instance: Peru exports anchovies and Ghana exports tuna, while Peruvians and Ghanaians suffer unspeakably from protein hunger. Cuba's communist monopoly devotes the prime land to sugar for export; the same happens under capitalism in the Dominican Republic. Other Latin American countries squander their topsoil on the production of coffee, tea or cocoa, all non-nutritious items for international trade, so that a tiny minority can reap the profits while the large majority have no food.

What's the solution?

I think it's in re-aligning people's minds away from "maximization of profits" and toward serving human needs. It's in re-aligning land-use so that every nation can produce ample food for the ordinary people, not luxury junk for the rich. It's in re-aligning political power so that everybody has their say.

These re-alignments will be bitterly opposed by the wealthier folks who already control the land, the food, and the political power. These wealthier folks may be the very ones who are saying, "Oh you poor hungry woman, we feel so sorry for you. We know just how to help you. Let's kill your kid."

April 19, 1978, *Prolifers for Survival*. P.O. Box 3316, Chapel Hill, NC 27514. Reprinted with permission.

A Single Parent of Six on Abortion and the Poor

by Lucien Miller

The following interview is with a single parent and mother of six children. She is a person well acquainted with poverty. Her experience of a life lived among the poor in Washington, D.C., is the inspiration for her work in the areas of health care and fair housing.

Lucien: Maybe the place to begin is with the question about your experience of poverty. What does being poor mean?

Response: You don't have choices. That's what it means. When you go to the store, you buy what you can afford. Being poor means not having a place to stay, or being in public shelters with your kids, or having them taken away from you. When you are poor, it is difficult to get help. Kids are more likely to go to jail. You can't give them things. Rich or middle class kids can always find things to do.

L: What about the pressures on poor women in Washington, D.C., especially those who have children?

Response: There are approximately 10,000 births in Washington, D.C. each year, mostly to people with lower incomes. The upper-income people moving back into the city, as a rule, don't have any children. These bureaucrat-professionals buy up the older homes and renovate them as townhouses. The low-income housing is incredibly bad or else unavailable, and is manipulated by the out-of-town rich. There is a real connection to the abortion clinics. If women have to give up their born children because they cannot rent any sort of housing for them, you can surely see how the system is meant to relieve us of our unborn ones. Corporations own the clinics. People you never see. They capitalize on the people. The slum landlords and the owners and operators of abortion clinics are the same kind.

L: What kind of housing for your family did you obtain when you came to Washington?

Response: When I came to Washington, we had no place to stay. Protective Services (welfare) put us in a motel. You sign an agreement that as soon as a place is available you will take it. The apartment we had to accept was privately owned by a housing corporation. There was a hole in one wall you could walk through from the outside, and the sink in the kitchen would fall down. It was below zero that year at times, and either they turned the heat off or there was never enough.

My youngest child was still a baby. People throughout the apartment building turned on their gas stoves to keep warm, but ours was next to the wall with the hole in it. The wind would blow the gas out, so I was afraid of turning on the stove for fear we'd be suffocated. We were really cold that year.

L: I take it there wasn't anything you could do about the living conditions?

Response: I went to Small Claims Court and tried to sue, but it was very hard to identify the person who was responsible. You could never deliver the suit. They have you over a barrel, like a starving person. What finally happened was that the Protective Services got behind on their welfare checks, so they piled up and I got them all together. I took that piled-up money and moved to Virginia so we wouldn't freeze.

L: Given the number of children born each year and the terrible housing, how do the Protective Services personnel look upon poor women who are pregnant? In your own experience, do social workers encourage abortion?

Response: The first questions asked are: are you black or white or pregnant? They couldn't tell looking at me. I suspect that with others they rush to get a Medicaid card so that the person can have an abortion. But I think I am different from a lot of people in not feeling any pressure to abort. There wasn't coercion from the social workers so much as from the whole system. With others, they ask questions to show you how difficult it will be for you to have the baby. The only pressure on me to stop having babies was from doctors.

L: Why was that?

Response: I feel that doctors are more likely to hold strong "elitist" opinions than are welfare workers. Once I had a bladder infection and when I went to see the doctor, he told me I should have my tubes tied. He didn't think I had a right to have more children. I had four kids then.

L: What about abortion clinics? Are they exploiting the poor?

Response: Some of them focus on the poor to make money off us. They get government money through our bodies, just like the landlords. They operate the same and exploit us the same. It's as if what we want is not good enough for us. It is hard to imagine a man with a $300,000 house, swimming pool and tennis courts really thinking of whether or not we want to live in the rotten rat-infested place he owns. And it's just as hard to think that this doctor running the abortion assembly line really truthfully believes that he is giving us what we want. Yet you hear them saying: "Poor people want it". "You're depriving them of their rights if you don't give them abortions," etc. That's bull! They aren't even thinking about what we want.

L: Is it your knowledge of exploitation that led you to oppose abortion?

Response: It is so obvious that abortion does nothing to redistribute the wealth or to improve the economic situation for the poor class. Abortion is overt bigotry. In other words, it's the view of those who say it saves money, that it's cheaper to get rid of the poor. This is the motive of a lot of so-called "liberals" who are behind abortion. They think they can do more for us by cutting us down to size. It's much easier for them to think in terms of "population control."

L: Could you talk about some of your personal reasons for working against abortion — I mean, what motivates you?

Response: I guess, first of all, I don't believe we can or should solve problems by destroying life. But there is an attitude behind the abortion mentality that I have always found very digusting. I read an article in a right to life journal last spring in which a history professor wrote that the people who make up "the backbone of pro-abortion opinion in America" are the well-to-do folks who have had all the children they want and who feel that their own teenage daughter would be "ruined" if she got pregnant. He hit the nail right on the head.

L: Maybe you are reacting in part to people who have a kind of "perfect product" morality regarding the correct number of children we are supposed to have and the acceptable circumstances under which they are to be born?

Response: People in my class feel uncomfortable around people who think like that, people who make you feel ashamed and defensive, as though you owed them an explanation for having children.

L: What would be your response to the middle class or rich folks' horror of a teenage pregnancy?

Response: I could count on all my fingers and toes the twelve year old mothers and twenty-five year old grandmothers I know. It's accepted, not something special, but a fact of life. Nobody ever says "unmarried mother." I hate that term. To me it comes down to my own brand of feminism which is opposite to those women who are anxious to define themselves and their children in relation to their men and that little piece of paper, the marriage certificate.

L: What about your experience as a member of the Right-to-Life movement?

Response: In the right-to-life movement, I work with all kinds of people who are against abortion. I agree with this opposition to abortion wholeheartedly. What I find incompatible is the fixation some pro-lifers have with "the family." The pro-family thing puts marriage first and kids second, and all else (like social justice) is excluded. It is the kind of mentality that defines children as "illegitimate." It is exactly the kind of structured thinking that motivates the typical pro-abortion attitude the history professor so precisely described. I would expect to find this sort of narrowness at a Planned Parenthod clinic, but it should be opposed, not endorsed, by right-to-lifers. If we want to pursue a pro-life social conscience, we cannot afford to increase intolerance toward any pregnant woman.

L: But you find the reverse is true?

Response: "Pro-family" is sometimes against daycare, welfare, work opportunities, and every logical and human alternative to abortion.

L: So in addition to working against abortion through the right-to-life movement, it seems that you perform a critical role within the movement as well.

Response: I think most of the people in right-to-life are missing the point. This is a very radical movement. Today there is automation, no jobs, and population control. As a work force we are becoming more obsolete. The pro-life movement is a radical movement to change the whole system. Being part of right-to-life really comes down to becoming anti-capitalistic. It includes the right to exist, but more importantly it means the right to be an equal part of.

L: How do you think you are received by others within the pro-life movement?

Response: Some of them think "right" more than "life". I do encounter some problems with certain conservative people in the right-to-life movement — the ones who are against sex education and who enthusiastically push adoption for babies born into "unauthorized" homes. I think most of the activist people really go along with me to the limited extent that they 'can understand where I am coming from. And there are others involved who are just like me — sort of "outside insiders." Some of the conservatives who are sincere are our most appreciative supporters, though, because they see that we are able to reach people who won't listen to them.

L: Does your involvement in the abortion issue also grow out of a concern for civil rights, the right to fair housing, for instance, which you discussed earlier?

Response: Yes. I'm concerned about an attitude which says, if your family can't fit into a one room flat, we'll cut you down to size so you can.

L: Were you yourself given hope by the civil rights movement of the 60's?

Response: Yes, we poor and members of minorities felt we had come a long way through the 60's. We thought there had really been changes. Yes, there is just as much poverty today, but at least it's no longer cool to be a bigot. That couldn't happen any more. But then abortion came along and that made me realize: "They're still thinking that way."

L: What about other women's issues since you joined the pro-life movement — have you been involved with them?

Response: After I got into pro-life, another woman and myself worked in California with the Coalition for Medical Rights. They are against population control and forced sterilization. The leftist feminist types. They are more against Planned Parenthood than even Right-to-Lifers are. They have produced great literature against Rockefeller, the symbol of population control. Planned Parenthood wants to control the population in Third World countries and apply the same mentality here. Basically, the people behind it want to save themselves money. It's imperialistic, racist, and everything else. They want to promote business conglomerates and make sure the resources in the Third World go to them. So my anti-abortion stance was tolerated by people in the Coalition, because they fully appreciated that I agreed with them.

L: These strong reservations regarding Planned Parenthood among the radical left are not about birth control, are they?

Response: There is a strong and powerful leftist movement against Planned Parenthood because of Planned Parenthood-World Population whose major objective is population control. As for birth control, I am for it because I think it is one of the necessary alternatives to abortion.

Taken from *Reflections*, P.O. Box 150, Amherst, MA 01002. Reprinted with permission.

A Matter of Welfare
by Elizabeth Moore Sobo

On June 30, 1980, the U.S. Supreme Court handed down another in its long and controversial series of opinions on the subject of human abortion. This time the court concluded that federal and state governments were under no Constitutional obligation to fund abortions under the Medicaid program. Anti-abortion groups claimed a victory, saying that taxpayers should not be forced to pay for abortions against their wishes. Abortion proponents, noting that the Congress and a majority of state legislatures have already gone on record in opposition to abortion funding, said that the ruling would drastically limit abortion access for poor women. Both responses reflected an accurate analysis of the court's action, and both were entirely predictable. What neither group noted, however, is that the welfare abortion controversy is as much a matter of welfare as it is a question of abortion.

Reasons cited in favor of funding abortions under Medicaid fall within two general headings: the equal access and the economic arguments. According to the former theory, rich women are able to "choose" abortions and to finance them for themselves, so the government ought to allow indigent women the same option by subsidizing the procedure with Medicaid dollars. The second theory sees poverty itself as a compelling reason to abort, and presents "evidence" to support a conclusion that both the poor themselves and the society as a whole will benefit from a welfare abortion program.

In order to understand the error of these arguments, it is necessary to relate the welfare-abortion question to a culture of inequality which is responsible for making poverty itself an institution that can be simultaneously tolerated and condemned by reformists. The economics of poverty and the economics of abortion are inseparable.

Poverty, as a personal experience, affects all facets of an individual's existence. It limits one's lifestyle in every conceivable way — not just physically, but socially, environmentally, culturally, and politically as well. It isolates its subjects from the mainstream of society, and it instills in them a sense of irrelevance, rejection, and hopelessness.

Because our nation is founded both on the idealism of individual equality and on the practical theory of competitive economics, poverty has yet another dimension. It serves as a yardstick by which the achievements of the non-poor may be measured. While poverty may be condemned as unfair, it nonetheless serves to reinforce the belief that individual success and individual worth are identical. And so, while the system may see a need to relieve poverty, it strongly militates against the actual elimination of poverty.

It is in this respect that the equal access theory in the abortion debate most clearly illustrates the error of contemporary reformist thinking. By proposing to provide equality of "choice" to the poor with free abortions, the argument carries an implicit assumption that the poor are equal in most (if not all) other respects. The theory thus reinforces the myth that one's personal abilities and one's personal choices are the primary factors which determine one's status in society.

But the myth of "choice" in abortion is apparent not only with regard to the needy. Because abortion undeniably involves a degree of physical and emotional pain, the abortion decision cannot be viewed apart from the factors that motivate it. Those factors — personal problems, social pressure, lack of support from family, society, or friends — suggest that the choice is never a truly voluntary one. It is more likely in fact that women submit to abortions, not so much because they have the choice, but because they feel that in their own circumstances, they have no choice at all.

For indigent women the decision is even less voluntary. When one considers the fact that poor women have been effectively denied access to the basic necessities of life, that adequate housing, nutrition, jobs and job training, and daycare services are generally out of reach, the offer of a "free" abortion seems far less altruistic. Poverty itself negates the right to make choices.

A variation of the equal access argument involves the prediction that a given number of poor women will opt for abortions anyway and, denied safe, legal ones, they will be driven to the "back-alley butcher." Although government statistics from those states which ceased to provide welfare abortions following a federal payment ban in 1977 tend to discredit this approach, it is still accepted as valid by a number of public officials, service and lobbying groups, and well-intentioned private citizens.

This, too is an argument based on a false premise; the misunderstanding here is primarily one of values. A well-known historian once commented that it is upper-middle-class couples, who have all the children they want and who fear their own teenage daughters would be "ruined" by an unplanned pregnancy, who form the backbone of pro-abortion opinion in America. Because the poor generally have not been assimilated into a culture which condemns large, woman-headed households, teenage motherhood, or births, apart from marriage or any unintended pregnancy does not create the personal crisis that is imagined by more affluent pro-abortionists.

Furthermore, material wealth and social status mean most to those who have achieved them. And the values of low-income people are proportionately more "people-centered." Thus the attitude toward children among disadvantaged classes, particularly minority groups, has been one of unqualified acceptance. Because childbearing is never explicitly condemned, the "right" of abortion — even in cases of near-insurmountable financial hardship — has never been viewed with anything close to the urgency attributed to it by those who subscribe to the "back-alley butcher" theory.

Like the equal access arguments, the economic aspects of abortion funding are similarly based on judgments which represent the values and interests of the upper classes. It was argued by the abortion funding advocates in the Supreme Court case that indigent women, as a direct consequence of their own economic deprivation, were subject to more frequent and more serious health problems during pregnancy and delivery, and that their children likewise were at a medical disadvantage. These facts were presented to the court as evidence that induced abortions were a "medical necessity" among the welfare population.

Not only did that argument fail to note that all poor people, not just pregnant women and infants, are adversely affected by poverty, but it neglected to take into consideration the fact that health conditions generating difficulties in natural birth are also likely to present problems in abortion surgery.

Ironically, those who argued on behalf of Medicaid abortion funds were willing to identify the environmental problems associated with economic hardship, but were silent with regard to any political or economic solution to these problems. In other words those women who lack adequate food, clothing, shelter, education, daycare, jobs, and other opportunities taken for granted by most Americans, are to be offered abortions precisely because these needs remain unmet. It is this kind of reasoning which has led a number of welfare rights advocates to conclude that human services to the poor will be diminished in direct proportion to the increased availability of abortions as a solution to human problems.

Abortion does nothing whatever to promote social and economic justice, nor does it compensate for the lack of it. But it does, indeed, undermine collective responsibility. Since abortion was made legal nationally in 1973, it has become less and less "logical" for the government (or the private sector) to respond to the needs of a mother for daycare or affordable family housing. Just as the consequence of a woman's decision to abort has become private and outside the realm of public interference, so has the consequence of her determination not to abort. More and more, she is left to fend for herself; more and more, she is blamed for her own situation.

The Medicaid abortion controversy, with all its apparent contradictions, has the unique potential to help us identify a difference between real and imagined charity. While funding abortions may seem a relatively simple way to avoid a more radical response to human needs, it can also be interpreted as an implicit denial of all those things we seek in the name of our children.

A true economic democracy cannot be created overnight, nor without considerable commitment and sacrifice on the part of many. But a positive approach to the interrelated issues of poverty and abortion might be a good place to start.

Reprinted with permission from *Sojourners*, P.O. Box 29272, Washington, D.C. 20017. Taken from the November, 1980 issue.

All Abortions Are Selective

by Jo McGowan

Amniocentesis, a medical procedure by which certain abnormalities in an unborn child can be detected, is fraught with moral dilemmas, the magnitude of which are only now being understood. The standard use of the test has been to provide women in high-risk categories — older women, women with a family history of genetic diseases, women who have contracted German measles in the first trimester of their pregnancies — with information about the well-being of their babies. If the test proves that abnormalities do exist, the option is to abort the child or carry it to term anyway.

The test by itself is not without risk to the child. It involves the precise insertion of a needle into the womb and withdrawing a small quantity of amniotic fluid which is then tested. There is always the chance of the needle going into the placenta or the child, causing severe damage or miscarriage. Women are advised that if they do not intend to have an abortion if the child is found to be defective, they would be better off not having the test at all. As such, it can be termed a "hunt and kill" method.

In the United States, where the first test came out, fears were expressed by many feminists in regard to one of the side aspects of the test: that, in addition to revealing defects, it could also reveal the sex of the child. They were afraid that such information would be used to abort baby girls simply because they were girls and irrespective of their physical and mental health. These fears were brushed aside by most people as unthinkable. Surely, they reasoned, we have gone well beyond the stage where the birth of a girl is a tragedy.

Not so in India. Recent reports in national newsmagazines tell startling stories of women undergoing the test for the sole purpose of discovering whether the child is a girl. If it is, it is promptly aborted. The reasons given are painfully familiar: the expense of marrying a daughter off, the need for sons to help in the family business and carry on the family name — in short, the age-old preference of boys over girls.

Feminists, naturally, have risen in anger. With morality and justice as their standards, they argue that it is "morally incorrect" to use the words of Dr. Kirpal Kaur, who performs abortions at the Guru Tegh Bahadur Medical College in Amritsar, to allow sex to be the determining factor in the decision to abort. In effect, as Manjulika Dubey points out in a recent article in *Mainstream*, using the test in this way affirms what has long been suspected in this country: that to be born female is to be genetically defective.

Both Ms. Dubey and Anjali Deshpande, author of a second article in the same magazine, draw attention to the steadily decreasing ratio of women to men in India (from 1,000:972 in 1901 to 1,000:935 in 1981). "If amniocentesis is misused on a large scale to weed out female fetuses, the ratio is bound to show a further decline," writes Ms. Deshpande. Ms. Dupey goes on to decry the failures of the feminist movement if it is possible that women could "reject their own kind and ... worship and covet power objectified in the male to the point of participating in *atrocities* against their own daughters" (emphasis added).

"Atrocity" is her term for abortion. "Female feticide" is Ms. Deshpande's. And from Vimla Ranadive, secretary of the All India Coordination Committee of Working Women: "It is like the Nazi's 'final solution' of exterminating the Jews and it only adds a touch of sophistication to the brutal practice."

"Atrocity," "female feticide," "brutal practice." Apt descriptions of abortion — but they ring a bit hollow coming from people who, in the next breath, assert that abortion rights must be safeguarded so that women can "control their lives."

What are we to make of all this? Without denying in any sense the depravity of killing baby girls simply because they are girls, I submit that the position feminists have taken on this issue is morally bankrupt, without substance of any kind.

Why? Because one cannot have it both ways. Once the abortion of any child, for any reason, is permitted, the abortion of all children becomes acceptable. If it is all right to kill a child because it is handicapped, or because its mother is unmarried, or because it is the third child in a family that only wanted two, why isn't it all right to kill it because it is a girl?

This process of aborting girls when boys are wanted has been termed "selective abortion," but in fact every abortion is a selective one. What changes from case to case are only the values of the parents, determining what they select and what they reject. Parents who only value physically and mentally normal children might reject a child who was retarded or who had hemophilia. Parents who value education and want to be able to provide their children with it might reject a third child if their resources could only educate two. Parents who value their time and freedom might reject *any* children they produced. And parents who value boys might well reject a child known to be a girl.

Feminists who have been so active in assuring women of the "right to choose" can hardly complain when those same women exercise their freedom to choose something with which feminists do not agree. Choice being such a highly personal affair, one can hardly expect everyone to choose the same things. But it is tragically ironic that what has been hailed as the "great liberator" of women may turn out instead to be the means of their destruction — a tool to make them, in Manjulika Dubey's words, an "endangered species."

Perhaps, however, something good may yet emerge from this "female feticide" outrage. Perhaps people, and feminists in particular, will finally realize what is actually at stake in an abortion, any abortion. Perhaps from this undeniable truth that it is wrong to kill girls will emerge the larger truth that it is wrong to kill anyone. Perhaps it will first be necessary for a special interest group to champion the cause of each particular group of children targeted for destruction: feminists for baby girls, disabled activists for handicapped babies, would-be adoptive parents for unwanted babies.

This would certainly be the long way round, but perhaps at the end of it all we would realize that the single unifying factor in all these cases is that the child to be aborted is, first and foremost, a human child and one of us, that to kill it is to kill that which makes us human, bringing us closer to the day when the entire race — male and female — is an endangered species.

This article was originally published in 1982 in *Indian Express*, and is reprinted with permission of the author.

Who Are You?

by Jean Blackwood

Who are you
Floating nameless in that secret sea?
Who are you
To make claims against humanity?
You, who have done nothing to earn equality?
When did you draw breath
Through a finely rolled
Stick of chopped, burning tobacco?
Where is your diploma
Testifying to daily attendance
In public school for twelve years?
How many steaks have you eaten?
Do you even know how to barbecue?
Have you ever watched tv?
Do you know who Walter Cronkite is, or even J.R.?

Have you ever been drafted
And learned to fight and kill
On command?
Ever paid on a mortgage?
Ever spoken so much
As one sarcastic word?
Ever paid any taxes,
Or complained about them?

The answers are all no,
I know;
You're not a bit like me.
You don't even have
A microwave oven!

And yet, I fear you,
You nothing,
Because if someone doesn't put a stop
To your damned **growing**
Pretty soon I'll have to **see** you.
And then you and your kind
Will gather round me
And start stealing.

First my cigarettes,
Then my steaks,
My tv,
My car,
My house...
You'll take my job!
You'll walk on my lawn
And push me out
Into the cold,
Nameless nothingness I came from.

I won't have it!
Who are you, anyway?
You can't come along
And take my microwave oven!
Then who would **I** be?

From *Beyond Beginning and Other Poems*, P.O. Box 490, Clarion, Penna 16214

Talk of 'Wanted Child' Makes for Doll Objects

by Sidney Callahan

I'd like to start a campaign against the idea of "the wanted child". This phrase is dangerous to children, even in small doses. The people who use the phrase in efforts to control population or sell family-planning programs are well-meaning, but they are sowing the seeds of subtle destruction.

The corruption involved is quite simple to grasp. If you start talking and thinking about a child as a "wanted child" you cannot help but put the idea into people's heads that children exist and have a right to exist only because someone wants them. And alas, the opposite conclusion is also there waiting for us: if it's an "unwanted child" it has no rights.

It's destructive of family life for parents even to think in these categories of wanted and unwanted children. By using the words you set up parents with too much power, including psychological power, over their children. Somehow the child is being measured by the parent's attitudes and being defined by the parent's feelings. We usually want only objects, and the fact of wanting them or not implies that we are superior, or at least engaged in a one-way relationship, to them.

In the same way, men have "wanted" women through the ages. Often a woman's position was precarious and rested on being wanted by some man. The unwanted woman could be cast off when she was no longer a desirable object. She did not have an intrinsic dignity beyond being wanted. That's what they mean in protests against being a sex object.

Well, talking about the "wanted child" is making a child a "doll object". When you want one, you make one or buy one, and it then has a right to exist as a glorified form of property. And woe be to the child who is no longer wanted, or who is imperfect in some way. Or who in the crunch, does not satisfy. Has satisfaction been given, sir? If not, the merchandise is returnable, you know.

The point I'm trying to stress, of course, is that old idea in our common culture that each human being has inviolable rights and dignity no matter what. If you're a Jew and they don't want you in Nazi Germany, it's Germany's shame. If you're a black and they don't want you in the club, that's the club's crime. If you're a woman and they don't want you in the job, it's their fault. The powerful (including parents) cannot be allowed to want and unwant people at will.

In family life, this idea of unique inviolable dignity and intrinsic value is especially needed. Since emotions are so strong and dependency needs are so urgent, the temptation to cop out is ever present. We don't hang in there because we always want to, or want something or somebody. The old parent, the sick spouse, the needy child are not always wanted.

So who cares what you want, or whether other people want you? Human beings are human beings. Every individual has his rights. A child's very existence is claim enough.

Reprinted by permission of the *National Catholic Reporter*, P.O. Box 281, Kansas City, MO 64141. This article was taken from the Dec. 3, 1971 issue. Reprinted with permission of the author.

Can They Defend Themselves?

Kesey On Un-Dead Old, Un-Born Young

[Excerpts from "An Impolite Interview with Ken Kesey" by Paul Krassner, Editor of the *Realist* (Vol. 90, Dec. '71):]

Q. Since you're against abortion, doesn't that put you in the position of saying that a girl or a woman must bear an unwanted child as punishment for ignorance or carelessness?

A. In as I feel abortions to be probably the worst worm in the revolutionary philosophy, a worm bound in time to suck the righteousness and the life from the work we are engaged in, I want to take this slowly and carefully. This is the story of Freddy Schrimpler:

As part of his training, a psychiatric aide must spend at least two weeks working the geriatric wards. These wards are concrete barns built, not for attempted cures or even for attempted treatments of the herds of terminal humanity that would otherwise be roaming the streets, drooling and disgusting the healthy citizenry, but for nothing more than shelter and sustenance, waiting rooms where old guys spend ten, twenty, sometimes thirty years waiting for their particular opening in the earth. At eight in the morning they are herded and wheeled into showers, then to Day Rooms where they are fed a toothless goo, then are plunked into sofas ripe with decades of daily malfunctions of worn-out sphincters, then fed again, and washed again, and their temperatures taken if they're still warm enough to register, and their impacted bowels dug free in the case of sphincters worn-out in the other direction, and their hair and cheesy old fingernails clipped (the clippings swept into a little pink and grey pile), and fed again and washed again, and then usually left alone through the long afternoons.

Some of these derelicts still have a lot going and enjoy trapping flies and other such morsels in the snare of their baited hands, and some engage in contented and garrulous conversations with practically anything, and some watch TV, but most of them lie motionless on the plastic covered sofas or in gurney beds, little clots of barely-breathing bones and skin under government sheets. Even the doctors call them vegetables.

In caring for these men something becomes immediately obvious to all the young aides undergoing their first real brush with responsibility. The thought is very explicit. After the first meal squeezed into a slack mouth, or after the first diaper change or catheter taping, every one of the trainees has thought this thought, and some have spoken it:

"Without our help these guys would die!"

And, after the hundredth feeding and diapering and changing, the next thought, though never spoken,is: "Why don't we just let them die?"

An awful question to find in your head, because even young aides know that age can happen to anyone. "This could I someday be!" But even fear of one's own future can't stop the asking: "Why don't we just let them die? What's wrong with letting nature take its own corpse? Why do humans feel they have the right to forestall the inevitable fate of others?" Freddy Schrimpler helped me find my answer:

Freddy was 70 or 80 years old and had been on the Geriatrics Ward for close to twenty years. From morning until bedtime he lay in the dayroom in a gurney bed against the wall, on his side under a sheet; his little head covered with a faint silver gossamer that seemed too delicate to be human hair — it looked more like a fungus mycelium joining the head to the pillow — and his mouth drooling a continual puddle at his cheek. Only his eyes moved, pale and bright blue they followed the activity in the ward like little caged birds. The only sound he made was a muffled squeeking back in his throat when he had dirtied his sheets and, since his bowels were usually impacted, like most of the inmates who couldn't move, this sound was made but rarely and even then seemed to exhaust him for hours.

One afternoon, as I made my rounds to probe with rectal thermometer at the folds of wasted gluteus maximus of these gurney bed specimens — hospital policy made it clear that the temperature of anything breathing, even vegetables, had to be logged once a month — I heard this stifled squeek. The squeek came again, slower and sounding remarkably like speech! I moved closer to the pink and toothless mouth, feeling his breath at my ear.

"Makes you....kinda nervous...don't it?" he squeeked. The voice was terribly strained and faltering, but even through the distortion you could clearly make out the unmistakable tone of intelligence and awareness and, most astonishingly, humor.

In the days that followed I brought my ear to that mouth as often as the nurses let me get away with it. He told me his story. A stroke years ago had suddenly clipped all the wires leading from the brain to the body.

He found that while he could hear and see perfectly, he couldn't send anything back out to the visitors that dropped by his hospital bed more and more infrequently. Finally they sent him to the VA, to this ward where, after years of effort, he had learned to make his little squeek. Sure, the doctors and nurses knew he could talk, but they were too busy to shoot the breeze and didn't really think he should exhaust himself by speaking. So he was left on his gurney to drift alone in his rudderless vessel with his shortwave unable to send. He wasn't crazy; in fact the only difference that I could see between Freddy and Buddha was in the incline of their lotus position. As I got to know him I spoke of the young aides' thoughts.

"Let a man die for his own good?" he squeeked, incredulous. "Never believe it. When a man...when anything...is ready to stop living...it stops. You watch..."

Before I left the ward, two of the vegetables died. They stopped eating and died, as though a decision of the whole being was reached and nothing man or medicine could do would turn this decision. As though the decision was cellularly unanimous (I remember a friend telling me about her attempted suicide; she lay down and placed a rag soaked in carbon tetrachloride over her face. But just before she went out completely there was a sudden clamor from all the rest of her: "Hey! Wait! What about us? Why weren't we consulted!?" And being a democratic girl at heart she rallied over mind's presumptuous choice. "Our mind has no right to kill our body," she told me after the attempt, "Not on the grounds of boredom, anyway...." and met with the satisfaction of all concerned.

Punishment of unwed mothers? Care of neither the old nor the young can be considered to be punishment for the able, not even the care of the un-dead old or the un-born young. These beings, regardless not only of race, creed and color but as well of size, situation or ability, must be treated as equals and their rights to life not only recognized but defended! Can they defend themselves?

You are you from conception, and that never changes no matter what physical changes your body takes. And the virile sport in the Mustang driving to work with his muscular forearm tanned and ready for a day's labor has not one microgram more right to his inalienable rights of life, liberty and the pursuit of happiness than has the three month's foetus riding in a sack of water or the vegetable rotting for twenty years in a gurney bed. Who's to know the value or extent of another's trip? How can we assume that the world through the windshield of that Mustang is any more rich or holy or even sane than the world before those pale blue eyes? How can abortion be anything but fascism again, back as a fad in a new intellectual garb with a new, and more helpless, victim?

I swear to you that abortions are a terrible karmic bummer, and to support them — except in cases where it is a *bona fide* toss-up between the child and the mother's life — is to harbor a worm of discrepancy.

Q. Well, that's really eloquent and mistypoo, but suppose Faye was raped and became pregnant in the process?

A. Nothing is changed. You don't plow under the corn because the seed was planted with a neighbor's shovel.

Q. I assume that it would be her decision, though?

A. Almost certainly. But I don't really feel right about speaking for her. Why don't you phone and ask?

[Krassner phones Kay Kesey in Oregon and reviews the dialogue. She asks: "Now, what's the question — if I were raped, would I get an abortion?" "That about sums it up." "No, I wouldn't."]

Q. But would she marry the rapist to give the child a name?....What would you have done in my place before abortion was legalized and someone with any unwanted pregnancy came to you for help, and you knew of a safe doctor as an alternative to some back-alley butcher?

A. I have been in your place and done what you did. I think now — not just because of religious stands but of what happened to the girls' heads as a result — that I did a great disservice because I was being asked for more than money or the name of a guy in Tiajuana. In the last few years, when asked the question, I've found myself able to talk the women out of it. I could have talked them out of it back then as well. There are girls with kids coming and no old man to carry his share of the load. Women sense far better than a man what the bearing and raising of a child means in terms of a lifetime commitment. It all comes down to a pact of support. And if the man pulls out his support first, how can he blame the woman for pulling out hers? Next time you're asked to choose between hygiene and a back-alley butcher, Paul, try choosing instead against both possibilities and for life instead.

From *The Realist* (Vol. 90, Dec. '71). Reprinted with permission.

sweet angels, Incorporated

by Mary Goggins

Albert Wibble, president of "sweet angels, Incorporated", was accustomed to placating irate customers. Back perfectly straight, shoulders firmly in place, he prepared to do battle with Mrs. Flatterly. If Mrs. Flatterly could have read his mind, she would have been pleased to discover a flicker of apprehension masquerading under his perfect posture. But Mrs. Flatterly wasn't a mind reader and didn't detect his vulnerability. Instead, she launched a direct frontal attack, her fashionable green hair bobbing frantically, her dulcet voice rising to a feverish pitch of hysteria.

"It's abominable, not at all what we specified when we signed the contract, and we don't intend to let sweet angels walk all over us — do we, Mr. Flatterly!" Her last remark was directed at a middle-aged man seated in a chair behind and to the left of her. The man shook his head sadly, whereupon Mrs. Flatterly again turned her wrath on Mr. Wibble.

"Mr. Flatterly and I are firm in our decision. We demand that you return our deposit and we also want compensation for the months of agony and torment we've suffered." Her voice broke with emotion. "We've waited — hoped — prayed that your company would honor its obligation to us — and *that* is not what we ordered." A black-haired, slant-eyed infant lying in a portable crib on Mr. Wibble's desk looked Mrs. Flatterly straight in the eyes and gurgled. A friendly, intuitive gurgle Wibble noted, most certainly an intelligent specimen in which sweet angels, Incorporated could take pride. Mrs. Flatterly frowned. "This is not the twentieth century, Mr. Wibble. There's no longer any excuse for such a mistake."

Wibble's fingers caressed the pencil in his hand. An authentic graphite instrument dating from the late 1900's, a lucky find chanced upon at an estate auction one propitious Sunday afternoon, the pencil had become Wibble's own personal talisman and he smiled inwardly as he lightly tapped it against the Corporate Archives Monitor in the middle of his desk. The display screen activated. Wibble cleared his throat and proceeded to take command of the situation.

"Uh-hum....I have your complete file here, Mr. and Mrs. Flatterly, and I've carefully gone over the contract entered into between yourselves and sweet angels, Incorporated. Quite frankly, I've found nothing to substantiate your complaint." He peered at the infant who was shoving all five fingers of its right hand down its throat. It gagged and removed the offending fingers. "Uh-hum, let me see now," Wibble said, returning his attention to the monitor. "The child is female, is it not?"

Mrs. Flatterly's eyes narrowed. "It is," she said.

"And you specifically requested a female, did you not? None of the 'surprise us' foolishness for you, am I right?"

"We requested a female, but we certainly didn't request an Oriental!"

Wibble dismissed her response with a wave of his hand. "According to a team of outside medical consultants — a team, I might add, which is accredited by the State Department of Controlled Births — the child is unencumbered by any physical defect or mental deficiency." Once again he referred to the display screen. "I might add that she has received a AAA rating for health and intelligence. You can't get a better rating than that." The Corporate Archives Monitor blinked off. "In truth," Wibble continued, "there is no good reason for your refusal to take possession of the child, and in fact, sweet angels, Incorporated has every right to charge storage and handling for the three months since you first refused delivery."

"What about the slanted eyes?" Mr. Flatterly cried, her voice shaking with rage. She leaned toward him and he felt her angry breath on his face. "I'll explain it, I'll explain it," she shouted. "Someone in your little factory got our mating pod mixed up with somebody else's, didn't they? They put our name on the wrong pod, didn't they?" Tears streamed down her cheeks and she sobbed loudly. "....and....we gave you such a pretty p-p-pink pod! It even had her name on it in gold....Joleen." She began to wail. "Our little girl, our dear sweet Joleen has gone to someone else and you want us to take this substitute. This one's not our very own — it's not ours — and we want our deposit back!"

Wibble stood up. His chin jutted out as he clasped his hands behind him and rocked back and forth. "Slander, Mrs. Flatterly, slander! Our quality control is scrupulous, madam. There is no way an error of such magnitude could take place. This child is yours."

"We are not Oriental, Mr. Wibble!" Mrs. Flatterly's voice reached a dangerous pitch that threatened to shatter the crystal decanter on Wibble's credenza. He sighed ungraciously.

"Perhaps somewhere in your lineage there is Eastern stock of which you are unaware but which, in this child, has reasserted itself," he said.

"If you and Mr. Flatterly will just permit the consultants to perform a few simple tests, I'm sure you'll find that the child is yours."

Mrs. Flatterly was shaking uncontrollably and pathetic choking sounds came from her throat. Wibble basked in the warm glow of victory.

Mr. Flatterly, who until now had appeared to be disinterested in the whole matter, reached for his wife's hand and patted it in an awkward attempt to console her. "Perhaps he's right, dear," he said, glancing at the infant in the crib. "She is a pretty little thing. It's possible we could become quite attached to her."

Mrs. Flatterly's twitching body stopped twitching. The struggle to bring her emotions under control was apparent in her face which was several shades paler than when she had arrived. She pressed her lips together and took a deep breath.

"Mr. Flatterly and I supplied sperm and eggs just as your company required. We assumed we were dealing with a reputable firm, so we patiently waited for sweet angels to produce the infant we ordered. We have not accepted delivery because the child is not ours." Her previous lack of composure disappeared completely as she continued. "Kindly be informed that if we are not reimbursed for the payments already made to sweet angels, Incorporated during the incubation period — and if we are not suitably compensated for the time wasted in waiting for sweet angels to fulfill its contract — and if we are not further compensated for the emotional distress inflicted on us by your slipshod organization — then rest assured, Mr. Wibble, we will take you and your company to court and sue you for every GEC you possess."

Wibble's expression became thoughtful as he sank into the soft cushion of his antique leather chair and considered the alternatives. He could pay her off or call her bluff. If she followed through, he could lose most of his gold exchange cards and it could take years to have them reinstated by the Federal Reserve Bank. Wibble looked into her eyes; they were cold, ruthless, unwavering. The anchordroid on the 6 O'Clock News would make the most of Mrs. Flatterly. Wibble could almost hear the placid baritone of the droid suitably programmed to betray just a trace of emotion...."Where is Joleen?....Broken hearted mother pleads for lost daughter....sweet angels, Incorporated accused of fraud...." The supple leather gave off a delicious aroma of success, reminding Wibble of the benefits of a lucrative business venture. His good luck charm tapped nervously on the monitor.

"Well?" Mrs. Flatterly was unrelenting as she glared at him from across the desk.

Wibble considered the matter a moment longer. He chose his words carefully.

"Our dear departed foundress, may she rest in eternal peace, had a vision, dear lady — a glorious vision of happy families loving and growing together in this wonderful land. I realize now that this child would not thrive in the environment of your home. Forcing you to take her woud break faith with our foundress' deepest wish and would be completely counter to our firm's basic objectives. Therefore, I'll instruct my attorneys to contact you within the week. I'm sure a settlement can be reached which you will find satisfactory and equitable."

The color returned to Mrs. Flatterly's cheeks as Wibble spoke. "I will, of course, make the final decision as to what is or is not equitable, Mr. Wibble. Are we in agreement on this point?"

"Agreed," he said.

"Then our discussion is complete," she said and, with that pronouncement, marched from the room with Mr. Flatterly close behind, leaving Wibble staring angrily at their backsides as the door shut behind them.

Wibble glared at the closed door and then at the infant who was contentedly chewing the toes of her right foot. He pressed a small button at the edge of the desk and a moment later his secretary entered the room. Wibble pointed to the child. "Transfer her to the factory outlet, and don't forget to feed the data on her to Accounting. Tell them to mark her down twenty percent to begin with. If she's still in inventory at the end of the month, we'll put her at half price."

The infant stopped chewing and turned her dark, almond eyes at him. The rare lead pencil snapped between Wibble's fingers. He looked down at the broken pieces in the palm of his hand. A vein popped in his forehead. "When you're finished with that," he said, "get Epweiler from Quality Control up here. There's been too damn many foul-ups the past few months."

Abortion and Child Abuse: Is There a Relationship?

by Monica M. Migliorino

Abortion's destruction of the bond between mother and child is one of the factors contributing to an increase in child abuse. Philip G. Ney, M.D. has done an extensive study on the relationship between abortion and child abuse. He discussed the results of his study at a symposium on the psychological aspects of abortion sponsored in 1978 by the Department of Obstetrics and Gynecology of the Stritch School of Medicine of Loyola University. Dr. Ney states:

> In all creatures, a signal of distress from the young will invite either parental care or aggression. The submissive baring of the neck will suddenly stop the dominant wolf's attack on the rival. On the other hand, a healthy seagull tied by one leg, flapping helplessly on the ground, invites the aggressive attack of the whole flock. There is a fine balance between caring and destruction. ...
>
> Whimpering, even across species, produces a tension in people, which is only relieved when the need is attended to or when the whimpering is forcibly, sometimes permanently, stopped. A woman, to abort her helpless young, has to overcome her instinctual impulse to attend to the little one's helplessness. Even though aborters are frequently told, "It's only a piece of tissue," no one can help seeing pictures of fetuses which are visibly human from early life. Even the seasoned aborter, seeing her limp fetus, experiences a profound psychological shock that can produce a serious illness. ...
>
> ... The aborting person must suppress the species preserving instinct. Having done so once, it's easier the next time. The suppressed response is less effective, even when the helplessness is that of a whimpering child. Therefore, more people are responding to the cries of distress with rage or neglect, rather than protection...[1]

Abortion contributes to child abuse through the suppression of the instinctual response of women to respond to a child's helplessness.

But Ney also demonstrates another factor, that abortion interferes with the maternal bonding between mother and child.

> The establishment of the mother-infant bond is a delicate business and can be easily influenced by subtle changes in mother or infant. ... Bonding develops throughout pregnancy and becomes set when the infant is born.[2]
>
> ... it would appear that those who abort their infants at any stage of pregnancy interrupt a very delicate mechanism and sever the developing bond that is critical for the infant's protection against the mother's carelessness or rage. It is hypothesized that, once bonding is interrupted in the primipara, there are long-lasting psychological changes which make it more difficult for the same bond to develop in subsequent pregnancies. For this reason, it is likely that abortion contributes to bonding failure, an important cause of child battering. Consequently, as rates of abortion increase, rates of battering will increase proportionately.[3]

Abortion also contributes to child abuse through guilt and anger that the mother may experience.

> Severe guilt is found in 2 to 23 percent, depending upon the type of study. These rates were found on surveys and questionnaires, but more detailed interviews find "without exception, there are feelings of guilt or profound regret."...Guilt is one of the major factors causing battering and infanticide. There are "intolerable feelings of self-hatred, which the parent takes out on the child." Abortion results in guilt, and guilt contributes to child battering.
>
> In both battering parents and women who abort, there is a significant lack of self-esteem. It appears that women who place no value on their finest creation do so because they have poor self-esteem. However, the abortion contributes to that lowered self-esteem, which contributes to child battering.[4]

The rupture of the maternal bond between mother and child brought on by an abortion is undoubtedly a contributing factor to women undergoing multiple abortions. As Ney indicated, once the maternal bond is broken, it is more difficult to develop in subsequent pregnancy.[5] With the bond ruptured by the first abortion, women find it easier to undergo a second, third, and even fourth abortion.

As one who has stood outside of abortion clinics to persuade women to keep their children I can testify that those women who had previous abortions were *actually more difficult* to convince than those who were seeking their first abortion. The difficulty seemed to be rooted in an inability to identify with the child. Many of the repeat aborters that we have spoken to manifested low self-esteem, pessimism, and a real lack of confidence that they could continue with the pregnancy and be good mothers. One study revealed that repeat abortion patients are more frequently dissatisfied with themselves, more often perceive themselves as victims of "bad luck" and more frequently express negative feelings toward the abortion.[6]

Martin Ekblad's study which was cited earlier in this article revealed that of the 479 women who had been granted abortion in a Swedish hospital, 25 percent had admitted that they had felt self-reproach for the operation or regretted the step.[7] Eleven percent (54 of the women) had serious self-reproach or regretted the operation.[8] Ekblad concluded that, "It is thus obvious that a legal abortion entails feelings of guilt and self-reproach in many women."[9] He also questioned the therapeutic role of abortion for a number of women and suggested that many should not have had the abortion.

We can see from this that more study is needed in the area of the relationship of child abuse to abortion.

1. Philip G. Ney, "Infant Abortion and Child Abuse: Cause and Effect," in *The Psychological Aspects of Abortion*, ed. by David Mall and Walter F. Watts, (Washington, D.C., University Publications of America, Inc., 1979), p. 26-27.
2. *Ibid*, p. 31.
3. *Ibid*, p. 32.
4. *Ibid*, p. 29
5. *Ibid*, p. 32.
6. Judith Leach, *Family Planning Perspectives*, Vol.9, No.1,(Jan.-Feb. 1977), p. 39.
7. Martin Ekblad, "Induced Abortion on Psychiatric Grounds: A Follow-Up Study of 479 Women," *Acta Psychiatrica et Neurologica Scandinavica*, (1955), p. 212.
8. *Ibid*.
9. *Ibid*.

Infanticide and the Oppression of Women

by Monica M. Migliorino

In Dongguan County in eastern Guangdong...a reporter from Hong Kong's left-wing newspaper Zheng Ming Ribio saw pregnant women herded into vehicles and taken to hospitals for abortions. "The vehicles were filled with wailing noises, and the scenes were bitterly distressing," he reported.

He wrote aboùt one woman who arrived at the hospital nine months pregnant and immediately received an injection. "Three hours later the baby was born — but then it stopped breathing," the reporter said. Some women were reportedly handcuffed, tied with ropes or placed in pig's baskets.[1]

Social scientist Stephen Mosher, author of *Broken Earth: The Rural Chinese* who lived with villagers in China's Guangdong Province relates:

While the birth of a son has always been a more important event than the arrival of a daughter, Peking's policy of one child per family has raised the stakes. For the peasantry birth has become a kind of Russian roulette: The arrival of a son heralds a relaxed and secure old age; the coming of a daughter portends poverty and slow starvation during one's declining years. It is not "feudal nonsense" but brutal economic reality that moves the parents to hope for a man-child.

If the child isn't male, then the choice is a stark one: Either kill or abandon the newborn female infant, reserving your one-child quota for the birth of a boy, or face a harrowing old age. It is no surprise that many peasants decide in favor of their own security, and trade the child's life for their own.[2]

Newsweek magazine of Feb. 21, 1983 reports:

Gruesome accounts of young girls drowned in rivers, suffocated in their sleep or simply abandoned in the fields have become a regular event in the Chinese press. They are part of an official crusade against the resurgence of one of China's oldest social vices, female infanticide.[3]

The above news items barely scratch the surface of documentation recently collected on the practice of forced sterilizations, abortion, and infanticide, particularly female infanticide, in China today. Very few individuals will argue that China does not have a population problem. However, the Chinese government's means of curbing the population has resulted in one of the most oppressive systems existing anywhere in the world. What compounds this oppression is that human rights organizations and governments of the free world have rarely spoken out on the travesty of the so-called birth control program in China. In April 1983 there were organized protests and a court case against a priest who had drowned some kittens but there is very little consciousness raising about the Chinese drowning their newborn daughters. Indeed, American money has indirectly aided in the Chinese birth control program. Economist Jacqueline Kasun in March 1984, testified before a Senate foreign relations subcommittee that "the Chinese population control program receives about $50 million a year from the United Nations, whose largest supporting donor is the United States." She charged that the two agencies involved in the Chinese program funded by U.S. tax money are the U.N. Fund for Population Activities and the International Planned Parenthood Federation.[4]

What needs to be realized is that any birth control program that does not take into account the inherent dignity of the human person will result (most often) in the oppression of two parties: the children who are killed in abortion and infanticide and the mothers whose children are murdered.

In the case of China where male children are more highly valued the degradation of the female class is even worse. What possible self-dignity could be left for a woman when her female powers of reproduction and any female child she may bear are viewed as social evils? The woman's dignity as a mother and the life of her child are both mutilated and destroyed.

Of course, it is easy to point fingers at China. However, in those countries where abortion is legal and touted as a right and paraded as a reproductive choice, the anti-life ethic that there is something evil and diseased about the procreative powers of women lurks beneath the surface of what appears to be a liberation. Willard Cates, former director of the Center for Disease Control in Atlanta, referred to unwanted pregancy as a "venereal disease." Welfare mothers are told that it is better for society that they abort their children since they are burdens for the taxpayer. Many unmarried women are encouraged or even forced by their family to abort in order to "save" the family's reputation and "spare them" the inconvenience of the unplanned, unwanted child. Women are also coerced into abortion by friends, family, and counselors who convince them that they cannot be good mothers — that they do not have it in themselves to make the necessary sacrifices connected with motherhood.

Perhaps China is the paridigm of population control's oppression of women but is the Western world really that much better? After all, how can we tell the Chinese how wrong they are when our own contraceptive and abortion practices denigrate the dignity of women?

The population problem of China needs a solution. However, a solution which is truly effective and liberating will probably never take root in this country — or anywhere else — until it is recognized that favoring males over females, viewing women and their reproductive powers as social liablities, and believing that the solution lies in killing human beings are intolerable.

The population control program in China not only kills infant girls. It kills their mothers too. In a sense the mothers are destroyed because the defining characteristics of their feminity — their physical and emotional life-giving and nurturing powers — are a target of oppression.

Until societies honor and respect the inherent nature of women, a truly liberating mode of population control cannot be implemented but will only represent a reign of tyranny.

1. Michele Vink, "Abortion and Birth Control in Canton, China", *The Wall Street Journal*, (Nov. 30, 1981).
2. Stephen Mosher, "Why Are Baby Girls Being Killed in China?" *The Wall Street Journal*, (July 25, 1983).
3. "Death to Baby Daughters", *Newsweek*, (Feb. 21, 1983), p. 23.
4. Mary Meehan, "Paying for China's Abortions", *The National Catholic Register*, (April 8, 1984), p. 8.

Handicap-ism

by Barbara Sieger

[Barb Sieger, Milwaukee chapter president for Feminists for Life of Wisconsin, went to Madison to participate in a committee hearing on Bill AB 148, which would prohibit abortions in public hospitals. Barb's testimony is somewhat different from the others who testified that day, however....Barb was born with spina bifida. What follows is her appeal.]

Fellow citizens of Wisconsin, I have heard the argument that abortion of the physically and mentally handicapped is a blessing because we cannot have a quality life. I say "we" because I am one of those who would have been aborted, under this thinking. As the argument goes, an abortion of the physically handicapped is an aesthetic and humane action taken by a civilized society to create a better world for all. The gas chambers of Nazi Germany and the labor camps in Soviet Russia are also comparable actions of a civilized society disposing of the unwanted and dissident. We say Hitler is a murderer, we say Stalin is a murderer, but we praise the lethal knife of the abortionist, the poisoned solutions in which untold millions die unseen inside mothers who do not understand in many cases, due to political propaganda, that a baby with a nervous system feels the pain of its own death. Were this murder to be committed against children outside the mother, millions would demand a death penalty for those wielding the knife, injecting the poison, as they did at the end for the butcher of Buchenwald.

Fellow citizens of Wisconsin, you who are empowered with the responsibility of law, please take a good look at me, not at the cosmetic of the non-handicapped, but at the beauty of God's creative love, a human being with emotions and feelings. Children, not blinded by society's prejudices, love me. Friends share experiences of their daily lives, including joys, sorrows and pains, and we celebrate the joy of life's experiences together. I feel the warmth of a gentle sun, and a rose brushed up against my cheek is as velvet to the touch to me as it is to you. Fresh air is as clean and the smell of rain as new to me as you. The seasons pass and I exalt in the crystal of winter and the luxury and abundance of summer. Music can bring me to tears or to laughter, and I feel the pulse of life throughout my being.

I ask you in the name of the countless millions like me who are being murdered for convenience of one sort or another is "quality of life" the clean murder by an abortionist, or is it the poetry and music of the cycles of human life, enjoyed in the richness of the earth's goodness? As one of those permitted to live, I beg for the lives of those who have not yet attained their voices. Those who vote on the laws are responsible for their consequences. Please vote life, not death.

[The bill which Barb Sieger gave such eloquent testimony for was not allowed out of the committee. -ed.]

Taken from the November 1983 issue of *Feminists For Life of Wisconsin Newsletter*, 1503 N. 47th St., Milwaukee, WI 53208

Panthers and Pussycats

by Gail Grenier Sweet

Child abuse is an epidemic which crosses all social boundaries. Yet it took years for health care professionals and the public to *see* it. Now, finally, many programs help both adults and children recognize and fight the problem.

Abuse of old people is an issue which is just beginning to come "out of the closet." As with child abuse, people are slow to uncover and admit to the extent and seriousness of "elder abuse." But gradually, Canadian and U.S. statistics are being compiled — statistics which indicate that a million or more old people suffer emotional and physical abuse every year.

There is an eerie similarity among the practices of sex selection of infants (through amniocentesis and abortion), infanticide, and elder abuse. That similarity is: THE VICTIMS ARE USUALLY FEMALE.

Screaming newspaper headlines have announced the policy of some doctors to abort babies on the basis of gender, at the mother's request. What happens is that amniocentesis shows the sex of the unborn baby to be "undesirable" — usually female — so the woman has the abortionist "fix" the problem. Many abortionists disapprove of this capricious reason for aborting. However, there are apparently enough doctors who are willing to perform the procedure, for whatever reason.

The scandal of infanticide in China has reached the newsrooms of America.

Chinese baby girls are sometimes "allowed" to die. This is because of severe governmental pressure upon the mothers to bear only one child. Because of the way Chinese society works, the "preferred" gender is male.

Euthanasia — the "good death" — is practiced in the United States, both covertly and openly, upon "defective" newborns and upon the elderly or infirm. Proponents of active euthanasia insist that it is "mercy-killing" or "death with dignity." Pro-lifers, however, insist that life is an inalienable right, that we must leave life alone from conception to natural death. "Natural death" means life unassisted by extra-ordinary aids such as elaborate machinery. However, *food* is not considered extraordinary, ever. Therefore, speeding death through withholding of food — even intravenous feeding — is usually held to be murder. Euthanasia is the most extreme form of elder abuse, just as abortion is the most extreme form of child abuse. And because, statistically, most old people are women, women are the most likely candidates for euthanasia. The old woman, like the fetus, is often voiceless, powerless, and *unwanted.*

On the basis of one Canadian study ("Protection of the Elderly" by Donna Shell, 1982), abused old people are most likely to be women aged 80-84 years. The study indicates that although there is indeed abuse of the elderly in institutions, only a small percentage of old people live in institutions. The abused old person has typically lived with a family member for ten or more years. Four other studies done from 1978-1981 confirm that family members are the most frequent abusers of elderly persons. The abusers are the sons, daughters, and spouses (and occasionally the neighbors) of the old person. The types of abuse most commonly found are first financial, followed by psychosocial (verbal/emotional), and then physical.

Now we have to wonder: why are most abused old people female? Is it *only* because more women than men live to a very old age? Or is there another, more sinister, reason? Can we look back to female infanticide and infant sex selection by abortion and wonder if one of the reasons old women are abused is that they *are* women?

Who are the abusers? Shell's study found abusers themselves are almost always elderly — over 60 years of age. This finding was in accord with three separate research projects conducted from 1979-1981.

Think about those abusers: They are men and women aged 60 or more. What triggers their abusiveness? It is a good guess that along with their own personal problems (stress, depression, alcoholism, and/or attitudes toward aging), there is something else going on inside their heads. Something about *women.* When they were growing up, the idea of female equality was unheard of, except in a very few cases. At the time of their birth, U.S. women had just been granted the right to vote! It is not farfetched to assume that these abusers see women as somewhat less "human" than men, less worthwhile. So when a woman becomes frail and vulnerable, she becomes even *less* valuable as a human being, in the eye of the abuser. This youth-oriented society has a "thing" about age to begin with, as Ronald Reagan found out when he fought to earn his second term as president. People forget about Churchill, Einstein, Picasso, Rubenstein — and also Sojourner Truth, the Peace Pilgrim, and Grandma Moses — and it becomes easy to stereotype all old people as "useless." How easy it then becomes to abuse them by withholding their social security checks, by punishing them with verbal barrages and isolation, or by direct physical assault.

How much easier it becomes to end their problems (and the problems of those who must care for them) with "mercy-killing."

What can be done? On a professional level, programs aimed at increasing awareness of elder abuse must be started. We need systems for reporting suspected abuse, and strict laws to protect old people.

On a personal level, hearts need to be touched and changed. People must be educated so they'll stop stereotyping old people and thinking of them as "disposable." The Grey Panthers are one group struggling to change dehumanizing attitudes towards old people. They have a network promoting pride and independence for old people. They have some pointers for us — especially us *women* — to consider. Basically, these pointers say "Be a panther and not a pussycat." A panther develops its own skills and muscles so it isn't handicapped or dependent. A pussycat has its claws removed and is trained to live in a house and be "petted."

How do the Grey Panthers view aging? They see it as an ongoing natural process that is shared by all living things. This attitude is well summed up in the words of Matilda White Riley, Sc.D. While serving as Associate Director for Social and Behavioral Science of the National Institute on Aging, she asserted that "aging is mutable and varies from one individual as well as from one social condition to another. Aging is not entirely fixed or determined by biology, but biological aging interacts with psychological and social aging, and this results in a great range of mutability."

Ms. White Riley believed that false stereotypes about aging persist and are perpetuated by old people and doctors. Classic data on aging must be challenged. For instance, it is a universally accepted myth that the aging process is an inevitable biological deterioration. This stereotype is based on data which compare differences between *old and young* at a given time, and therefore, do not reflect the *process* of aging. On the other hand, comparisons of data against *peers* suggest that peers who are going to be old in the future will be healthier, in some respects, than peers already old today.

Therefore, we must throw out the stereotype of unavoidable decline and replace it with the more realistic view of the potential for health in old age.

Before she died, Dolly Carlson shared her thoughts with me on how to be a panther rather than a pussycat. Ms. Carlson was an activist for old people. She indicated that the biggest trouble group is women in their early 60's. Many of these women have no skills or jobs, and they can't get money from the government until they are 65. They may not even be able to move into subsidized housing. Because of the way they were raised, these women are embarassed to talk about age. They are plagued by the pervading concept that old women are unattractive. (We are seeing some change in this concept as the "baby boom" generation grows older.)

Symptoms of agism are apparent in the agist words all around us, such as "70 years young"; "senior citizen"; "golden ager"; and "older adult." Grey Panthers stress that we should promote a positive attitude toward age — for instance, it's fine to say "I'm 70 years *old*." It's up to us to make it okay to be an "old woman." Ms. Carlson suggested looking at a picture of an old person and thinking: "Can I believe this will happen to me?" and "How will I feel about it when it does happen?

Panther activism means forcing inequities into the public arena. Grey Panthers are against forced retirement. They believe, for instance, that a good plan is a 20-hour work week for people over 60. They're against inequities in the social security system. They resent housing old people like rabbits in "projects;" they feel it would be better off to give an old person money with which to find his or her own housing. Panthers hate senior centers which are "adult playpens," where old people are given junk food to eat and encouraged to make craft items out of egg cartons. Instead, senior centers should be run by the old people themselves. They should have real *power* over their activities.

Both Ms. White Riley and Ms. Carlson have urged women to be assertive feminists — a necessity if you're going to be "a successful old woman." Ms. Carlson saw a feminist as a woman who thinks opportunities and responsibilities should be the same for women and for men. A woman should be in charge of her life, financial and otherwise. Women and men should make decisions *together*. Of course the question arises: how do you retrain an old man who is set in his views on the inequality of women? Ms. Carlson advised teaching men about women gradually and gracefully. Let men know about women's situation and they'll gradually understand.

Everyone has fears about old age. Knowing about elder abuse doesn't do much to alleviate those fears! Here are Ms. Carlson's suggestions for coping with those feelings:

HEALTH: Don't smoke; get exercise and don't be overweight. Use common sense. If you improve the life of your arteries and veins, you'll have true health.

BOREDOM: There's much to do after 70 — political party work, for instance. You can also enroll in one course per semester — it's good mental exercise and you meet other people.

FINANCIAL SECURITY: As far as social security is concerned, wives typically get one half of what husbands get. Try to make some provisions for financial security — through savings, job training, and so on. If you are married, most likely your husband will die ten years before you do. Be concerned about those ten years. Check into your financial status. Some wives unwisely assume that they have a meal ticket for the rest of their lives just because they are married. Many women in their 50's are devastated when their husbands divorce them. They find themselves with less money than they could get on welfare.

LONELINESS: Loneliness is something we'll all probably experience before we die. Maybe it won't be that bad. We need to find ways to be alone that aren't so excruciating — more coping mechanisms for living alone.

CRIME: Most old people feel better living in apartments. Or they get a big dog or someone to live with. It's a good idea to walk in pairs or groups. Old people can have a full social life in the *daytime*. They can retire at 9 PM and arise at 5 AM if they wish.

Ms. Carlson stressed the need to reorder our priorities. Ask yourself what will be important in your old age. It's wiser to store up treasures of your own resources than to seek happiness from physical beauty or material possessions.

Matilda White Riley encouraged us to influence the alternatives for older women by living our own lives as change agents and working actively to change the future. As we have seen, these changes will come only when we alter our own attitudes and when we become activists for Grey Panther goals.

Nukes Abort Everybody
by Juli Loesch

Great moments from Mae West: "Ah could nevah accept such familiarities from a perfect stranger," she insists with a pout. Pausing thoughtfully, she brightens: "But then, nobody's perfect."

I can't resist paraphrasing a Jesuit political scientist's recent published comments on modern war: "I could never justify the wholesale destruction of innocent civilians," he seems to say, righteously: "But then, nobody's innocent!"

The argument is that because the totalitarian state can politicize the entire population and mobilize it for warmaking purposes — including the elderly, the sick and the children — it is questionable whether these people are actually innocent.

To begin with, it must be recognized that the majority of adults, even in a totalitarian, war-making society, are involved in pursuits which are blameless. The farmer farms. The mother mothers. The just man, as Hopkins says, justices. That they do so in a communist or Nazi or fascist context does not obviate their objective participation in just activities.

Further, the totalitarian systems are evil precisely because they subordinate all individual human rights to a political end. The Jesuit's argument lays the rhetorical foundation for direct attacks on these people (remember, under no circumstances may we for any reason directly attack the innocent) because their human dignity has supposedly collapsed to the point that they are now mere instruments of the state.

But if the totalitarian state is wrong for using these people as instruments, is it not also wrong to kill them as instruments? Concretely: If the communists are wrong for enslaving them, are we better because we kill the slaves?

Merciless notion: that because the enemy has "politicized" the entire nation, we have the right to destroy the entire nation. The former is totalitarianism. The latter has always been called genocide. But what do we call it now? I'm not quite up with the modern way of thinking!

Without abandoning the "old women and children" whose innocence — and therefore immunity from attack — is being questioned, I would like to voice a defense for the most helpless victim of totalitarian logic: the unborn child.

I don't know how the communists mobilize their three-year-olds, making the toddlers "in some sense" responsible for their own form of rule; but I will hazard the theory that the unborn, at least, are innocent.

And the unborn would suffer, and massively, as a result of acts of nuclear war. The fact that arrangements have been made to kill everyone else around them simultaneously hardly justifies things.

The sensitivity of the unborn to radiation is so pronounced — and so exceeds that of adults — that we can accurately say that the destructive effect of radioactive fallout is primarily abortifacient.

The extent to which this is ignored in contemporary literature on nuclear war is striking. The unborn child, because of his or her extremely rapid rate of cell division, is 50 to 100 times more vulnerable to this "radiation curettage" than already born brothers and sisters.

Of course, if you don't regard an embryonic death as a "real" death, this hardly changes the equation of proportionality.

But if you do regard an embryonic death as real, then the Just War picture flies all out of proportion. Because not only are all of the "enemy embryos" well within the radius of destruction; and not only must we add the millions of unborn in neighboring countries who would be subjected to the fallout hazards; but we are stretching the icy hand of death over the children, grandchildren and great-grandchildren of the future. Genetic assault on this generation is assault on their progeny forever.

Of course today's children are innocent. And, of course, tomorrow's are, too.

Sometimes I tire of all this talk of innocence. We humans have far more solidarity in sin than in innocence. We are all sufferers from Original Sin, a kind of genetic defect of the soul, a mutation from God's good design.

And all of us, the born, also have the solidarity of actual sin as well. We can prepare encyclopedias of "justification" for every entry that the Devil can list.

Mass killing of innocent human lives? Look under "A" for abortion. Aha! Here's a convenient notion — they're not "really" human. Or look under "N" for nuclear war. Another convenient notion — they're not "really" innocent!

If I ever become pope — don't worry, there's no chance — I would take the name Pope Guilty the First. You will find me first in line begging for mercy from God — and protection from learned touters of total war.

Originally "Innocent Children" reprinted from the *National Catholic Register*, January 10, 1982. Permission to reprint by the author.

On Planned Parenthood

by Jean Blackwood

Some seeds are sown by human hands
   in rows and plots
     of fine design
But seeds are sown

             by wind

   and chance

                  as well.
Here and there the turnips grow,
But everywhere grasses blow.
I like the world this way.

From *Beyond Beginning and Other Poems*, P.O. Box 490 Clarion, Penna 16214

Section Four: Violence Against Women

Playboy and Naral Host Fundraiser

by Elizabeth Moore Sobo

On Saturday, October 20, the Chicago Playboy Mansion hosted a gala fundraiser for NARAL (National Abortion Rights Action League). Advance publicity and personal invitations told the world that Playboy would be covering all expenses in order that the guests' $50 donations may go, in their entirety, to the NARAL operating account. "Make checks payable to the National Abortion Rights Action League," reads the invitation, with the checks to be sent to the Playboy Foundation.

Sponsors included Representative Cardiss Collins of Illinois and talk show host Phil Donahue. An appearance by special guest Midge Costanza was promised.

Even more interesting was an accompanying list of pro-abortion groups which the Playboy Foundation said it was "supporting through grants and technical assistance." These groups were: Abortion Rights Action League; Campaign for Choice, ACLU Foundation; Catholics for a Free Choice; Center for Constitutional Rights; Illinois Pro-Choice Alliance; Ms. Foundation Pro-Choice Project; National Abortion Federation NARAL; Parents Aid Center (Bill Baird); Religious Coalition for Abortion Rights; Roger Baldwin Foundation of the ACLU; and the Voters for Choice.

"The Playboy Foundation is the activist arm of *Playboy Magazine's* philosophy," proclaimed the abortion fundraising flyer. And so, abortion took its rightful place as a fixture in the most universally detested form of male chauvinism, the Playboy philosophy.

National Right to Life News, November, 1979. Reprinted with the permission of the *National Right to Life News*. Suite 402, 419 7th Street N.W., Washington, D.C. 20004

Pornography: A Booming Business
by Lorraine Williams

       •

The film *Not a Love Story* shows the need of the porn consumer to try to awaken his deadened responses by ever more violent means — culminating in the "snuff" movie in which a woman is abused and murdered before our eyes. Anything is possible after the viewer sees a reprint of a cover of *Hustler* showing the body of a naked woman being processed through a kitchen meat grinder with a pile of red mincemeat beside it, the remains of the top half of her body.

The income from porn has increased from 5 million dollars to 5 billion dollars in the last 12 years.

From Lorraine Williams' movie review in *The Human,* November 1982. Reprinted with permission.

A Rose to:

J.W. Marriott Jr., president of the Marriott Corp., who instructed all of his hotel gift shops to discontinue the display and sale of pornographic magazines. He said in a letter to a patron, "The moral value of such a policy outweighs the financial loss of revenue." The Marriott hotel chain is one of the largest in the United States.

From *The Interim,* August, 1984, 215 Victoria St., Suite 505, Toronto, Ontario, Canada M5B 1T9

Pornography and the Sexual Revolution

by Judy Shea

A real sexual revolution will be possible when feminists finally see the link between pornography and abortion. Unfortunately pro-abortion thinking distorts the current feminist analysis of pornography.

The women's movement correctly attacks the obscene material in our society which implicitly condones rape; but the problem of violence against women will remain inextricable until *all* forms of violence against women are recognized. Many feminists refuse to accept that the violent ethic of abortion is doing serious damage to women and that the proliferation of pornography and the million-plus abortions a year are inexorably connected.

It is no accident that the greatest apologist for pornography in our culture, Hugh Hefner, is also enthusiastic about abortion on demand. Hefner's misogynistic playboy philosophy inevitably leads to the destructive, dewomanizing practice of abortion. As its core the playboy ethic is anti-woman and anti-child.

The reality of the possibility of pregnancy and childbirth interferes with the Hefner dream of multiple partners and everlasting orgies. The Hefner playboy is incapable of relating to a mature woman who ovulates, menstruates, conceives and lactates. In fact, he's quite puritanical about the messy, dirty processes of human reproduction. He likes his bunnies "clean" and sterile. If his bunny mysteriously gets pregnant, she can take care of that like magic with a clean, sterile abortion. The biological reality of the combined fertility of women and men which might result in the creation of a new human being must be denied. In the Hefner dream world there is no need for the commitment it would take to nurture new life.

For women the playboy dream has become a nightmare. The phony sexual revolution which tolerates and even celebrates the dehumanization of women in pornography promotes the mutilation of women in rape and abortion. For Linda Lovelace, "star" of *Deep Throat*, the "revolution" meant cruelty and injury almost beyond our comprehension. In her book, *Ordeal*,* she describes how she was treated like an animal by her husband/tormentor whose hero is Hugh Hefner.

Eventually in her "rise" to fame managed by her sadistic husband, they arrive at the Playboy mansion and encounter the great strategist of the sexual revolution, Hugh Hefner. It seems Hugh is quite a connoisseur of porn/animal flicks so one night the careful arrangements are made for Hefner to observe Linda with a dog. Since to our fun-loving playboys there is little difference between women and animals, a bunny and a dog are a good match. In all fairness to H.H. it must be pointed out that when he found out later that Linda was forced by her husband to participate, he felt badly. Apparently it unburdens the playboy's conscience to believe the bunnies want it and like it. It sometimes ruins the playboy's fantasy if she isn't enjoying what is done to her.

He feels better believing it is his bunny's "choice." Our playboy doesn't want to be labelled a male chauvinist you-know-what.

After all, he's into feminism. He supports abortion on demand, doesn't he?

*Lovelace, Linda. *Ordeal.* Citadel Press, 1980.
Taken from the Spring 1981 *Minnesota Feminists For Life Newsletter,* 2815 West 38th Street, Minneapolis, MN 55410. Reprinted with permission.

The Best Defense
by Judith P. Woodburn

"Put a can of hairspray in your purse." This was what my mother had called all the way from Chicago on a warm June afternoon to tell me. A can of hairspray.

My hair is usually a bit disheveled, but my mother had long ago given up offering me beauty tips. This was serious: she had heard about the guy Milwaukeans were calling the East Side Slasher and she was telling me how to protect myself.

At the time, that motherly bit of advice (gleaned, I assumed, from an article in *Reader's Digest* or some such thing) caused in me the same reaction that her reminding me to finish my milk had caused in me as a child — a warm, safe feeling of being fussed over, even though there didn't seem to be much to be gained by obeying her.

It struck me as somewhat absurd: I couldn't envision myself fishing around in my purse for a can of hairspray when an attacker was bearing down on me, and I certainly couldn't see myself walking around Downtown Milwaukee at night with an aerosol can in my hand. After all, what rapist or other criminal seriously bent on doing me harm would be deterred by a quick spritz of Final Net?

My doubt, really, was nothing new. One of the earliest lessons I ever received in the futility of self-defense —for women, anyway —came from my brothers. "Hit me as hard as you can," one of them would say, girding his gut for my girlish punch. Even when I tried to spare my dignity and refuse, knowing full well what the outcome would be, he somehow managed to goad me into it.

"Go on, hit me." So I would. I would ball up my 10-year-old fist and bash him one. He'd smile. *Of course you can't hurt me.* He thought he was invincible, or at least he wanted me to think so. And I did.

I realize that, in light of all the women who have been raped, slashed or beaten in the past few months, and in light of the justifiable sense of outrage and mourning those crimes have evoked in the community, these stories may sound a bit more trivial and facetious than I intend them to. I apologize for that; perhaps it's the journalistic equivalent of nervous laughter. But every word is true, and what it really boils down to is this: up until not too long ago, I believed that, short of being armed with a pistol, there was absolutely nothing any woman could do in defense against any criminal. Or, to take it to its logical extension, against any man. Ever. And I suspect that, deep down, my mother and a lot of other women share that sense of futility too.

If by now it hasn't become clear, this is a story about rape and other kinds of violent attacks on women, from the standpoint of what women can do to stop them. I first decided to take a physical self-defense course and to write about it in June, after the East Side Slasher had struck too close to home for the fifth time. His territory seemed to be the blocks adjoining my office building, and one of the women here had already taken to carrying a two-foot length of pipe in her car for protection. To the best of anyone's knowledge, the slasher was not a rapist, but he had a knife and he was using it, and that was frightening enough for me.

In July, when an 18-year-old Brookfield woman was so brutally assaulted, and women and girls seemed to be getting attacked almost daily on the bike path, I became all the more motivated.

Initially, I had intended to write a "how-to" piece with tips on self-protection: you know, kick here, punch here, do this if he grabs you there. My motivations for doing this, I confess, were rooted more in a vague sense of feminist responsibility (and the sense that this would be a good story topic) than in any concrete sense of conviction that it would really work. It wasn't long before I realized something my instructor had pointed out right at the start — that all this punching, kicking and jabbing I was practicing wouldn't do me a bit of good unless I had the right attitude. I seriously had to *believe* that I could assert myself against an attacker and prevail, at least long enough to get away. And perhaps more importantly, I also had to believe that it was *okay* for me to do so.

Cultivating these beliefs proved to be more troublesome than I would have expected — more difficult, even, than the physical part of the course. And the more I read and learned about women and self-defense, the more I discovered that I was hardly alone in this. So instead of talking merely about techniques for blocking punches and escaping from wrist grabs, I am also talking about attitudes and ideas, and the infinite number of ways in which they affect what we can and cannot do for ourselves — and the kinds of choices we can make.

The best way to start is by telling you a story. It is completely true, except that, naturally, I've changed the woman's name to protect her privacy and safety.

I'll call her Debbie Porter. It's late November, about midnight, and Debbie, a tall, slender 42-year-old schoolteacher is in her nightclothes, writing letters and listening to music. Suddenly there's a loud thump at the back of her house. Her cats are acting spooked. She gets up to check on the noise, turns on the outdoor lights and sees nothing. So she goes back to her writing.

Meanwhile, an intruder has scaled up the side of the house to a second-story balcony. He has pulled a ski hat down completely over his face and is quietly lifting the phone off the hook. Carefully, stealthily, he heads down the stairs, gauging each step through the cloudy mesh of his knit hat.

Debbie decides to go to upstairs to bed. She heads toward the hallway and stops short. Standing in front of her is the faceless figure — holding a knife in one hand, a lamp in the other. She does not know this, but he is already wanted for several rapes in the City of Milwaukee.

Stop. Think about what might happen next. Think about what *usually* happens next in stories like this.

"At first I thought, I'm dreaming," she tells me later, reconstructing the events of the evening. "And then I thought, well this is a joke, someone's playing a joke on me. And then I thought, oh my God, there's a man there."

After a few seconds of shock that seem like hours. Debbie remembers something from the self-defense course she is taking: *the eyes are vulnerable. Go for the eyes.* Where *are* his eyes? The ski hat has no holes for eyes, nose or mouth. She can only guess. She raises her hands, her fingers spread wide in claws, and aims them at his face.

"Get the hell out of my house," she intones over and over again in a voice so guttural it scarcely sounds human. She takes a step forward.

He steps backward.

She steps forward again.

"GET...THE HELL...OUT...OF MY HOUSE!"

The intruder continues backing up through the hallway, making in his throat what Debbie later will describe as "monster" noises. Finally, she is able to slam a door in his face. She runs to safety at a neighbor's house, where she telephones the police.

Unless you are personally acquainted with Debbie Porter, you've probably never heard this story before. But her story is important to me and I feel sort of revolutionary telling it, because compared with all the bloody, tragic, true-life tales of crime and violence out there, it is pretty anticlimactic stuff. And a horror that *didn't* happen is usually not news.

I am hard-pressed, in fact, to remember any writing on the issue of sexual assault in the popular media that doesn't begin with the story of one of the many thousands of women who are victimized by rapists each year. (The Sexual Assault Treatment Center at Family Hospital, which sees most of the city's reported rape cases, treats between two and three rape victims a day, every day of the year, in Milwaukee alone. And experts there say that's only a small fraction of the number of rapes that actually occur and go unreported.)

Of course, these kinds of stories are essential for many reasons. First, they evoke empathy for the victim, or at least they should. Second, they make people angry, which is often a catalyst for action. And third, they remind people of their own vulnerability and the utterly nondiscriminatory nature of violence: it's only when we become aware that we're all potential victims that we will actually take steps to protect ourselves. I think these emotions are what one woman was hoping to arouse when she suggested at a community action meeting that Milwaukee follow the example of another city by placing prominent stickers at the scene of every sexual assault. Like the epitaph on a tombstone, the stickers would announce:

"A WOMAN
WAS RAPED HERE."

But the problem is that these constant reminders also evoke within many of us a deep sense of fear and powerlessness — the kind of helplessness that paralyzes us, the kind of expectations of doom that cause us, sometimes, to surrender when we don't have to. And then there's one more statistic, one more violent reminder, one more reason to be afraid. It's a vicious and dangerous cycle, and it's been going on for a long, long time.

In her book, *Against Our Will*, which in 1975 became one of the definitive studies of rape in our culture, Susan Brownmiller identified the various historical and mythological traditions that rapists and victims have fallen into over the years. As the stories are told and retold, she noted, real-life rapists tend to take on larger-than-life characteristics. They wind up in the minds of many as anti-heroes, the invincible "supermen of sadistic sex." Their real names are shed and they are bestowed with Mickey Spillane-type titles. Who remembers the Boston Strangler's full name? Or the Ski Mask Rapist's, for that matter? I even recall hearing someone joke once that Milwaukee must be the "big league" to have a criminal of such repute.

The same goes for the female victims in popular lore, except that the glamorization happens in reverse. Their strengths are minimized to the point of being nonexistent and their helplessness is blown out of proportion. In fiction, it's Little Red Riding Hood in the jaws of the wolf and Fay Wray swooning in the grasp of King Kong. In real life, we remember who Sharon Tate was and what happened to her. But I'll wager that few recall Corazon Amuraro, who rolled under a bed and escaped Richard Speck's bloodletting. We'll not soon forget the 18-year-old woman from Brookfield, whose terrible experience made headlines throughout the country, but Debbie Porter, I suspect, will fade all too rapidly from our thoughts. It's strange, but women seem to be so much more *memorable* when they have been damaged somehow.

Suffice it to say that precious little lore, if you want to call it that, has been established for the image of a strong woman who thwarts a rape, escapes, or otherwise prevails over her attacker. Instead, just about every sexual assault experience that we do hear of — every story that we assimilate into our view of How the World Works — ends up being one of violence and defeat, and we start believing (if we haven't been convinced already) that being a victim is a terminal condition. That we can try to *hide* from an attack by locking our doors, getting home at a reasonable hour, taking our full names off the mailboxes, and maybe even tucking a can of hairspray in our palms, but that if a bad man ever does get through our arsenal it is hopeless.

Debbie Schmitz, a social worker and counselor at Family Hospital's Sexual Assault Treatment Center, tells me that even women who are skilled in the martial arts or who have had rape prevention training find it difficult or impossible to put their self-defense skills to use when they encounter threatening situations. "I had one woman who knew judo," she says. "She was a black belt. But she froze and couldn't respond."

Many times this response may be because of an intuitive feeling that tells a woman that fighting back would endanger her more. There *are* times when fighting back physically could present more risk than it eliminates, and the ultimate goal of a woman in any violent situation should not be to escape, but simply to *survive* in the best condition possible.

Women, of course, should never be made to feel obligated to fight back. (This would have the atavistic effect of returning us to the days when, to protect their "virtue," women were required to fight back even to the point of death, if it came to that. In order to be believed, they were also required to sport some kind of injury that would demonstrate how valiantly they had resisted.)

There is also a legitimate concern that emphasis on a woman's ability to defend herself might be twisted into blaming the victim for her victimization: if she can fight back, then why didn't she? And if she did fight back, why didn't she succeed? I think one of the philosophical reasons for not heavily stressing self-defense in community programs that deal with rape is that if you put too much emphasis on self-defense, it can tend to shift all the responsibility to women and detract from the real issue — which is effecting the social changes necessary to get men to stop attacking women in the first place. The Sexual Assault Counseling Unit of the District Attorney's Office, for example, does not give out tips on self-defense because they fear that it might imply that women who didn't or couldn't follow the tips were somehow to blame for what happened to them. And if women fear they are going to be blamed, they might not be as inclined to report or prosecute the rape.

Unfortunately, the lack of such information and the disproportionate publicity of the so-called "sensational" sexual assault cases may give women an inflated sense of fear in sexual assault situations. And this, combined with the fact that from their earliest days women have been told that it's not nice to say no, that's it's not okay to resist, effectively deprives women of even being able to make the *choice* to fight back if the situation seems conducive to it.

The facts, according to a study published in 1982, are that about 73 percent of reported rapes occur without a weapon, and that when weapons are involved a gun is involved only 34 percent of the time. Contrary to the myths of "Stranger Danger" we hear from the time we are children, as many as 50 percent of sexual assaults are committed by somebody the victim knows or at least has met before. And unlike many of the graphically violent cases that make headlines, around 50 percent of assaults occur not on a secluded sidewalk or parking lot somewhere, but in the victim's own home.

Most experts in the field also agree that a meek and fearful response to an attacker is *not* likely to mollify him and cause him to "go easy" on a victim. Research seems to indicate that meekness and fear are exactly what the attacker seeks. Two studies published in 1980 by Dr. Pauline Bart of the University of Illinois Medical Center, and Dr. Jennie McIntyre of the Bureau of Social Science Research, Inc., Washington, both indicate that women who immediately and actively resisted an attacker were more likely to escape, while those who were passive or tried to talk their way out were less likely to escape. (Active resistance techniques include running away, yelling, saying "no" forcefully or even being physically assertive in some way.) On the other hand, Juana Sabatino, a sexuality educator at the Sixteenth Street Community Health Center and black belt in karate who teaches rape prevention and self defense in Milwaukee, notes that "passive" resistance, which usually involves such acts as crying, pleading or fainting, seems to correlate very high with extreme violence.

In the flyer on self-defense that Family Hospital's Sexual Assault Treatment Center hands out, some of the first words of advice are: "If more women would get angry instead of scared there would be fewer rapes and assaults ... We've been socialized to 'remain calm,' but this usually doesn't work, because this is exactly the type of vulnerable woman the assaulter is going after. If we react opposite of what they think we will, at least we have a chance."

But the problem with this — as with many of the issues surrounding rape — is that most of the public's conceptions are not based on facts but on the images and ideas that are most prevalent in movies, newspapers and the 10 o'clock news.

I have to admit that I approached my first self-defense class with a good deal of ambivalence. In my high school, "she's so nice" was one of the highest accolades that could ever be bestowed on one of our gender. It was even ranked above being "smart " or "cute" (although being cute certainly did help you seem nicer). Niceness is one of those notions that has stuck with me into adulthood, and even though it has become generally acceptable for a nice woman to be self-sufficient in a lot of areas, self-defense still doesn't seem to be one of them.

Kneeing a man in the testicles is not nice. Punching him in the Adam's apple is not nice. When I wasn't privately doubting that these techniques would actually work, I was secretly fearing that knowing them would turn me into a tough broad or a bellicose punk prone to inflicting pain on people at the slightest provocation.

On a more subconscious level, I think I also feared that knowing these things would make me less attractive to men. (Try as I might not to, I still worry about these things.) When I told my father I was taking the course, he commented "What are you doing a stupid thing like that for?" When I told a male friend about what I was learning he would warn me not to get "overconfident," and I began to suspect (whether it was justified or not) that his caution was motivated less by his concern for me than by a fear that I might become tougher than he was. I think this might be one reason why more women don't care to learn self-defense or study the martial arts: for so long we have been told that the way to become "safe" is to be adorable to a power figure who will protect us. Under that logic, learning self-defense skills, if it costs a woman the affection of a man, would have the net effect of making her — psychologically speaking, anyway — *less* safe.

Strangely enough, the course proved to be its own self-cure for most of my fears. My instructor, Rick Reshel, has a second-degree black belt in karate, and one of the first things he stressed was that effective self-defense meant being assertive, not aggressive, That actual physical self-defense was a last resort to be used only when other types of resistance — like yelling, or saying no, or running away — either did not work or were not possible. The goal wasn't necessarily to completely waste somebody, but merely to incapacitate him long enough to get away. And the whole idea behing learning self-defense was essentially a *peaceful* one: the better I got at it, the less likely it would be that I would ever need it. (This, bad karate movies starring Bruce Lee notwithstanding, is the philosophy underlying the martial arts in general.)

"Rapists," Rick told me, "generally do not choose women as victims if they look confident and capable of defending themselves. They look for somebody they are sure they can dominate."

Like most women learning self-defense skills, I had to start pretty much from scratch because there was little in my childhood (other than those wildly unegalitarian punching sessions with my brothers) to prepare me for real fighting. This later occurred to me as ironic: As Linda Tschirhart Sanford and Mary Ellen Donovan said in their book, *Women and Self Esteem,*in our society, it's the women who are the most vulnerable to being physically violated but it's boys who seem to get the most preparation for defending themselves against it.

Over the 10-week course, however, I learned the basics well. I learned what a sturdy fighting stance is, and how to balance myself to take a blow. How to make a fist, and, instead of allowing my wrist to flop, to drive straight through with my punch. How to put the weight of my body behind my strikes, and how to "think through" my target so the blows would penetrate instead of glancing off.

Because I was taking the lessons privately, I also had the chance to do some sparring with Rick — practicing my snap kicks and punches on a human, moving target (well-padded, of course). And this was where I got my first taste of an emotion that I have never felt before: the deep sense of satisfaction that comes with a well-placed punch.

I realize that by telling the story this way and by talking about Debbie Porter, I am engaged as much in the art of myth-making as I am in conventional journalism. As a woman who made a choice and resisted successfully, Debbie stands as the antithesis of most of what we have been led to believe throughout our lives, and I confess that what I'm trying to do here is to even out the lopsided picture we've been given by making her into just a little bit of a hero.

I can't ignore the fact that Debbie Porter never really did have to strike an intruder, and that she admits she really doesn't know what she would have done if the circumstances had been any different — if the man had been bigger, for example, or if he had managed to sneak up behind her.

I also can't gloss over the very important fact that, in a lot of ways, Debbie was still very much a victim. Because her attacker was prevented from completing his mission, she was very afraid that he might return and she was forced to move from the place she had called home for 12 years. She spent months of sleepless nights with a scissors under her pillow and a brace under her bedroom door.

But in another equally real sense, Debbie did prevail, and I even wish that I could tell you her real name so that she'd seem more believable. I have sat at her dining room table. I have petted her cats, and her voice is on my tape recorder. For me she is real and tangible proof that the notion of resistance — of "fighting back" — will not remain the way one male friend of mine described it not too long ago: "Rhetorically useful, but practically speaking not really very feasible."

This is the epilogue. It's very late at night. I've just about finished researching this story, and my friend Diane is telling me she wants to take a self-defense class because of the disturbing series of nightmares she's been having lately. I know exactly what she's talking about because as far back as about the age of 12, I can remember having the same dream over and over again: I am inside a house. Sometimes it's my house, sometimes it's the house where I used to babysit. I am alone. Then there is a sound — not a loud sound, really — at the window, and I see a hand, maybe, or the top of someone's head poking into the room. It is sinister and terrifying, and I am frozen with fear. I cannot move, and I cannot scream.

This dream, because it has come to me so often in the night, and because it is so unnervingly realistic, had at one time convinced me that this was exactly how I would respond in real life.

Susan Brownmiller had a name for it. She called it "paralysis of will." Our reflexes become paralyzed, she theorized, because we've been conditioned not to react. I tend to think of it more in terms of the title of an old Harlan Ellison science fiction novel I saw once: *I Have No Mouth and I Must Scream.* I have never read the book, but the image has stuck with me ever since.

Now, after taking a self-defense course, after hours of drills in a damp basement karate studio, after learning some of the facts about rape, even after hearing Debbie Porter tell her story, I cannot honestly say that the image still doesn't lurk somewhere deep within my subconscious, And I cannot honestly predict how I would respond if my nightmare were to become a reality. But what I want to believe — and what I think I must believe if I'm going to get on with it and live at all comfortably in this world — is that, at the very least, I can make some kind of choice.

Reprinted from *Milwaukee Magazine,* September, 1984.

Can You Really Protect Yourself Against Assault?

by Denyse Handler

This is primarily a chapter of personal experience. I am not an "expert witness" of any kind on the subject of assault. But I know the feeling of being set upon suddenly by a violent thug; I have been attacked three times in the past twelve years. That tends to cause one to form an inevitable interest in the subject, mainly from the point of view of carefully evaluating strategies for prevention or quick extrication from a difficult situation; my observations will be mainly practical.

There are two main schools of thought on how to avoid assault: First, there is the Hai Karate! school, popular among some feminists. Sisters, defend yourselves! Smash rape, rapists, etc! Guns, knives, aerosol spray cans of mace, these should be your everyday purse companions. Approach every social situation as if it were a battlefield.

The trouble with all this is that a social situation is *not* a battlefield. If most of us thought that there was any chance we would be attacked on any given evening, we wouldn't have gone out at all — or, speaking for myself, I'd go out in battledress, not an evening gown and carry a rifle rather than a purse (don't forget the canteen and the first aid kit.) But seriously, we do not really expect to be attacked, nor should we. Hence, if we are attacked, it is a surprise and we have only a half second (maybe) to decide what to do about it. I will return to that latter point later, as it is crucial for developing an effective response to the problem.

What about weapons? If you have a gun, you might not reach it in time. If you keep a gun ready to hand for any emergency, the most likely casualty will be you, one of these days, shooting off your toe. Knives, toxic sprays, etc. escalate the battle without necessarily giving you a better margin of success. Your assailant may be much more skilled than you are at wresting control of and using these things; you may be providing him with a weapon he had forgotten to bring. In fact, I would hazard a guess that unless you are quite sure that you can disable your opponent instantly, weapons that escalate the battle will not improve your margin.

More helpfully, the Hai Karate! school also suggests self-defense courses. These have the great advantage of improving a woman's capabilities, and her attitude to her own capabilities without posing any added threat to her. This attitude business is quite important, since, as we will see later, it may provide the key to reducing the risk of attack. It may even repel your assailant (though don't count on it.) Self-defense above all teaches you to think during an attack. But you don't know and can't know just what you will do when the attack is for real. (And your assailant may have taken the course too.)

The other major theory for avoiding sexual assault is the one promoted by some anti-feminist groups: the It Never Happens to Virtuous Women school. The idea is that if you don't wear provocative clothing, perfume, etc., act modestly, and do look appealingly helpless, it just won't happen.

How valid would that approach have been for me? I dress conservatively, wearing mid-calf length dresses most of the time. The first time I was attacked, I was wearing a parka that looked a great deal like a bear's winter coat. The second time I was wearing a long grey quilted winter dress and a long-sleeved sweater underneath it — most unattractive, actually, because I dress for warmth, not fashion, on cold winter days. The third time was in in the summer in Minnesota — I was wearing a mid-calf length summer dress with the neckline up to the jugular. No make-up, no jewelry, no perfume. I was in all cases minding my own business, walking to work or washing clothes in a public laundromat. I don't know if I looked appealing or not; I was attacked from behind, rather suddenly, by people, whom I realized later, were stalking me for a short period of time.

Really, the only thing that made me seem a good prospect to my assailants was that I was small, looked timid and was all alone. Assailants, like carnivores, have basic and simple attitudes — they are looking for the minimum risk situation: *that* is what "turns them on".

Of course, the Virtuous Women school would have an easy answer for my situation — as a married woman, I shouldn't have been working, right, and then I could have stayed at home and tatted doilies instead of being attacked while walking to work. And I should never have been washing clothes in a public laundry (we couldn't afford machines at the time) or alone, without my husband (so who was going to look after the kids while I was gone?). Certainly, the Virtuous Women wouldn't advocate that *he* should have washed the clothes, as it might affect his masculinity. I must conlude therefore that the Virtuous Women school does not have answers to the problem either, for anyone who is not wealthy enough to avoid it simply by spending money. Even that, of course, won't protect you from the assailant who breaks into your upper crust fortress, if you have one.

The wealth issue is important because, as we are already aware, a disproportionate number of assaults are committed on poor, black and very young women. Some of the very young are foolish teen-agers taking chances that they have been repeatedly told are too high-risk (such as hitchhiking alone and accepting a ride with a group of guys, too often a classic preventable tragedy). But in most cases the disparity lies in the fact that the poor simply must take chances that the rich don't have to take. There is not time here to deal with the social justice factors involved in the prevention of sexual assault, except to say that it underscores one of the very serious flaws in the Virtuous Women approach. Whether one is virtuous or not, one runs a much greater risk if one is poor.

I do not remember being very brave or clever when I was attacked. But I have an instinctive tendency to become savagely aggressive when threatened (shades of prehistory?). This is not courage, it is lunacy. I suppose my assailants may have thought I was mad. I screamed horribly and attacked them and they ran away. I chased one to the foot of an alley into which he disappeared, along with my winter coat. Only a sudden surge of common sense prevented me from chasing after him to get it back. (I didn't, and froze on the way home.) But I learned a valuable lesson: assailants are bullies at heart, which means that, aside from anything else, it is no fun for them if the intended victim doesn't act the part.

This gave me an insight into an incident which occurred when I was fifteen. My sister and I were lying in bed late one Saturday night and she was already asleep. I heard a shuffling sound out on the balcony and then became aware that someone was fumbling with the door knob. Being young and fearless, I went to the door and when the second-storey man (as I guess he must have been) opened the door I confronted him suddenly with "Who are you? What are you doing here? You've no business here. Get out!", a neatly worked out practical syllogism which had him scurrying over the side of the balcony and across neighbours' back yards within seconds. Of course it was foolhardy, and with all I've heard since, I doubt I would do it today. But the point is that what scared him was his own failure to elicit fear. I was no real threat to him.

The advice of both schools of thought, Hai Karate! and Virtuous Women, suffers from the same problem: they assume that you will have ages to decide what to do. Of course you won't. During the half-second in which you become aware of an assailant, you are likely to do the thing most natural to yourself, whatever that is. The good advice you've received, which you have not already incorporated into your overall way of living, is likely to become the stuff of "I should have ...." The worst thing to do is to cringe, plead or act "nice". This literally turns the assailant on: it is exactly the response he was hoping for. Yet some women are like that. Unless they change their outlook on themselves as women they will always be like that. They are used to cringing, whining and pleading in their dealings with men. Some women actually do what the assailant tells them, without being forced to, physically. Of course, if you are used to taking orders from men all your life, then, when your are in a state of shock, what could be more natural?

This is why I think that changing one's instinctive outlook regarding male-female relationships is so important: simply not acting like a predictable victim may take the fun out of it for the assailant. This matters because he may then elect simply to commit some indecency, such as urinating in your presence or on you, then leave. That's gross, of course, but it is better than a continued assault.

The police often counsel women not to resist, for fear that the assailant will then kill. I think that this is understandable from a police point of view: they would rather investigate an assault than a homicide. But failure to resist may make it difficult to prove assault; in any event, this advice makes women prepare to be precisely the easy victims the assailant is looking for. I suppose each situation has to be judged on its risks and its merits. Some authors have suggested shouting "Fire!" or giving orders, such as "You better leave quick. This area is patrolled". One seventy-year-old Florida woman got rid of a would-be assailant by laughing and saying "What? Me? At my age?" I would not suggest insulting or arguing with the assailant on the grounds that he is probably used to altercations that end in violence. All you really are trying to do is to give enough of the "wrong" type of signals that he begins to suspect that it won't be any fun after all.

The after-effects of being attacked are almost as difficult as the situation itself. Although I was not harmed in the incidents themselves I found that the biggest problems for me were loss of trust and panic attacks. It is no defense against the irrationality of trusting no one and nothing to argue that "it can't happen again." Unfortunately, it can happen again. It happened several times to me. There is no warning when it does. Fear of the panic itself is as big a problem as fear of another incident. Long after one has stopped fearing the attack, one fears the long hours of fear, when one is alone at night. Long after one has stopped replaying the incident again and again in one's mind, one is jolted by hearing of another one on a news broadcast.

How can one help a friend in this situation? At first, she needs most to recover a sense of normalcy, a sense that in general strangers are not enemies and she will not be attacked. It would be psychologically disastrous for her to be attacked again soon, especially under similar circumstances. (I myself developed a severe laundromat phobia because two separate incidents had occurred in laundromats. We ended up having to get laundry machines at home because my family grew tired of my panicky approach to being alone in public washing facilities.) It's probably best to go along with the need for security at first but then to gently discourage an obsessive attitude to it. It will just get worse and worse, because one is never safe from one's own fears.

It comes down, as we all know, to a question of personal and social attitudes. There is much to be said about the changes that are needed before we will get a handle on this problem, changes that must occur in many different sectors. I just want to end on a note of reflection: Few people want women to be assaulted. But many would prefer that we be passive and run the risk rather than that we avoid it by becoming self-directive. Neither the Hai Karate school nor the Virtuous Women school can help with this: both are reacting to the problem rather than addressing it. Being feminine doesn't mean being in purdah and being self-directive does not mean being armed to the teeth, ready for any kind of trouble. A pro-life feminism should be able to steer clear of these futile opposites and affirm that there is hope — for the woman who need not be a victim, for the man who need not be an aggressor and the society that need not be full of hostages to fear.

Accepting the Unjust
by Mary Meehan

"Rape" and "abortion" are two of the cruelest words in our language, representing two of the worst realities of our time. What do we say when the first is used to justify the second?

It is not enough to say that relatively few children are conceived through rape, or that it is wrong to remedy violence with more violence. Both are true, but they do not fully meet the feelings of fear, disgust, humiliation and great injustice that rape victims undergo.

So deep is the sense of injustice, and so widely is it shared by non-victims, that many people find it hard to say that abortion should be barred in rape cases. Dr. Mildred Jefferson, a longtime prolife activist, remarked that the revulsion people feel for the crime of rape carries over to the rape victim and to any child who "may have resulted from the unwelcome union." She added: "For some people of strong religious bent, rape becomes an unpardonable sin which taints sinner and victim alike. The child is never thought of as an entity deserving of consideration — only a blot to be removed."

Yet the child has done no wrong and should not be punished for the father's crime. Rape is no longer punished by execution of the rapist (certainly a change for the better), but now the child is executed instead. What does this say about our sense of justice? And what happened to our commitment to equality if we say that some children's right to life depends on the circumstances of their conception?

Accepting abortion for rape also makes it harder to protect other innocent children. Thus Georgia, in 1968, became one of the first states to allow abortion for rape and certain other hard cases. The lawyer who defended the Georgia statute before the U.S. Supreme Court had difficulty proving her state's commitment to protect the unborn in view of the exceptions allowed. Justice Thurgood Marshall underlined the problem when he asked, "Is there any other statute in Georgia which says under certain conditions you can kill somebody?" The Supreme Court struck down the Georgia law in one of its 1973 decisions.

The history of the Georgia statute also showed that some of the support for abortion in rape cases is due to racial bigotry. In urging segregationist Gov. Lester Maddox to support the 1968 bill, lobbyists for the state medical association asked him how he would feel if a white girl were raped by a black man and pregnancy resulted.

Rape is a terrible crime, one of the worst; but it does not become more or less of a crime according to the race of the man who commits it. Abortion proponents who appeal to bigotry when speaking of rape (or when attacking welfare mothers) undoubtedly pick up support this way, but they should not be proud of it.

Having said all of this, however, we are still faced with the problem of a woman who has been victimized by crime and who is pregnant as a result of that crime. Besides the usual discomfort and restrictions of pregnancy, she may feel great anger and hatred toward her assailant and may find it hard to avoid feeling the same way toward the child she carries. If she is married, she has her husband's attitudes to worry about in addition to her own. If she is unmarried, she has the problem of explaining the pregnancy to family and friends. And there are the financial costs of pregnancy to worry about...and the process of adoption.

What do we say about all of this? It seems to me that honesty requires us to say that it is unjust that a woman must carry to term a child conceived through rape, *but that it is a far greater injustice to kill the child.* There is no way to avoid injustice in this situation; the best we can do is reduce it. The first injustice, which lasts for nine months of a life, can be relieved both relieved financially and psychologically. But the second injustice ends a life, and there is no remedy for that.

Some states now provide financial aid to crime victims. Certainly such aid should cover the obstetrical and hospital costs of pregnancy when it results from rape. When public aid is not currently available, private aid should be. Pro-life doctors and pregnancy aid centers should be especially generous and sensitive in handling these cases.

Psychological support, especially from the woman's family and friends, is enormously important. They should stand by her and say clearly that, no matter what the circumstances of conception, there should *never* be any embarrassment about bringing a child into the world. There should never be anything but pride in that.

It is also important to assure the woman that crime is not hereditary and that, in fact, rape is one of the rare cases in which good can come from evil. Thus journalist Jerry Hulse, in his book *Jody* (McGraw-Hill, 1976), explains that doctors urgently needed a family medical history for his wife, who was adopted. Hulse found her natural mother, who revealed that she had been raped at the age of 15 and, as a result, had given birth to twins — Hulse's wife and a boy who was reared by his grandparents. The mother had not wanted to give up either child. She was happy to be reunited with her daughter, as the twins were to be reunited with each other.

To say that good can come from evil is not to accept the evil itself. A young prolifer put it well when she said: "The answer to rape is not abortion, it's stopping rape." Ways to do this include: 1) changing outrageous male attitudes, especially those promoted by the pornography industry; 2) training women for self-defense, 3) participating in "Take Back the Night" marches.

The unborn have a right to life and to freedom from assault. So do women.

Courtesy *National Catholic Register*, April 18, 1982. Reprinted with permission. 1901 Avenue of the Stars, Suite 1511, Los Angeles, CA 90067

A Letter to the Editor
We Have Seen

January 12, 1984
To the Editor:

Everyone gets upset by rape, child prostitution, incest. Some people even advocate abortion as a "solution" when a raped woman becomes pregnant — although this "solution" punishes two innocent victims (the mother and the child), rather than the criminal: the rapist.

Why don't citizens examine some of the *causes* of rape and child abuse in their own communities?

I'm tired of seeing pornographic magazines openly displayed in liquor stores and bookstores. If store owners cherish the revenue from these publications, they should keep them face down behind the counter, available ONLY BY REQUEST.

I enclose a photo layout of a very young girl and 11 ads from a "soft core" porno magazine which I found — not in a sex bookstore in downtown Milwaukee — but in a liquor store in my own village of Menomonee Falls. The ads brag about "little movies," "all subjects — all ages," "cherry popper," "wet little sister," "sweet cherrys [sic]," "posed and candid young girl pictures," "schoolgirl sex," "virgin orgy," and so on. Several of these ads include photos of 11-12 year old girls in disgusting poses. One ad promotes a magazine called *Incest.* I reluctantly bought the magazine so I could clip this evidence and send it in to the newspaper...in the hope that it will shock some people into action.

Were these children kidnapped and forced to pose? Did their mothers take them to the studio? Were they runaways trying to earn some money? Does anyone really care? IF YOU care, then please call the owners of the stores you patronize...and if nothing is changed don't reward them with your dollars any more. Every dollar is a vote.

Then, if you have the courage, examine possible causes of twisted attitudes in your own living room. Do you subscribe to cable TV channels which regularly run R-rated "soft porn" movies? If so, do you think your children never see them? Or do you think that they remain unaffected by this trash? Do you subscribe to pornographic magazines and leave them around for your sons and daughters to find?

I include one ad which doesn't portray young girls but which illustrates my point about pornography and its relation to sexual assault. The ad depicts a nude woman tied up, with the headline "ROPED AND RAPED." Whoever says pornography doesn't encourage rape must be nuts.

For the sake of all our children, please act now to eliminate some of the causes of sex crimes in your own community and home.

Sincerely,

Gail Grenier Sweet

From the January 19, 1984 MENOMONEE FALLS NEWS. Also the January 24, 1984 *Milwaukee Sentinel.* Used with permission.

And...A Letter to the Editor
We are Still Waiting to See

Ms. Magazine
370 Lexington Avenue
New York, N.Y. 10017

December 1978

To the Editor:

I belatedly finished the November issue. The articles on erotica and pornography were well written and welcome. I appreciated it even more in this holiday season as the media reported that a few women had returned the Andrea della Robbia Christmas postage stamps because the naked baby Jesus was "obscene". Deliver us.

In light of the feature story, I found it ironic that the Lichtenstein article on the St. Paul fire-bombing (Highland Park Planned Parenthood) should mention "a local philanthropist" donating $200,000 to pay for Planned Parenthood abortions. It is common knowledge here in the Twin Cities that the "local philanthropist" is Benjamin Berger, town pornographer.

Sincerely,

Paulette Joyer

Taken from the May 1979 *Minnesota Feminists For Life Newsletter*, 2815 West 38th Street, Minneapolis MN 55410. Reprinted with permission.

Section Five:
Giving Life:
Activism & Strategies

I feel that presenting alternatives to violence is the *most important* thing we can do in this book.

However, there are so many alternatives — and people have so many different talents — that to cover alternatives would require another book.

Therefore, I've stuck to the general rather than the particular in this chapter. For more specific ideas on alternatives to abortion, for instance, I refer the reader to each year's January issue of *National Right to Life News* — always a special issue on many different alternatives.

A word of caution: in seeking alternatives to abortion, let's not ignore women who are seeking *alternatives in birth.* Specifically, a woman has the right to choose *home birth,* an age-old tradition. Feminists must continue to fight for control of the childbirth experience. In the hospital environment, we must insist that doctors and nurses treat birthing women with the greatest respect.

— Gail Grenier Sweet

Why I Did Not Want a Baby Shower

by Jean Blackwood

You wanted to gather like modern magi,
Gift-bearing and resonating "ah"s
For my new son.
Thank you.

But this child needs no gift.
He is here, alive and loved.
Would you not gather instead for the others,
Unloved, unborn, unnoticed,
Clinging to life in hostile wombs,
Soon to be surprised by death
And drowned in an ocean saltier than tears?

Must we always be like babes ourselves,
Our senses gross and untuned,
Aware only of the larger forms
That move across our line of sight,
Our hands clumsily grabbing
And our mouths noisy with kisses?

Let us grow to a finer love!
One that feels deep
And sees in darkness
And cares when there is no caress.

Forgive me, if I seem not to value kindness.
I only mean to say
Do not suffocate your love
In little places.

From *Beyond Beginning and Other Poems*. Reprinted with permission from Low-Key Press, P.O. Box 490, *Clarion*, Penna. 16214

Our Bodies, Their Lives
by Juli Loesch

There is a common room, a kind of unfurnished vestibule, where pro-choicers and pro-lifers brush past each other as they head out to the street to their respective banner and placards. They pass; their eyes meet for a moment; and then they hit the revolving door which deals them out: right, left, right, left.

Into this corridor I want to bring some decent chairs, a pitcher of beer, and a tray where we can lay aside our Right to Life and Right to Choose buttons — at least for the time being. Not that our slogans are false; they are, all of them, true in their way. But at some time, we need to share more deeply from each others' experience.

I'm nearly an anarchist in any case, and the legal aspects of abortion are particularly ambivalent for me. Whatever the law , no unborn child has any security which does not flow from a woman having the desire to foster its life, and the means to do so. These essential conditions can never be produced by coercion on a pregnant woman. I want to unburden this essay of any legal/illegal controversy — assume liberty to choose, right or wrong — and rather discuss abortion itself.

Unquestionably, abortion does two things: it empties a uterus; and it kills an embryo or fetus. Pro-choicers tend to focus on the first aspect, and the pro-lifers on the second; they develop their arguments from the one-half or the other.

Yet there is considerable sympathy in each of the "camps" for the perceptions of the other. Many pro-lifers believe that a woman does have the right to physical autonomy; that it is dehumanizing to regard a woman's body as being primarily at the service of somebody else; a "vessel," as they say. A similar proportion of pro-choicers recognize that it is dehumanizing to regard a new human life as a mere disposable growth: a "tumor" as they say. There are many who are profoundly dissatisfied at having to trade off one life for another, and who long for more inclusive solutions.

I keep thinking of that indispensable requirement, "a woman's control of her own body," and of the unacceptable risks which endanger that control.

I remember 7 or 8 years ago, lying on my bed with tears of anguish streaming because — my menstrual period was late. I thought I was pregnant. (Luckily, I was not.) But after two or three episodes of this kind, I began to feel real anger about my situation. There was thrombosis in my medical history, so that I shouldn't take the Pill; besides, why put something into my body every day that I'd hesitate to put into my compost pile? The IUD was out; I've had no children and am afraid of tubal pregnancies. Foams, sprays, plugs and rubbers, jellies and jams, that's what I was using. The failure rate is too high. Why be thrown into anxiety every time my period was late?

Motherhood? Not then, not now, maybe not ever. Abortion? Adoption?

One thing I knew: the whole situation was out of control. Say a woman doesn't want to get pregnant; and say she keeps participating in actions that could get her pregnant. *Who's in control then?* I thought about abortion: how simple. "...And then you pass a piece of gray tissue." "Pass." Like excretion. "A piece," When it's not a piece, it's a whole organism. "Of tissue." Come, let's be accurate: an organism which has, at eight weeks, a heart pumping blood (his or her own blood, not mine); organs, systems, and readable electric brain activity (his or her brain, not mine). At ten weeks, swallowing, squinting: spontaneous movement.

Not wanting my body to be the place where a killing is done (and who "wants" death-before-birth?), I was up against hard decisions.

All around me were the casualties of the sexual revolution. In the bad old days, if an unmarried woman got pregnant, the father-of-the-child was expected to accept some degree of accountability: if not the (sometimes OK, sometimes awful) shotgun marriage, then at least some meaningful degree of support. Now, the responsible thing is to put up the cash for an abortion ("No hard feelings, OK?"); and if the man actually goes to the clinic with the woman — if he holds her hand — why, he's a prince!

This may all sound quite acceptable, until you think of the actual social realities. *Aborting* comes to be seen as an honorable alternative to *supporting.* And if the woman, for some reason, ends up having the baby after all, the man may feel perfectly justified in saying: "Hell, I did my duty. I offered to pay for an abortion. Don't expect me to help support it."

If there are any who doubt that this is what's going on, I suggest that they get to know some women who have been through it. For the past six years I've helped staff Hospitality House and the Pax Center, both of which offer emergency housing/crisis sanctuary to women. Abused wives, abused children; runaways, throw-aways. I have seen the abortion mentality provide a neat justification for the financial and emotional abandonment of women who, for one reason or another, did *not* destroy the unexpected child.

A more equal sharing by women and men of the care for children is absolutely essential. I want young men to learn to be babysitters as well as baseball players. I hope to see a growing number of liberated fathers who are attentive and nurturant to human lives at every stage, and not just remote money/authority figures.

But we have created a situation in which a man, if he wishes, can easily shift the *total* obligation on to women. He can *buy* his way out of accountability by making "The Offer" for "The Procedure." So the matter of children, which should be two people's decision and responsibility, becomes one person's decision and responsibility. The man's *sexual* role then implies — exactly nothing: no relationship. How quickly "woman's right to choose" comes to serve "man's right to use."

In the way, society at large find it easier to say, "Lady, we feel no sense of obligation: so just be sensible and terminate your problem, and everyone will breathe easier." (How often have I heard that a welfare abortion is so much cheaper and easier than a welfare childbirth — and in four years, daycare — and in sixteen years —)

As Tillie Olsen observes in her powerful book, *Silences*, we live "in a society hostile to growing life" — a society becoming ever more so because of its fondness for disposability: the runaway father, the flushaway pregnancy, the throw-away teenage daughter.

So this is the sexual *status quo*. This is what needs to be challenged with all our force. I think what many men hoped for (women, too) in promoting a "sexual revolution" was that women would change, would become more loose and groovy. What's needed now is that the *men* must change. We need to campaign among men for responsible attitudes and behavior with regard to sexuality, parenthood, and human relations generally, raise consciousness in men about sexism and domination. Men must relinquish the privilege of their caste and become nurturers of our children.

Fine idea. Swell. What do we do till then? (I mean, besides struggle, organize, agitate, build a whole new world, and so forth.)

We all agree that preventing unwanted conception is infinitely preferable to the destruction of a kid you've already started. Despite all talk to the contrary, we don't have to continue taking these unacceptable risks while we "wait" for white-coated researchers to develop the super-pill that solves all problems. We have some safe, effective choices already.

One is to choose not to have sex. Celibacy is becoming a real option for more and more of us.

Sexual intercourse is being wrongly used to fill a real need for what used to be called *social* intercourse: affection and friendship. The misplaced use of sex is often an emotional rip-off for *both* partners, who were seeking to be "close" and ended up in a bruised and bruising — or at best ambiguous — affair.

Another is Natural Family Planning. The couple avoids reproductive contact during the five or six days per cycle when, by intelligent self-examination, the woman knows she's fertile.

This is not the old "calendar rhythm" system. It's a truly feminist method: it's safe for the woman; it's effective; it doesn't cost money; it requires cooperation from the male partner; and it's the *only* birth control method which cannot be used coercively by the state.

This is the kind of program which increasing numbers of pro-choicers and pro-lifers could cooperate with. It enables us to reject the presuppositions which have driven American women to endanger their health with synthetic hormones and IUDs, plus destory 1.3 million new lives every year. We oppose both the medical/surgical assault upon these women's bodies, and the indignities to human life in its earliest stages.

The development of cooperative, fertility-aware sexuality is something society must do on a massive scale. We deserve, demand, have a right to — can create — something better than the abortion industry's "cure" for our unique condition of impregnability, whether that abortionist be in the back alley or the plush front office.

I would still actively oppose any attempt to criminalize abortion. That is, it would be outrageous to send girls and women who have had abortions, plus their abortionists, to jail.

But we're in-between times. The old structures (the patriarchal family, the taboos against sexual experience) are falling and good riddance; but the new structures (the mutual community, feminist sexual ethics) haven't yet been fully developed. I sincerely fear that an aggressive pro-abortion philosophy could hinder the development of these humane new structures, by encouraging the privatization of pregnancy as one of those "female problems" and a proliferation of gynecological surgery by the millions as the "solution".

In that common-room, that unfurnished vestibule where pro-choicers and pro-lifers met on their way to the street and dividing barricades, I would like to put chairs and a pitcher of beer and a sign: Pro-Choicers for Life, Pro-Lifers for Choice. Come, sit a bit, discuss what kind of society we want to build together. Let's see if we can strengthen the woman's right to choose, and the new life's right to live at the same time. Is there hope in that? Can we encourage each other? We have a right to choose. Can we choose life?

Taken from *The Catholic Agitator*, 632 N. Britanica St., Los Angeles, CA 90033. Reprinted with permission of the author.

Contraception:
Any Happy Medium Possible?

by Gail Grenier Sweet

An old saying claims that East and West shall never meet. That may be true of two radically different cultures, but it shouldn't be true of pro-choicers and pro-lifers when it comes to the contraception issue. Unfortunately, prejudice and coverups cloud the issue on both sides.

First, consider the pro-life view. Pro-lifers come from all areas of the political and religious spectrums. Some believe in non-violent protest such as "sitting in" at abortion clinics. Some do street counseling of women approaching the clinics for their appointments. Others do pre- and post-abortion medical testing and counseling at their own prolife clinics. A few groups seek housing and emotional support for women in crisis pregnancies and for single mothers and their children. And there is a large segment of the prolife movement which dedicates itself solely to educating the public about the realities of abortion, infanticide, and euthanasia.

Now, for the most part, these different prolife groups co-exist peacefully. The prevailing philosophy is "We all have different talents; we can all help in different ways." There is little feeling of competition among the various organizations, because they're all hitting the problem from different angles.

However, there is a big problem and it appears to be growing into a rift which threatens the very life of the prolife movement. That problem is CONTRACEPTION. Some pro-life activists agree with Dr. Landrum Shettles, who writes from a medical background in his book *Rites of Life.* Dr. Shettles urges pro-lifers to be pro-contraception, as long as the form used is not abortifacient. He explains why the IUD, "morning-after," "month-after" and "once-a-month" pills, and progesterone only oral contraceptives taken daily are abortifacient — either destroying the fertilized egg or preventing its implantation in the womb.

A fairly large segment of pro-lifers, however, oppose *any* type of contraceptive device or drug. They approve only of Natural Family Planning for married couples; for single women, chastity is the only option. If these pro-lifers encounter a pro-life group which does not take this same stand, they brand that group as "not really pro-life."

This is judgmentalism at its very worst, and most dangerous. It reminds me of some teachers I met during my first year of teaching junior high school students. These older teachers continually moaned about how today's students weren't like they were "in the old days." Personally, I found my students delightful and full of enthusiasm. *I accepted them where they were,* and we proceeded from there. I felt that I was successful as one who taught — and learned — a lot. Prolifers who insist that single girls and women act like females did "in the old days" (i.e. be chaste) are not accepting them where they are, *today.* And because of this close-minded judgmentalism, they will get nowhere if they try to counsel or teach these young women. *Acceptance* is the first, crucial step.

Does this mean that I approve of the promiscuity which is often common today? Does that mean that I would "push" contraceptives on young girls? Does that mean that I would not teach both boys and girls the value of virginity? Of course not! I'm a pro-lifer who believes in contraception. However, I've taught sex-ed classes to sixth graders through my church, and believe me, I stressed virginity. More important, though, I taught students about the heavy responsibility of raising children. I taught fetal development. I taught about self-confidence and self-respect.

I believe that self-esteem is the best form of birth control. Obviously, easy access to contraceptives hasn't stopped the tide of unwanted pregnancies, abortion, and venereal disease. We're awash in an epidemic of all of these. But at any time a young woman chooses to become sexually active, and for any reason, I believe she should have the freedom to use non-abortifacient birth control (and so should her partner). The simple truth is that no matter how ideal chastity is, not everyone has that value. The truth is that although contraception is against some people's religion, it isn't against everyone's religion!

As a matter of fact, Alternatives to Abortion International has no policy on contraception. Many groups which are members of AAI state simply, "If you want to use birth control, see your doctor." In addition, these groups will recommend that the client talk with a doctor who would prescribe a birth control device but *never* perform an abortion.

Medical people, you see, understand the difference between preventing conception and killing. It's time that all right-to-lifers learned this distinction, too. If they don't, they are likely to tear apart the movement which means the most to them.

Now let's examine contraception from the pro-choice stand. There has been some curious double-think going on in this area. On one hand, pro-choice feminist leaders have warned women of the many physical harms that may result from the use of birth control pills and some IUDs. They have placed big ads in metropolitan newspapers, in *Time*, and *Ms.*, offering to take legal action on women's behalf if they are past users of the Dalkon Shield IUD.

On the other hand, pro-choice feminists misconstrue the Human Life Amendment as a threat to the availability of these very same drugs and devices. Their goal, of course, is to build opposition to a constitutional amendment that would prohibit abortion. So they talk out of both sides of their mouths.

What *is* the truth about contraceptives? The facts are there for all to discover, and it's the *facts* which both pro-life and pro-choice feminists should be concerned with. Similarly, we must all uncover the truth about dangers to women in the abortion procedure. (Dangers to the fetus are obvious!) There is no honor in covering up the truth in the interests of protecting women's so-called freedom to choose. If "the procedure" — and if the Pill and IUD — are dangerous to women, let the truth be known!

In a recent year, a huge U.S. media blitz proclaimed the Pill as "safe." Barbara Seaman, co-founder of the Women's Health Network, and author of *The Doctor's Case Against the Pill*, led a campaign to challenge the study upon which the media blitz was based. Turns out that the "study" was funded, interpreted, and promoted by drug companies (Searle, Mead Johnson, Ortho, Parke Davis and Syntex) which manufacture the Pill! Eventually five companies were cited for violating the Pharmaceutical

Manufacturers Assocation Code of Ethics.

Unfortunately, much damage may have been done in the interim if women believed what they heard. Encouraging results from the study were reported, but alarming findings were omitted! In addition, the method used during the study was nothing less than scientifically shoddy.

In mid-1984, in a landmark decision, the Supreme Court of Ontario awarded Pauline Buchan of Mississauga over $800,000, plus legal costs, against Ortho Pharmaceutical (Canada) Limited. She is one of the women who have personally experienced the sometimes devastating "side-effects" of the Pill. She suffered a stroke when she was only in her early 20's — 34 days after she started taking Ortho Novum 1/50. She suffered permanent brain damage and partial paralysis of her left arm and leg, and she is unable to seek permanent employment outside her home. Her case was the first such action by a consumer against a birth-control pill manufacturer in Canada.

Study after study has shown that the oral contraceptive pill increases some women's chances of strokes and other serious maladies. Yet Dr. Earl Plunkett, a member of the Canadian federal government committee studying the Pill in 1970, told the court that they had been "concerned about alarming the public unnecessarily." He said the committee concluded it was "irrational" to warn of "unproven" dangers that might affect only a few women.

Ortho in the United States spells out in greater detail the dangers of the Pill in its informational pamphlet. We can only hope that women will be given credit for some intelligence and always be given the information they need to give "informed consent" before using the Pill or any other contraceptive drug or device.

Sadly, the same type of cover-up that has gone on concerning contraception continues to go on when it comes to abortion. Young girls and women who go for "counseling" at abortion clinics are seldom, if ever, told the facts about fetal development and about possible physical and emotional dangers to themselves from the procedure. I must admit I'd be a little suspicious of conflict of interest if the one who counselled me also stood to make money from my situation.

In 1979, the *Chicago Sun-Times* printed a gruesome exposé of abortion clinics which proved that "legal" doesn't necessarily mean "safe." Horror stories haven't abated. In fact, recent years have shown an increase in reportings of the abortionist's worst fear — the "aborted" baby born suffering, but *alive.* Women like Nancyjo

Mann, founder of WEBA (Women Exploited by Abortion) shout out about the mental agony they went through during and after their abortions. Numerous studies of the emotional sequelae of abortion have shown that women suffer guilt and remorse after this "safe, harmless" procedure. But many pro-choice feminists choose to shut out the cries of their sisters. They fear that if they admit to the havoc that abortion wreaks upon women, they will endanger their own cause — that wonderful "right to choose."

It's time to end the cover-ups. We've lived through the horrors caused by Thalidomide and DES. Thalidomide, once thought to be a harmless sleeping pill or remedy for morning sickness, caused crippling birth defects beyond anyone's imagination. DES, prescribed by doctors in the 1950's to help women carry their babies to term, resulted in infertility and cancers among the children of the women who took it.

Women need to know the truth. Too much harm has come to them through pharmaceutical tampering with their bodies. Women have the right to easy access to understandable education about birth control — Natural Family Planning being about the best thing going. Pro-choice feminists who say they care about women's right to choose have to be willing to share information about safe, non-abortificient birth control. There's no money to be made in teaching women the truth — and that's why the teaching probably will not come from anyone who has money to be made from drugs, devices, and abortions. Women have to depend upon each other.

Pro-lifers and pro-choicers must bridge the contraceptive impasse and recognize that safe, non-abortifacient contraception is every woman's right. That's reproductive freedom that we could all agree on!

Ken Kesey on the 'Unwanted Child'

Ken Kesey writes: "...my eldest daughter is adopted. She could have been terminated before birth if Faye and I hadn't been hustling to adopt a kid and connected with the pregnant mother. And if we hadn't connected we could have frittered on for years through the agencies, waiting for an available child. Adopting is tough, the lines are long and black market babies go high. Thus, I came to realize: There is no such thing as an "unwanted" child...there are only unwanting parents."

From a December 28, 1983 letter to a Feminists For Life of Wisconsin member.

Post-Abortion Counseling

by Patricia Fernandez

Pregnancy Aftermath Helpline, Inc. is a 24-hour telephone hotline based in Milwaukee, Wisconsin, for persons with problems after an abortion, miscarriage, or adoption. It was begun in November, 1976, by Feminists for Life of Wisconsin who were aware from their own and others' experience, that problems do not necessarily disappear when a difficult pregnancy is ended. In open-ended calls from persons voluntarily contacting the Helpline, counselors give free, non-judgmental support and make referrals to sensitive and appropriate community resources. An anonymous data sheet is kept on every call received.

The accompanying chart is an analysis of abortion sequelae in 58 post-abortion calls from the first two years of Pregnancy Aftermath Helpline's operation. During this timespan the Helpline received 95 post-abortion calls, 25 from persons other than the woman herself and 70 from women who reported having one or more abortions. In the 58 calls analyzed, the women calling made the direct connection between their symptoms and their abortions.

Pregnancy Aftermath Helpline's approach to counseling women after an abortion usually involves some clarification of the individual's value system. After the caller has had an uninterrupted opportunity to tell about her situation and all her attendant feelings and to verbalize what the abortion means to her, she is ready to begin dealing with these feelings. It would seem, from our experience on the Helpline, that women deal with their post-abortion feelings of depression and anxiety in a variety of ways.[1] One method is denial. Two women who published separate newspaper accounts of their abortion experiences reported immediate feelings of relief but both mentioned the necessity of blotting the whole thing out of their minds in order to keep going, perhaps in the same way some people postpone dealing with grief after the death of a loved one. Doubtless many people can continue this way indefinitely, but many others call five, ten, and fifteen years after an abortion to report feelings of depression and anxiety stemming from the abortion. "I was O.K. for a while...."

Another form of denial is avoiding taking any responsiblity for choosing abortion. "I had no choice" is a frequent comment, although holding that statement up to the light usually brings about a reassessment from the woman herself. Many women disavow responsibility even for their pregnancy: "I don't know what happened; we were doing everythig possible to avoid pregnancy." For these women, a significant step in achieving some peace of mind is realizing that dealing with their feelings requires taking charge of their lives and accepting appropriate responsibility for their actions.

The last form of denial accepts the fact of the abortion but denies the involvement of life. "It's just like birth control." The woman who makes this statement can ask herself if such severe anxiety accompanies or follows other methods of birth control. "It's not killing." When this statement is truly based on ignorance of the basic biological facts of conception, the woman is usually not experiencing feelings of depression and anxiety and will not make genuine distress calls.

Generally, however, the women who call do so precisely because of their sense that a specific child of a specific age is not here today because of the action they chose to take. The particular state of pregnancy during which the abortion was performed so far has not been mentioned by callers as having any signifance in this respect.

Once a woman deals with denial, she can then face the source of her anxiety: a basic conflict between her actions and the values she professes. Where there is no conflict, there is no anxiety.

The woman who is knowledgeable about the biological facts of life, and is unable or unwilling to suppress or postpone her feelings, sometimes reacts by changing her values to reduce the conflict between values and actions. "Sure it's life, but we don't have the absolute right to life. I don't. You don't." The implication is that life itself has no inherent worth, so its destruction is not a serious matter. Others will quantify the value of life. "I wanted that baby, but it would have been unfair to bring a child into the world without two parents who wanted him." This approach does not make for much personal security since one's own value then depends on the attitudes of others. The thought behind all of this is, "If that child's existence is worth so little, what does this say for mine?"

However, most women who call the Helpline are unwilling to solve their conflict by reducing their appreciation of life. Since women report feelings of lowered self-esteem after an abortion — "I don't feel very good about myself." "I just hate myself for what I've done." — they are interested in raising their self-image and in feeling more comfortable with themselves.

The "life-itself-has-no-value" approach might leave them with the necessity of proving their worth through goal-oriented activities that never end, driving them on to achieving greater and greater "worth," or competing fiercely with others to achieve more importance, if only relatively so. This unsatisfying drive may itself be a function of tenacious self-hate, although these women may also see fit to let go of this self-hate at some later date. One woman reached the peak of her career only to discover that, "Suddenly it just doesn't seem very important any more. I wish I had my baby." At this point she began to deal constructively with her self-image.

Callers are able to reaffirm their values that life, including their own, is to be cherished and nurtured and consequently feel they have good reason to give up hating themselves for what they have done. They are able to say that their actions did not fit the values they have always held or want to hold now and begin forgiving themselves, viewing themselves at least as compassionately as they would view a friend in similar circumstances.

Most women at this point still seem to need some form of restitution to "make up" for what has been done. This need can be met and self-esteem enhanced at the same time. Women can make a list of things they have to offer the world — and pick out what seems to them to be the expression of their own best talent or ability and develop this to its fullest in order to offer back to the world some life-giving energy to replace that which they took out. This can also serve as a way of giving themselves permission to develop talents and pay attention to their own needs in the future.

PSYCHOLOGICIAL SEQUELAE

Type of Distress	Number of Incidence
Guilt	22
Anxiety	16
Depression	15
Sense of Loss	11
Anger	11
Change in Relationship with Boyfriend	11
Crying	11
Feeling Misled by Misinformation or Lack of Information	10
Deterioration of Self Image	7
Regret or Remorse	7
Nightmares	7
Anxiety about Possible Infertility	7
Aloneness/Alienation	6
Marital Problems	6
Physical Concerns	5
Surprise at Emotional Reaction	4
Disturbance in Sleep Patterns	4
Phantom Child	3
Flashbacks	2
Likely Psychotic Reactions	2
Hopelessness	2
Helplessness	1
Powerlessness	1
Change in Friendship (other than boyfriends)	1

Monte H. Liebman, M.D. and Jolie Siebold Zimmer, "Abortion Sequelae: Fact and Fallacy," *The Psychological Aspects of Abortion*, David Mall and Walter F. Watts, M.D., eds. University Publications, 1979.

For more information on the work of Pregnancy Aftermath Helpline, Inc., contact us at 4742 North Sheffield Avenue, Milwaukee, WI 53211.

[1] Abortion affects persons other than the woman. Family members and others have also called the Helpline expressing problems such as depression, guilt, and anxiety in coping with an abortion.

Taken from the Fall 1981 issue of *Heartbeat*, 2606 1/2 West 8th Street, Los Angeles, CA 90057. Reprinted with permission.

You're Sorry You Had an Abortion — But Where Do You Go?

by Felicity Coulter

For some women pregnancy doesn't end happily. It can end in abortion, miscarriage or eventual placement of the child for adoption. The subsequent physical, emotional and psychological disruption of a woman's life poses many adjustments for her and for those who love and care for her and desire her well-being.

Talking to someone about the experience — someone who is receptive and non-judgmental — is often the first step in making these adjustments. But just who would you talk to if you are having problems following an abortion? Would you feel comfortable returning to your doctor who performed it or the psychiatrist who referred you? If you didn't understand the continuing distress and depression you were feeling months after the miscarriage, how could you begin to express it to someone else? Or the overwhelming need to hear about your child that you had to place for adoption?

Pregnancy Aftermath Helpline of Toronto began its 24 hour counseling service in December 1980, offering help and understanding to women who had experienced these crises. Personal referrals and the example of the first PAH in Milwaukee convinced us that there was a real need for this service in Toronto. Recent books and articles in psychiatric journals were bringing to light deeper aspects of the trauma of crisis pregnancy aftermath, yet there did not appear to be existing services to adequately deal with these problems.

Pro-life organizations, such as Birthright, an emergency pregnancy distress service, were picking up on these kinds of calls and attempted to help women handle these crises. But none of these services provided 24 hour counseling, nor were they set up specifically to assist callers with these difficulties.

What was needed was a helpline, staffed with women who understood the depth of feelings associated with pregnancy aftermath and who could respond in a warm, supportive manner. Thus Pregnancy Aftermath Helpline of Toronto was born.

Knowing that the need is there is one thing. Getting the financial and organizational support necessary to begin a service is another thing. It was at this point that a happy coincidence occurred.

Mary Lassance Parthun, then Volunteer Co-ordinator and Director of Public Relations for Catholic Family Services, Toronto in conjunction with the senior administration of that agency, offered to sponsor the Helpline for one year on a project basis.

Mary Parthun began supervising and training the core group of volunteers that were initially selected. Catholic Family Services provided a computerized telephone answering service allowing the volunteer staff to take calls during the evenings and on weekends at their own home, in addition to assigning a social worker to handle calls during the day. PAH, considered as a separate service under the 'umbrella' of Catholic Family Services has its own mandate, that of providing consultation, support and if needed, referral to selected community resources, to women experiencing a crisis pregnancy aftermath. Both services operate, however from a base which affirms the value of life.

Letters seeking referrals were sent to doctors, psychiatrists and clergy. Brochures advertising the Helpline were circulated to hospitals, clinics, libraries, drug stores — any place we felt we could reach women who needed someone to listen.

Women — and men — did call.

Of the 85 calls received by the Helpline between December 1980 and May 1981, 24 were about abortion. The callers expressed in various ways what Dr. Ian Kent stressed in his report to the Annual Meeting of the Canadian Psychiatric Association, that is, the importance of the woman being able "to bring her feelings of ambivalence about the abortion, her commitment to life and feeling of love for the unborn child to the surface."[1]

This appears particularly difficult for women to do in our present social atmosphere where there seems to be "the intention by all concerned to turn abortion into a non-event and (where) in many instances attempts at follow up are regarded as an impertinence if not betrayal."[2]

Feelings of guilt, anger and depression over a past abortion cannot easily be expressed by a woman to her family, who may have considered it as the best solution, to a boyfriend who paid for it, or to a husband who felt another child was financially impossible, particularly if these relationships have become strained.

But these feelings must find expression and be received in an affirming, accepting and non-judgmental manner if the woman is to come to terms with the situation, gain healing and a resumption of healthy relationships.

Evidence from the 24 abortion-related calls shows that the decision to have an abortion was precipitated more by pressure from family, boyfriend and husband than out of freedom of choice for the mother or a feminist viewpoint — that this is the best thing for me to do, as a woman, at this point in my life.

For instance, a woman whom we will call Mrs. Graham was pregnant and wanted to have the baby. Her husband did not and remained adamant in spite of professional counselling. Finally, the obstetrician advised Mr. Graham, "If she were my wife, I would let her have the baby". That was his only alternative for Mrs. Graham before he proceeded on her husband's demand to recommend an abortion on psychiatric grounds. Other alternatives, for instance refusing to submit to the husband's pressure out of consideration of Mrs. Graham's wishes or suggesting further counselling or professional intervention, were not considered.

Beside the 24 abortion related calls between December 1980 and May 1981, volunteers and staff handled 22 calls related to pregnancy, 7 dealing with a miscarriage, 7 involving depression and 4 about a problem marital stituation. One call was received regarding the placement of a child for adoption.

The remaining 20 calls ranged from information on services to enquiries about accommodation and missing persons.

Of the 85 calls, 43 were taken by the volunteer staff in the evenings and on the weekends. Ten of these were received between 11 p.m. and 8 a.m. On the basis of this information we decided that our original idea of a need for a 24-hour counselling service was confirmed.

Felicity Coulter has been a volunteer with Pregnancy Aftermath Helpline. She works at the University of Toronto.

[1] Kent I. 1977. Emotional Sequelae of Therapeutic Abortion. Paper presented to the 27th Annual Meeting of the Canadian Psychiatric Association in Saskatoon, September 1977.

[2] Myre Sim, M.D., and Robert Neisser, M.D, *"Post-Abortive Psychoses: A Report from Two Centers."* The Psychological Aspects of Abortion, David Mall and Walter F. Watts, M.D. (ed.) University of America, 1979.

Taken from the Aug./Sept. 1981 issue of *The Human* (1973-1984). Reprinted with permission of the author.

HOPE Network — Belief into Action

by Gail Grenier Sweet

Is it true that people who are against abortion only care about the baby until it's born? What happens to the single mother who chooses to give her baby life? Will she become a victim of isolation? Because she is isolated, will she be more likely to take her feelings of frustration out on her child? If the woman again becomes pregnant, will she then opt for abortion, since she believes that there's no one on her side?

Without hope, life is pretty meaningless. *But* without life, there is no hope. HOPE Network is an example of respect for life in ACTION...and proof that pro life feminists DO care about the baby after it's born — and DO care about the lonely single mother, too.

Begun in August of 1982 as a project of the Grenier Foundation, HOPE Network started out as Hope House. For four months, volunteers ran this supportive group residence for four single mothers and five children in Milwaukee, Wisconsin. When the homeowner decided to rent the dwelling instead to an associate, Hope House ended...but HOPE Network blossomed.

A working board of directors has been formed and a part-time coordinator has been hired, Funds are provided by the Grenier Foundation and private donors; no tax money is involved. The present focus of HOPE Network is its sponsor program.

A HOPE Network sponsor is a person who celebrates the joy of children and wishes to share that joy with a single mother and her child(ren). The sponsor is screened and matched geographically with the client. Giving supportive friendship RATHER THAN financial assistance, the sponsor helps the client in the areas of Holistic/Opportunities/Parenting/Education (HOPE). The goals are that the single mom will find friendship; feel a part of her community; and learn to use the wonderful free and inexpensive resources in her neighborhood.

New sponsors are trained at workshops where they meet other experienced sponsors, They continue to learn from each other through telephone calls and occasional sponsor support group meetings, In this truly grassroots effort, ideas are constantly exchanged: what works? what doesn't?

Sponsors seek ways to empower the single mother to improve things rather than just enable her to go on living as before. They seek to bolster her self-esteem and encourage her to take control over her own life. With more self-respect, confidence, and education, chances of a repeat pregnancy are probably lessened. But should a pregnancy again occur, the single mother knows she is loved and accepted. Abortion will not be sought out of desperate loneliness.

The single mother often needs to increase her self-esteem, true. But we've also found that she needs help in the areas of (1) money management; (2) parenting education; (3) having fun with and without baby; and (4) feeling part of her community. HOPE Network's sponsor program attempts to meet those needs.

Other smaller projects are a Single Parent Resource Directory which is available to all sponsors and clients. It lists many places and people that can help the single mom. It's an example of HOPE Network's efforts to encourage cooperation and communication among all the helping agencies in town. The Network also continues to promote the gathering and distribution of used baby clothing and household necessities.

We have to create visible, concrete community support systems NOW for women in crisis pregnancies.

Taken from the January 1984 RIGHT TO LIFE NEWS. Used with permission.

A Plea for Changes in the Workplace

by Nancy Randolph Pearcey

The press is doing its best to cast abortion as a New Right issue. A recent example is the attempted exposé of the financial connection between the Right-to-Life movement and the New Right in Connie Paige's *The Right-To-Lifers.*[1] Yet the defense of the unborn is properly seen as a civil rights issue, and growing numbers of liberals, with their traditional concern for civil rights, are coming to a pro-life position. One such group are the pro-life feminists.

"Pro-life *what* —?" is most people's first response. The group known as Feminists for life of America was organized by women compelled to leave the National Organization for Women (NOW) for their outspoken opposition to abortion. Although they promote women's rights, they do not believe those rights include the decision of life or death over the unborn. They acknowledge the difficulties of unexpected pregnancy, but they propose alternative solutions.

Industrialization and Women

Abortion has assumed a central position in the agenda of the mainstream women's movement largely because of the high price women pay to bear children. Although the intrinsic rewards of rearing children are great, women also pay a price in terms of loss of education, economic, social, and cultural opportunities. To understand why this occurs, we must examine the very structure of industrialized society. By removing work from the home, the industrial revolution created a gap between the private sphere of the home and the public sphere of business, politics, finance, and academia. As a result, women who stay home to care for young children are isolated from the major functions of society.

This becomes clearer if we compare ourselves with preindustrial societies, including Western culture into the 18th century. When work was performed in or near the home, the result was an integration of life and labor which allowed all women to be involved in economically productive work. A woman was able to participate in a business or craft alongside her husband as she managed her household. She was not excluded from contact with the outside world, for the world came into her home in the form of customers, business contacts, clients, patients, students and apprentices.[2] Such interplay of a family with society allowed a man to enjoy greater balance as well, his role as husband and father integrating with his role as work partner and job foreman.[3] Child care was not restricted to mothers, but was shared by fathers and members of the extended family, permitting "everyone to do some of everything."

Most of the functions once performed in the home — from education to food preservation, from home industries to health care — have been turned over to big industry to be directed by (male) experts. In the words of Dorothy Sayers,

> ....men took over the women's jobs by transferring them from the home to the factory. The mediaeval woman had effective power and a measure of real (though not political) equality, for she had control of many industries — spinning, weaving, baking, brewing, distilling, perfumery, preserving, pickling — in which she worked with head as well as hands, in command of her own domestic staff...but modern civilisation has taken all these pleasant and profitable activities out of the home, where the women looked after them, and handed them over to big industry, to be directed and organized by men at the head of large

factories. Even the dairy-maid in her simple bonnet has gone, to be replaced by a male mechanic in charge of a mechanical milking plant.[4]

As the home was stripped of many of its functions, women at home were squeezed out of most of their traditional occupations. They no longer needed to know a variety of skills related to areas such as food processing and textile manufacture; the only major tasks left to them were childcare and housework.

At the same time that they were suffering a tremendous narrowing of the scope of their activities, women were left with sole responsibility for the household. As industries left the home, husbands and the childless were forced to follow. Women then had to actually *perform* many tasks they had once *directed* in a managerial position over an extended family and servants, who were no longer there. In short, women were caught from two sides: as the home was impoverished, housework acquired the monotony it is known for today; yet, with no one to share household tasks and childcare, women were not free to leave home to regain their former occupations.[5]

When the home ceased to be the center of production, women found themselves removed from the mainstream of society. Work and home became polarized by gender: work was no longer the family industry but the "father's job"; home was reduced from being the center of society to being "woman's place."

Against the backdrop of this historical sketch, it becomes evident that feminism is not a protest against conditions intrinsic to motherhood or the family *per se*, as some opponents believe. If we assume that the role of women remained stable over long periods of time, it is difficult "to explain why, in the early 19th century, it suddenly became onerous."[6] The women's movement is rather a response to a great reduction in the opportunities open to women, and grows out of a genuine need among women for a more balanced involvement in both family and society.

Bridging the Gap

The gap between the private sphere of home and the public sphere of business and culture is difficult to bridge. Workplaces, educational institutions, and many cultural activities are not set up to allow women (or men) to participate and still have their children close by; neither are most work or educational programs designed to be performed at home. Thus neither mothers nor fathers are able to integrate their work with their parenting responsibilities, as they did in pre-industrial societies.

Ideals such as both parents of young children working part-time to share financial and childcare responsibilities remain no more than ideals for most people because part-time positions are scarce, the salaries shamefully low, and benefits non-existent. Companies have also been reluctant to experiment with job-sharing, flex-time, and other variations on the forty-hour week which might help parents juggle commitments. As a result, most fathers are forced to work full-time, becoming virtually weekend parents, and mothers must either follow suit or choose full-time parenting.

Whichever choice she makes, a mother pays a price. If her husband earns enough so that she can stay home, she must give up her career or educational goals; her prior education or job experience may seem wasted; age-segregation in many cultural activities precludes her taking her children along to conferences, concerts, volunteer activities, etc., forcing her to give those up, too, unless she can afford a sitter; and, of course, there is frequently financial strain from the loss of her income. Even the woman deeply committed to being home to raise her children may find, when thus isolated from the mainstream of society, that she falls prey to the nameless depression which Betty Friedan documented so well in *The Feminine Mystique*.

Many women today are literally frightened by the prospect of losing the salary, status and fulfillment they derive from their jobs, and hurry back to work after brief maternity leaves. And, of course, many women also join the work force because they need to contribute to the family sustenance. Yet in the work force, most women face largely low-pay, low-status jobs, childcare expenses, and the anguish of leaving children in the care of others, and the double burden of job and housework.

In pre-industrial societies, women did not have to choose between work and childrearing. They were able to "have it all," as the slogan goes. In light of the difficult choices a woman faces today when she becomes a mother, it is understandable why "control over reproduction" has become a central issue to the women's movement. As a society, we have begun to accept abortion as a solution for the woman with conflicts between childcare and school, job or whatever. These conflicts, however, are rooted in the historic and economic developments which have created the gap isolating mothers from society. Abortion ignores the cause and treats the symptom: instead of suggesting a way out of the isolation mothers face, it offers a way out of motherhood.

Accepting abortion is a short-term solution which only delays the implementation of real reforms. What women need is not the quick expedient of abortion; they need community support to allow them to experience pregnancy, birth, and parenthood with dignity. They need fathers more involved in childrearing, decent maternity and paternity leaves, the active assistance of supportive institutions such as churches, freedom from the isolation of nuclear family living, institutions flexible to the needs of families, part-time work with decent salaries, work adapted to performance at home, respect and support for mothers coming back into the work force, and good part-time education and job training.[7]

Those of us who work to stop abortion can only provide genuine solutions if we address the *cause* of distress pregnancies, finding ways to reintegrate work and home. This is not to deny that some women have abortions for other reasons; nor is it to suggest that parenthood should not involve sacrifice — it always will, just as it will always offer great satisfaction in return. But we must make ourselves aware of the pressures women face which are unique to our age. Pro-life feminists have rallied to presenting the ethical arguments against abortion, and to supporting women in crisis pregnancies.

We must now go a step further and address ourselves to changing those structures of modern society which make childrearing costly and thus make abortion seem an attractive alternative.

[1]See the review of *The Right-to-Lifers* by Juli Loesch in *Sisterlife*, Newsletter of Feminists for Life of America, December, 1983, pp. 3-4.

[2]Alice S. Rossi, "Equality Between the Sexes: An Immodest Proposal," *Readings on the Changing Family* (New Jersey: Prentice-Hall, 1973) p. 145.

[3]Ross P. Scherer, "The American Family in the Midst of Socio-Economic Technological Change," *Family Relationships and the Church*, Oscar E. Feucht, editor (St. Louis: Concordia 1970), p. 140.

[4]Dorothy L. Sayers, "Are Women Human?" *A Matter of Eternity* Grand Rapids MI: William B. Eerdmans Publishing Co., 1973) pp. 42-43 and 24.

[5]This development as it occurred in North America is very thoroughly traced in Nancy F. Cott, *The Bonds of Womanhood* (New Haven: Yale University Press, 1977)

[6]William L. O'Neill, *The Woman Movement* (Chicago: Quadrangle Books, 1969), p. 17.

[7]Some reference books for women choosing to work from their home are:

Marjorie McVicar and Julia F. Craig, *Minding My Own Business* (NY: Richard Marek Publishers, 1981).

Arlene Rose Cardozo, *Woman At Home* (Garden City, NJ: Doubleday, 1976)

Jeremy Joan Hewes, *Worksteads, Living and Working in the Same Place* (Garden City, NJ: Doubleday, 1981).

Marian Behr and Wendy Lazar, *Women Working Home* (Norward, NJ: WWH Press, 1981).

Population Controllers
Getting Needed Control

by Judy Shea

The population control lobby was dealt a severe blow by the Reagan administration at the International Conference on Population in Mexico City in August 1984.

At this point only the planned parenthood zealots and right-to-life activists fully appreciate the implications of the new pro-life policy advocated by the White House.

Since the sixties when a small group of ZPG/NPG fanatics were finally able to convince the U.S. government to fund their numerous and ubiquitous programs, the population control enthusiasts have pretty much had their own way. They had done a superb job of persuading the public that the most serious problem in the world today is overpopulation and that the U.S. ought to actively encourage all the Third World nations to drastically reduce their birthrates by any means short of infanticide (but including abortion on demand). This is not to say that they were exactly thrilled with the fertility of American women. They believed the U.S. would also benefit from reducing its population by lowering its birthrate and severely restricting immigration. (Besides, it wouldn't have looked good to have the USA ranting about the unwashed fertile masses of the developing countries unless we, too, promised to change our reproductive habits — charges of racism might surface.)

The fact that there was very little, if any, scientific evidence to back up their claim that a Malthusian nightmare was just around the corner certainly didn't bother them. After all, it seemed just as plain as day and perfectly logical to the gullible that the more humans you have on this planet, the more problems you have, and you just might be able to get a handle on this mess by preventing the birth of a few million babies, or — think big — a few billion.

Naturally, there were a lot of high-minded, quasi-scientific books written on the subject, like Paul Ehrlich's *The Population Bomb*. My goodness, you couldn't turn on the Tonight Show without seeing Paul discussing his vasectomy (for the cause) with Johnny. By then the population people had hooked up with the environmental movement and what they all had to say was becoming "conventional wisdom." Everybody just *knew* in their bones there were too many people on this earth.

And didn't it make people positively shiver to hear Paul talk about how bad things were in India? He had actually "felt" the population explosion and who could argue with that?

> "I came to understand the population explosion emotionally one stinking hot night in Delhi...The streets seemed alive with people. People eating, people washing, people sleeping, people visiting, arguing, and screaming. People thrusting their hands through the taxi window begging. People defecating and urinating. People clinging to buses. People herding animals. People, people, people.
> (from *The Population Bomb*)

Landsakes, it was practically impossible for Ehrlich and regular Americans with their standard of living to understand why these people would even want to exist. They certainly weren't anything like us.

So it came to pass that the U.S. government became more than willing to bankroll the many ingenious schemes of the population control network — no questions asked.

Since this was a *bona fide* crisis the family planning agencies figured they had to get tough. It wasn't easy working with the poor. The poor didn't seem to understand about optimum population levels and per capita income, and they were really stubborn about wanting to have babies. The planned parenthood bureaucrats kept dishing out their standard pap in press releases about how they were merely trying to give them more options — but they knew better — they were trying to convince them not to *want* so many children. They knew they'd have to resort to coercion to get results. They were just being realistic. And anyway the poor couldn't *really* want all those children. Furthermore, the family planners had such a nice way with words. How had one of them explained what they were up to?

> "You cannot, indeed must not, tread heavy-booted into people's bedrooms, however poor they might be. But you

can help structure people's choices so that they make prudent decisions concerning family size."

(Pranay Gupte, *Minneapolis Star and Tribune,*
August 7, 1984)

Stuff right out of *1984.*

Everything was moving along as well as could be expected "in the field," except that some people were starting to question their tactics. Right-to-lifers began the protests and even some feminists spoke up. Germaine Greer did a complete about-face on the population question and wrote a book condemning the whole population control movement. She was right on target when she pointed out that people throughout history have actually figured out ways not to have babies without the help of Planned Parenthood (even—gasp!!—resorting to such quaint methods as abstinence).

But Germaine's book didn't bother the Movement too much. They could just dismiss her as another crackpot feminist.

However, a statement prepared at the White House Office of Policy Development for the Population Conference in Mexico this year, that was another matter. The Reagan administration had announced it would no longer fund family planning programs abroad if they provide or actively promote abortion as a birth control method. The policy: "Attempts to use abortion, involuntary sterilization or other coercive measures in family planning must be shunned, whether exercised against families within a society, or against nations..."

Policies like that could really screw things up for those folks in the business of "structuring people's choices." Let's hope so.

Reprinted with permission from the newsletter of Minnesota Feminists for Life, Inc. 2815 West 38th St., Minneapolis, MN, 55410.

Counseling the Sexual Assault Victim

by Pam Cira

No one would have ever known about what her friend's brother had done that night. He said not to tell so she didn't. After all, he is big. He was 18. And she was only 4. But one day her mom noticed a foul-smelling discharge in her daughter's underpants. A trip to the hospital and a culture test confirmed the doctor's suspicions — Cindy had gonorrhea. Mom was dumbfounded. Dad was ready to kill. Little Cindy was scared and confused. They came into my office with their shock, their anger, their fears, their confusion. My job — to help them sort through the crisis their lives were thrown in. To help make some sense out of this horror-filled mess.

The crisis of sexual assault profoundly affects victims and their families. The shock, the disbelief that this could happen, that it has happened is shattered by reality. Cindy's fears were intense and needed to be understood. She didn't do anything wrong. She "told" and she was safe. He wouldn't hurt her anymore. Mom wasn't hurt by her. Dad wasn't mad at her. But dad's anger had to be dealt with. He was so caught up in "getting the guy," he seemed to have forgotten his daughter. I urged him to direct his energy toward Cindy.

"She's the one you care for, the one you love. Her assailant doesn't deserve all your attention. Cindy does, and she needs it." I told him.

Fears of the court system had to be dealt with. Information on court procedures had to be accurate, clear and extensive. I had to provide information on the emotional cycles of depression and the nightmares as well.

"Cindy might have trouble sleeping or eating during the next few weeks or months. These problems might come and go and return again," I told her parents. They needed to see how their reactions affected their daughter. How they could foster her confusion and guilt. She needed their reassurances that she was wonderful, that they loved her, and that her whole life lay ahead of her — a happy, healthy life.

*   *   *

Some friends had just left Mary's house moments before. She thought the knock on the door was Kim returning for her forgotten cigarettes. Mary opened the door, but it wasn't Kim. A stranger pushed his way into Mary's house. He stayed long enough to rape her. And long enough to leave behind a woman feeling shattered.

During the next few weeks, I met with Mary several times. She was working through her feelings, handling her fears well, and had done a terrific job of testifying at the preliminary hearing, when — boom. Mary discovered that she was pregnant. The only possible "father" was her rapist. She was told to get an abortion — by both her mother and the hospital social worker. I asked her what she thought and she expressed some concerns about abortion. She had had one several years before, at her mother's insistence, and had regretted it since. She also knew her fiancé would not want her to abort. But the social worker at the hospital had already made the appointment for her. I suggested she talk to her fiancé. After all, it was an important decision and she was going to spend the rest of her life not only with her decision but with her fiancé as well.

I didn't hear from Mary for nearly 2 months. No one answered whenever I called. Then one day she called me. She had just gotten back in town. She was ready for the trial. And she had a new name. Mary had decided to tell her fiancé about the pregnancy. They moved their wedding up a year and had gotten married. She did not have the abortion and was much relieved that she had withstood the pressures of her mom and the other social worker. She had, however, miscarried, 2 weeks before the wedding. She was adjusting to that loss.

Mary was doing well — she had regained control of her life. She had discovered a courage in herself that she never knew existed. When the hospital social worker chastised her for not aborting, saying "So you're going to let this boyfriend run your life!", Mary responded, "No, I'm just not going to let *you* run my life." For Mary, the nightmare of the rape also held an opportunity for self-discovery, She still had fears but she now had the confidence to live with them.

*   *   *

Joe thought they were his friends. He and these two women had socialized on numerous occasions. One night, though, after he was invited to dinner, they attacked him. Some men laugh at the thought of a man being sexually assaulted by a woman. Or by two women. "Hey, who would complain?"

Joe complained. He had been beaten so severely with pans and sticks that he was hospitalized for several days. A broomstick and some bottles had been shoved up into his rectum. Yes, Joe complained.

He had a hard time dealing with his vulnerability. He was a man in his 30's. How could this happen? His ego, like most male egos, had been developed without a thought to sexual vulnerability. We talked about that. We talked about his fears and guilt feelings. He was surprised to discover that his reactions were very similar to those of female victims. We worked through his depression cycles. Joe testified successfully at both the preliminary hearing and the trial with new insights and a strong sense of self-respect.

*   *   *

During the five years of working at the district attorney's office with sexual assault victims and their families, I dealt with over 1,000 clients. To say the above situations were typical would be a lie, There is no such thing as "typical sexual assault." Each case is different. But the feelings of fear, guilt and anger are fairly universal. Cycles of depression and nightmares are common.

When I first started my job, I expected to see people shattered — like shells of human beings quaking inside of bodies. What I found were courageous women and men. People in crisis who could find in themselves the strength to go on — and to go on with new insights into themselves, new compassion for others, and new confidence in their abilities to cope. I though I would nurture them. I found that their nurturing of me made that job more rewarding, more enriching than anything I could have imagined. I am forever grateful for the glimpse I've had into their lives and spirits, and for the opportunity to have been there when they needed me.

Incest: A Time to Heal

by Linda Macki Williams

"Never for the sake of peace and quiet, deny your own experience and convictions."
Dag Hammerskjold

Incest is a subject that has been talked about for the last couple of years. The emphasis has always been on prevention and as someone who has done community education in the area, I'm all for that. But as someone who also experienced it, I say, another time has come. It's time to reach out to others like myself and say it's a time to heal.

My friend looked at me sadly as we talked about our past incest experiences. "What bothers me the most, she said, is that I don't know who or what I could have been if it hadn't happened."

I knew what she was saying. She was saying that something was missing from our childhoods — something called innocence. As incest victims we were robbed of our innocence.

The loss of innocence is a very real one. When people ask what it was like to be an incest victim, I tell them it was like having my leg cut off of my body when I was four years old. The skin grew over the stump. No new leg grew back and so I learned to accommodate.

As someone who experienced incest, I learned to view the world and my place in it from a different perspective. There were many more times than I can count when I wasn't sure I even *had* a place in it. There were many years that were painful and life seemed overwhelming. I was trying to walk with one leg, with no one showing me how, and trying to fake it as if I was walking on two legs. That's what incest was like.

I can remember one day in the second grade: I had just overheard how babies were made — what a man and woman did to conceive one. But I had not learned the other facts about menstruation and sperm.

That day I sat quietly on a swing at the school playground listening to two other children banter back and forth on who Santa Claus really was, while I wondered about something else. I was afraid I was going to have a baby and I didn't know quite how I was ever going to explain it to anyone. No one would understand what was going on in my life.

People often ask why I didn't tell or why I didn't stop the incest. I can only answer that by saying that I was a little girl who was afraid of getting hurt more.

I thought like a little girl. I didn't have any answers about life and I certainly wasn't into creative problem solving at ages 4, 5, 6, and 7. Like a little child who has just lost a leg I was in pain and all I could concentrate on at the time was the pain. I couldn't see anything beyond the hurt I was feeling. Stifled by the hurt I felt, I could not stop the incest.

Finally when I was ten years old, I entered a Catholic school where rights and wrongs were sorted out. It was then that I began to realize the full implication of what had been going on all those years. I was exactly ten the last time my uncle approached me for sex.

I remember I wanted to go to Communion the next day and I asked him to leave me alone. This sex stuff was a sin. He still came at me and I ran into a closet, crying just to get away from him. He never came after me again. He must have thought I had gone bananas.

There I was in that closet crying, understanding the social taboo, feeling guilty and overwhelmed with the sense that I was never going to be like the other girls my age.

Incest victims often don't tell anyone of the incest. There is the fear that no one will ever understand. I believed that I was the only little girl in the whole world to have gone through such an experience.

I grew up with a stump and stumbled through life, never sure of my own femininity, always feeling different from other women and terrified of my sexuality.

It wasn't until I had a little girl of my own that I discovered recovering from incest is not something that just happens to you. Incest recovery is something to work towards. Just like the child who has lost a leg must be rehabilitated, incest victims need time to recover and to accommodate for the gap in childhood innocence. They need to learn to trust, to know they have a place in the world and that they are just as important as anyone else.

When I was a child, I always waited and prayed and prayed and prayed that some older person would rescue me from my fate. But no one ever came. Then when I grew up I realized that the villain, the perpetrator was still on the loose. The rescuer had not come. If there was ever to be a rescuer it would have to be me and that was scary.

I had always wondered if men who assaulted children sexually lost their steam as they got older. I wanted to believe that they did so I wouldn't have to tell my special secret.   But in my heart I wasn't sure.

When another female child was born into our family I finally had to say something. Breaking the silence about the incest was the beginning of my own recovery. For years I had accommodated, pretending to have the innocence I never had. Now the time was to explain my knowledge.

I wasn't out for revenge. I just wanted to make sure another little girl would not meet my fate. It was an extremely painful time and in my family, in other cases, the family did not want to acknowledge the situation. Doing that would mean they would have to change some of their relationships. It was just too hard for them. But at last the secret was out. And slowly, in private there were those who came to me and said my story was believed.

The secret was out, and the years of terror that someone would find out were gone. I talk to my own children rather freely about the incest and have told them they can come to me any time if anyone ever approaches them. I don't worry about them now that the secret is out and that's a good feeling.

Breaking the silence was only the first step however. There were others to follow. For years I felt guilt and shame. One day I followed a dear friend's advice. She said, look at a little girl. Anyone who would sexually assault a little girl is sick. And one day as I watched a child playing it finally sank in. I had always felt myself to be of less value than anyone else because of the incest. Suddenly I was on some sort of a different mind set. First I could think about my uncle and say "You poor sick miserable bastard" and I realized that I could forgive him.

And then I could forgive myself. I could forgive myself, not for being a part of the incest (because incest was something that happened to me not something I did), but I forgave myself for being so hard on me.

Forgiveness is a really freeing experience. Prayer was important for me in my recovery. However, it wasn't the kind of prayer filled with "Dear Sweet Jesus, here I am, your humble servant."

It was a real tongue lashing filled with "Where were you when I needed you and how could you have let this happen?" Prayer let me express my anger and anger is that emotion which allows us to affirm our values. My anger said that incest was damn wrong.

Yet through all my angry prayers an answer came often through the mother of a friend or through a peer or even a teacher. At the most difficult and confusing times, someone appeared to guide me through the worst of it.

I, like my friend have wondered at times who I would have been had not the incest taken place. Could I have gone on to achieve greater things if I didn't have to put so much energy into overcoming the pain I felt most of my life? At some point I reached a level where it didn't matter. Maybe it was the time when I talked to another victim who broke down in tears because someone finally understood her pain. Maybe it was the time I convinced someone else that suicide wasn't worth it. Or maybe it was when I was talking to a group of mothers and I realized that some good was coming from my own personal story.

"Never for the sake of peace and quiet deny your own experience or convictions." Incest was part of my life's experience, not a happy part, but a part.

My conviction is that it is wrong. Yet out of it I believe I have become a more caring person, more sensitive to the needs of others and more forgiving.

The Bible says that there is an appointed time for everything, and a time for every purpose under the heavens. A time to be born and a time to die... and well, you know... a time to heal. Recovering from incest is a difficult process...a process different for everyone. Through my process I found peace and in my peace I wish to offer others hope.

The Center

by Donna Eddy

Look within yourself
    See
Deep within yourself
    Feel
To the very center
    Touch
The core
    Listen
Listen to the voices inside
They know
Listen to your soul

What is it that you need?
What can you give?

Deep within
    a longing
    longings
Needs, desires, prayers

There is but
    One Longing
        and many longings
    One Need
        and many needs
    One Desire
        and many desires
    One Prayer
        and many prayers

Listen to
Touch
Feel
See
Be

It is not selfish
    to be whole

Ocean of Life

by Gail Grenier Sweet

The flatlands are an ocean:
Waves of lost days in mute earth.

Hills rise up,
    encircle,
    protect
    the land.

In shallow stoney soil
    a cactus clings to life:
Roots spread far,
    catching water from
    light rains and
    quick floods.
Stems hoard water,
    make food...
Large fragrant blossoms
    open at night
    hidden from sight
    blooming only for the joy
    of the One who creates.

A woman, nearby,
    watches over her small ones.
Like the hills she protects them.
Like the cactus she shores up her strength...
    Few know her true beauty.
The children run and laugh
    in the circle of her gaze,
    unaware of her love's depth.

Some day
    when the quick flood comes,
    they will understand.

The woman's day
    will not be lost
    in mute earth.

Teach Me To Die

by Deanna K. Edwards

Sunlight filters through my window
 Falling from the sky
 Time slips like a silent stranger
Softly passing by
Life goes on in busy circles
Leaving me behind
Memories like portraits
Fill the attic of my mind

CHORUS:
Teach me to die
Hold on to my hand
I have so many questions
Things I don't understand
Teach me to die
Give all you can give
If you'll teach me of dying
I will teach you how to live

I know that it isn't easy,
Seeing me this way
And it hurts to watch me
Lying here day after day
Trade your fear of parting
For the Faith that knows no pain
Don't be afraid to say "Goodbye"
I know we'll meet again!

CHORUS:

Used by permission of Rock Canyon Publishers — 11514 Ventura Blvd., Suite A, Studio City, CA 91604 — from
the album *Peacebird* by Deanna Edwards.

Epilogue

For Everything There is a Season, For Every Soul There is a Reason

by Gail Grenier Sweet

It was a glorious August day and I felt glad to be alive. I basked in back yard fresh air and sunshine with my kids. Then the phone call came that tore my life apart.

My brother David spoke on the other end of the line:

"Gail," he stammered, "come — home — NOW." He sounded like he was strangling. I felt confused.

"What's wrong, David? Are you all right?"

Again the choking voice: "Come — home — NOW."

"Okay, I'll be right there," I assured him. I hung up the phone and my stomach churned in sickened fear. What could be wrong with David? It was such an odd request: to come "home." David was 18 and lived at home with my parents, but I hadn't lived with them for six years. *This* was my home, ten miles away.

I raced next door to ask my neighbor for help.

"Maureen, can you watch Charlie and Brian for a while?"

"Sure...what's the matter?" She must have read my face.

"I don't know. My brother David just called me and asked me to come home right away. He wouldn't tell me the problem... I'm afraid he had a drug O.D. or something. I had never heard him sound that way, like he was crying and couldn't breathe."

"Is he home alone?" Maureen asked.

"Uh-huh. He stayed home while my folks went on a fishing trip with our little brother George."

Maureen's face fell, and whatever she was thinking, she didn't say.

I felt as if there was no blood left in my face. I kissed my little boys goodbye and ran to the car. As I put the key in the ignition, I reminded myself to calm down. Usually I'm almost mechanically calm and rational in crisis. But this was different, because I didn't *know* what was wrong.

The ten miles to my parents' house was the longest I ever drove. My mind tortured me with outrageous and horrible imaginings. Drug O.D....house burned down...I tried to comfort myself with the thought that the unknown is always more frightening than the known.

As I tried to keep my speed under 60 MPH, I pictured David's girlfriend Laura dying in a plane crash. She was in Hawaii visiting her brother. We all loved Laura like a sister. *But no*, I thought, *the truth can't possibly be as bad as my fears.*

I was wrong.

At last I drove into Mum and Pop's familar driveway. Everything looked normal. The house hadn't burned down. No beer bottles were strewn on the lawn. The trees weren't strung with toilet paper. The day was quiet and sunny and birds were chirping. Mum's flowers bloomed in cheerful profusion.

I ran into the house. No one was on the main floor. I flew down the steps into the family room, where I found David and my sister Sally. They were at opposite ends of the room, as if something invisible and enormous were wedged in between them. They were both red-eyed and teary-faced, looking at me with such pain that I didn't know what to say.

Finally I blurted, "David, is — Laura — dead?"

Sally burst into loud sobs. David looked as if he were in agony. He gazed straight into my eyes and said the words my heart has played over a thousand times since:

"No," he said, "Mum and Pop and George."

*   *   *

Three days later we had the vigil for my parents and my brother George. It was a muggy night, and hundreds of people filed through the funeral home. I remember Mum and Pop saying that young people always have big funerals.

I spent three hours comforting people, some of whom I hardly knew. Again and again two red eyes and a handkerchief approached me. Again and again two damp arms encircled me in a trembling hug.

Over and over the same words spun around me through my numb fog:

"Why did it have to be them?"

"It's such a tragedy."

"They were so young and full of life."

"I still can't believe it. Such a terrible accident."

"I don't know what to say."

"And Georgie was so young. Why was he born?"

I felt the people's love for my parents and brother, but not yet their anger. My father had taught me to accept death; he was fond of saying "when your number's up, it's up." That philosophy helped me now, although anger would set in later when I could *feel* things again. In a week I would want to kick in the walls to release my rage, but during the vigil that Friday night I was still under emotional anesthesia.

I looked at the three caskets resting in the funeral home, quiet and unmoving on the floor. Closed caskets, made of the finest woods, smooth, warm and gleaming. I felt a comfort from that perfect wood ...nature's beautiful design, magnificent grain. A silent statement. When all the visitors had left, I laid my face on each casket in turn. I wrapped my arms around each one and hugged it long and hard. The wood felt warm against my face. I let the tears flow.

* * *

August 1985 marks seven years since Mum and Pop and George left our world. Sometimes I wonder if the pain and tears will ever end. I ache still as I type this and I don't want to think about them because the memories bring more pain.

But there is something I must write out. Something for all those angry people, all those hurting people who wondered why George was born.

I cannot tell them why George died at age 13, or why my mother died at 48 and my father at 51. I don't presume to know the plan of life. But I can tell them that George's life wasn't wasted. I can tell them one of the reasons I believe George was born. You see, George saved my mother's life...just by being there in her womb.

Let me explain. My mother was a strong health woman who believed in *never* going to the doctor. She simply refused to get sick. But when she recognized signs of pregnancy for the fifth time, she made the familiar trip to her doctor, Nate.

If Mum hadn't been pregnant with George, she never would have gone to see Nate for a pelvic exam and Pap test. She probably would not have discovered she had cancer...until too late. And chances are high that she would have died long before seeing her children grow up.

But George *was* there, and Mum *did* go to the doctor, and Nate *did* find the cancer. Perhaps it was a miracle that George could be carried and born safely. Perhaps it was a miracle that Nate could remove the cancerous growth from Mum's body a short time after George's birth. She was 35 then, and the cancer never returned... another miracle, perhaps.

George was an inventor and musician and troublemaker and jokester. He liked to hide a rubber worm in the cottage cheese cartons that Mum opened faithfully for lunch every day. He brought lots of laughter into our lives. And he brought pain, too, for Mum and Pop had a mild case of "parent burnout" and had run out of patience for certain typical youthful stunts.

My brothers and sister and I liked to tell George the story of how he saved our mother's life. We told him how we might have lost her when we were very young, if it hadn't been for him. George never used to say much when we told him, but his eyes would twinkle and his chest would swell a little. I'm thankful that we never kept our gratitude from George.

So now all the angry people know...I'm sure the Creator had a plan in George's conception. We were given a beautiful brother we enjoyed for 13 years. And George gave us our mother in the years we really needed her.

It's true that my sons will never know their funny uncle with the rubber worms in the cottage cheese cartons. And they'll never be able to soak up the wisdom of their grandparents, except from what I can tell them. They'll have to wait till another life, as I will, to see Mum and Pop and George again. Sometimes when I sit in the summer sun with my children, I think about these things. And I hope I can teach them to accept life's plan...that for everything there is a season, and for every soul there is a reason.

Taken from the April 1984 issue of MARRIAGE AND FAMILY LIVING, Abbey Press, St. Meinrad, IN. Reprinted with permission.

Feminists For Life
Statement of Purpose

Our organization takes two stands: (1) Full equality for women in all areas; (2) The right of every baby to be born. We demand an end to all legal, social, and economic discrimination against women, including mass media stereotypes. We recognize all people as individuals with equal rights, including the unborn. We believe it is inconsistent to demand rights for ourselves and to deny them to the unborn. Without the right to life all other rights are meaningless. Futhermore, since roughly 50 percent of the unborn are female, half the abortions kill our sisters.

We hope to see an end to pro-abortion stands in other feminist organizations. By diverting time and energy into abortion legalisation, these groups have de-emphasized the struggle for legal and social equality. In addition, they have deterred many potential feminists from joining the movement.

We are an independent organization. We accept men on an equal basis with women. Our goals now follow:

(1) To encourage prolife feminists to join the feminist movement. We provide a forum for women who feel that joining a pro-abortion feminist organization would compromise their principles.

(2) To empower the female to identify with and take pride in herself as female, to secure equality of rights under the law, and to understand and retain our historical and cultural heritage.

(3) To encourage women to become educated in pregnancy, childbirth , and other aspects of female sexuality.

(4) To help others become knowledgeable on both sides of the abortion debate.

(5) To encourage efforts to alleviate the problems in society which cause women to seek abortions.

(6) To develop strategies for teaching the female how to develop affirming techniques in the world without sacrificing warmth and nurturance in the home. To develop strategies for teaching males how to be nurturant toward children without sacrificing their self-image or their ability to function in the world.

(7) To take an active part in eliminating sexual stereotyping.

Feminists for Life of America 811 East 47th St. Kansas City, Mo. 64110

The following is an open letter from Pregnancy Aftermath Helpline to women who have suffered following abortion: Immediately afterward is a letter to women who have released a child for adoption.

Dear Sister Who Has Had an Abortion,

We realize that the decision to have an abortion is often painfully difficult, filled with pressure from circumstances from those close to you, and from plans gone awry. We sympathize with you.

We also realize that an abortion may not always solve a woman's underlying problems such as dealing with a non-supportive sexual partner, continuing an education or career, coping with financial binds, or being manoeuvered by parents, boyfriends or friends.

Although women are rarely forewarned, emotional disturbances sometimes occur after an abortion. These reactions can cloud a woman's feelings and her ability to move into a fulfilling life after her abortion.

We've learned a lot talking to women who have called our hotline. Pregnancy Aftermath Helpline is a free, 24-hour telephone hotline for persons who need help after abortions, miscarriages, or adoptions. As volunteers we've learned that emotional distress after an abortion can be serious, that abortions can do violence to a woman's view of herself, her relationships, and her future.

If you are having trouble working through the aftermath of abortion, here are some suggestions you might want to consider:

(1) Talk with someone you trust about your feelings. Bringing your reactions and emotions to the verbal level is the first step in handling them in a rational way.

(2) Review your attitudes and re-establish the facts about fertilization, conception, and pregnancy.

(3) Make restitution. Women who have bad feelings about their decision to abort feel it helps them to replace the energy they took from the world. Plan and do something that puts your own life force to work in the work in a positive way.

(4) Call Pregnancy Aftermath Helpline, (414) 445-2131, anytime after your abortion. If you are having problems, take heart. There is a way to work through any difficulty with help from people who care. Pregnancy Aftermath Helpline's trained volunteers are always available — ready to listen, to give you non-judgmental support and appropriate referrals.

Sincerely,

The Counselors of Pregnancy
Aftermath Helpline
4742 North Sheffield Avenue
Milwaukee WI 53211
(414) 445-2131

Dear Sister Who Placed a Child for Adoption

by Pam Cira

The experience of placing a child for adoption includes some sharp pains and deep joys. The process a woman goes through to arrive at an adoption decision is both terribly difficult and greatly enriching. She needs support and care in making her decision and integrating it into her life. We offer that support and care. We are the counselors of Pregnancy Aftermath Helpline, a telephone hotline to help those with concerns following abortions, miscarriages or placing children for adoption.

Perhaps the hardest decision you'll ever make will be whether to keep or release a child you bear. Perhaps you've never thought about it before — but now that you know you're pregnant, you must ask yourself if you are prepared to raise a child. Your family and friends may have some strong opinions on what you should do. During your pregnancy you will grow to love your baby. You will want what is best for you and your child. And you must answer a very tough question: "Am I what is best for this baby?" You will struggle with your answer and probably change your mind many times during your pregnancy. But you can decide. And ultimately you will decide what is best for both of you.

For several months after you give birth you can expect emotions to be fairly extreme. The lows will be much more pervasive than the highs. Common reactions include: sense of loss (baby is gone), grief over that loss, loneliness (no one understands), alienation (no one will talk about the baby), need to talk (about birth and child), relief that struggle of decision is over and happiness about baby's start in life.

You will never forget your child and your decision will remain a part of your life. The emotional extremes will be tempered with time, and good feelings can become more pervasive than painful ones. Common reactions include: need to talk about child, think about and miss child (especially on birthdays and holidays), hope to meet child when an adult, care about child and adoptive family, growth in self-confidence, deeper understanding of love, and deeper understanding of relationships.

There are several things you can do to help get through some of these hard times. You may find it important to cry, and crying can be an effective emotional outlet. You may find writing helpful — keeping a journal (diary), writing poems, or writing a letter to the baby. You may need to read books or articles that deal with adoption issues to help you find words for your own feelings. You may be the kind of person who needs to keep busy while working through your feelings, or you may be the type who needs solitude and quiet to sort things out. But no matter how else you deal with your pre and/or post-adoption struggles, you will probably want and need to talk with others who share your adoption experience.

We at Pregnancy Aftermath Helpline understand your needs and want to help. We know that no one can take away your pain, but we can help ease the sting of it and help you grow through it. We know that many may not understand your hopes and dreams for your relinquished child, but we are here to listen and share in them.

Alphabetical Biography

Consuelo M. Beck-Sagué, M.D. is a pediatrician with the Chicago Department of Health. She was formerly organizer of The Teenage Sexuality Project and in that capacity performed abortions and did research on adolescents' attitudes and the effects of abortion on adolescents. "The result of that research and my own experiences during my pregnancy as an intern was that I became an opponent of constitutionally protected abortion. I belong to Peaceful Solutions of Chicago, a group devoted to non-violent alternatives to nuclear weapons and abortion."

Ginny Desmond Billinger lives in Minneapolis and has served on the Minnesota Feminists for Life board since 1981, as well as being secretary-treasurer of Feminists for Life of America from 1982 to 1984.

Jean Blackwood joined the pro-life movement in 1971 as co-founder of Cleveland Area Students for Life. She has been active as an essayist and poet and is the author of *Beyond Beginning and other Poems.* Currently working on a Master's Degree in Library Science, she is the wife of author Gary Blackwood and mother of two adopted sons, Gareth, 9 and Giles, 3.

Rosemary Bottcher is an analytical chemist whose major professional interest is protection of the environment. "I am an anti-choice fanatic on the issue of pollution". She wrote a column for the *Tallahassee* Democrat for a number of years and writes occasionally for *National Right to Life News.* She and her husband, an attorney who specializes in environmental protection, have four children, one of whom is adopted.

Sidney Callahan, Ph.D., is a psychologist, author and mother of six. She received her education at Bryn Mawr, B.A., (1955), Sarah Lawrence, M.A. (1971) and City University of New York, Ph.D. (1980) over a 25 year period.

Pam Cira was a counselor in the Sexual Assault Counseling Unit at the District Attorney's Office in Milwaukee County for five years. From 1978 to 1982 she was president of Feminists for Life of America.

Richard Cohen is a syndicated columnist for *The Washington Post.* His column appears thrice-weekly on the op-ed page and is syndicated to other newspapers. He is married to Barbara Cohen, a news executive with NBC. They have a son, a dog and a tremendous mortgage.

Felicity Coulter of Toronto was one of the pioneers of post-abortion counseling. She has also been active in pregnancy distress counseling.

Daphne deJong is a writer who lives in New Zealand with her husband and five children, one of these an adopted Chinese orphan. She founded the original Feminists for Life of New Zealand in 1975. She publishes popular novels under a pen name.

Tom Diaz, the Supreme Court correspondent and federal columnist for the *Washington Times*, writes from time to time about life issues.

Donna Eddy's main interests are the role of women in politics, religion and liturgy. A delegate to the 1972 Democratic National Convention for McGovern, she is currently co-chairing a progressive Catholic liturgy at Holy Rosary Church in Milwaukee. She has been published in the *American Poetry Anthology, Milwaukee Road Review,* and *Crossroads.*

Deanna K. Edwards is a singer-composer and volunteer music therapist. She travels thousands of miles throughout the United States and Canada. Her music, composed for the sick, dying and elderly, is for everyone who has ever laughed — ever cried — ever been afraid of the unknown.

Patricia Fernandez, a mother of four, is a telephone counselor and law student.

Judie Gillespie can't figure out whether she is still a Chicagoan, where she grew up, or a Milwaukeean, where she now resides with her husband and three sons. She is co-director of the pro-life effort of the Archdiocese of Milwaukee. She often wonders why there is a need for her job. "Doesn't the world realize that life is the greatest gift?"

Kathleen M. Glover has based her commitments on a strong belief in the value of human life. She founded a "Birthright" chapter, and currently is a member of Feminists for Life, the Waukesha, Wi. Peace Council, and co-ordinator of the Waukesha "Loaves and Fishes" meal program. She is a part-time obstetrical nurse and a full-time homemaker with four children.

Mary Goggins is a short story writer from Wauwatosa, Wisconsin.

Denyse Handler is a Toronto-based freelance journalist who has written for the Toronto *Star* and the *New York Times.* She did editorial work on this collection.

Paulette Joyer, a Minneapolis resident, edited the Minnesota Feminists for Life newsletter from 1977 to 1984. She was vice president of the chapter and also of Feminists for Life of America. She edited *Sisterlife* from 1982 to 1984.

Ken Kesey lives in Oregon with his wife and children, one of whom is adopted. He is the author of *One Flew Over the Cuckoo's Nest, Sometimes a Great Notion,* and *Kesey's Garage Sale.*

Cecilia Voss Koch is a teacher, not only to her three sons, but also to a broad range of other people, from the severely retarded to college freshmen. She is a member of Feminists for Life.

Paul Krassner was editor of *The Realist* (1958-1974) for which he received the Feminist Party Media Workshop Award. The complete interview with Ken Kesey appears in *Best of the Realist.*

Juli Loesch is an anti-war activist, former boycott organizer for the United Farm Workers, a contributing editor for the *New Oxford Review* and freelance writer. She is founder of Prolifers for Survival (P.S.), an international effort to bring together peace and pro-life activists to oppose abortion and nuclear war. "I used to call myself a feminist, but now like Alice Walker I call myself a womanist."

Sandra K. Mahkorn M.D. is chief resident in family medicine at Louisiana State University Medical Center. She is also a psychologist who has counseled troubled adolescents and victims of sexual assault.

Susan Maronek has an M.A. in sociology. A past member of St. Joan's International Alliance (a Catholic feminist organization), she is presently a member of Feminists for Life, Pro Lifers for Survival and Women's Ordination Conference. Her main interest is inclusive liturgy.

Jo McGowan is a writer and apprentice midwife, living in India with her husband Ravi and their son.

Mary Meehan is a freelance writer whose work has been published in *Commonweal, The Human, Life Review, Inquiry, The Progressive, The Washington Post* and elsewhere.

Monica M. Migliorino holds a Masters degree in Theology from Loyola University in Chicago and has begun work toward a Ph.D. in Theology from Marquette University. Ms. Migliorino has been active in the pro life movement since 1977.

Lucien Miller, professor of Comparative Literature, University of Massachusetts, Amherst, is also a Permanent Deacon, Diocese of Springfield, Massachusetts. Ordained in January 1983, he is married and has three children. He chairs the Pro Life Commission of the Diocese of Springfield. He is also the editor of *Reflections* (post-abortion newsletter) and chaplain of the Newman Center, University of Massachusetts, Amherst.

Nancy Randolph Pearcey is a professional writer working part time from her home while raising a beautiful five year old son. She was secretary of Feminists for Life of Missouri for 1982. She now lives in Toronto, where she and her husband are studying at the Institute for Christian Studies.

Judy Shea lives in Minneapolis and is an instructor in natural family planning, also a member of Feminists for Life since 1974 and president of Minnesota Feminists for Life since 1977.

Barbara Sieger is president of Feminists for Life of Wisconsin.

Elizabeth Moore Sobo ("s" as in "sugar") is the mother of seven children and is now working in legal aid for Haitian political asylum seekers who have fled the violent dictatorship of Jean-Claude Duvalier; she is also the producer of a weekly radio program on WDNA in Miami, "Africana".

Paula Sutcliffe lives near Milwaukee, Wisconsin. She does crisis pregnancy and post-abortion counseling. She has "one husband and three children."

Gail Grenier Sweet, a member of Feminists for Life since 1979, is a writer living in rural Wisconsin with her husband and three children. She has published a book of poetry and cartoons entitled *Looking In, Looking Out.*

Linda Mackie Williams is a journalist and communications consultant. She has done community education in the sensitive area of sexual assault, incest and child abuse. She is married and the mother of two children, living with her family in West Allis, Wisconsin.

Lorraine Williams, M.S.W., conducts a part-time private practice in marital and individual counseling. She is also a freelance writer and editor, wife of a Canadian member of Parliament (Ontario) and mother of five children.

Judith P. Woodburn is an editor of *Milwaukee Magazine.* She is coming to terms with the fact that the feminist position on abortion is not monolithic. Her story on self-defense shows one of the many ways in which women can be strong.